The Winnipeg General Strike of 1919
An Illustrated History

The Winnipeg General Strike of 1919
An Illustrated History

J.M. Bumsted

WATSON DWYER
PUBLISHING LIMITED

Designed by Doowah Design Inc.

Published with the assistance of the Manitoba Arts Council and The Canada Council.

Printed in Canada by Hignell Printing Ltd.

Canadian Cataloguing in Publication Data

Bumsted, J. M., 1938 -

    The Winnipeg General Strike of 1919

    Includes bibliographical references and index.

    ISBN 0-920486-40-1

1. General Strike, Winnipeg, Man., 1919.

2. General Strike, Winnipeg, Man., 1919 — Pictorial works.

I. Title

HD5330.W5B85 1994   331.89'29712743   C94-920058-1

Dedicated to
HELEN M. BURGESS

Front Cover photos
Left photograph: C.N.R. car men on strike, demonstration at the Legislative Building, 1914.
Right photograph: Great War Veterans' Association parade, 4 June 1919.
Inset photograph left: detail from back cover photo. Inset photograph right: detail from photo, page 75.

Back Cover photo
Transcona Shops workers, c. 1915.

Title page photo
The Royal North-West Mounted Police and the Militia on
Main Street, just south of City Hall, after the charge, 21 June 1919

Map
Map on page ix based on information provided by
the Manitoba Labor Education Centre

Acknowledgements
The majority of the photographs in this book are by L. B. Foote
who chronicled Winnipeg life and events from 1902 to 1948.

LEWIS FOOTE,
C. 1943

Photographs are from the
Provincial Archives of Manitoba except for the following:

Page 32
Archives and Special Collections,
University if Manitoba.

Page 17, 28 (left), 34 (left), 35 (right), 53 (right)
Western Canada Pictorial Index.

Page 88
Alan L. Crossin.

The publisher expresses its appreciation to
these institutions and to Mr. Crossin for permission
to publish their photographs.

✣ CONTENTS ✣

⚜ Winnipeg General Strike 1919 ⚜

■ Working Class Winnipeg

1 C.P.R. Station

2 Vulcan Iron Works

3 Selkirk Avenue

4 Working Class Housing

5 All Peoples' Mission

6 Ukrainian Labor Temple

7 Residences of the arrested Strike leaders

8 C.P.R. Weston Shops

9 Woseley

● Cresentwood
Home of the Committee of 1000

9 J.H. Ashdown residence

10 T.R. Deacon residence

11 General Ketchen's residence

12 Residences of the members of the Committee of 1000 and the Board of Trade

13 Ft. Osborne Barracks

14 The Legislature

15 Broadway and the Manitoba Club

16 Board of Trade

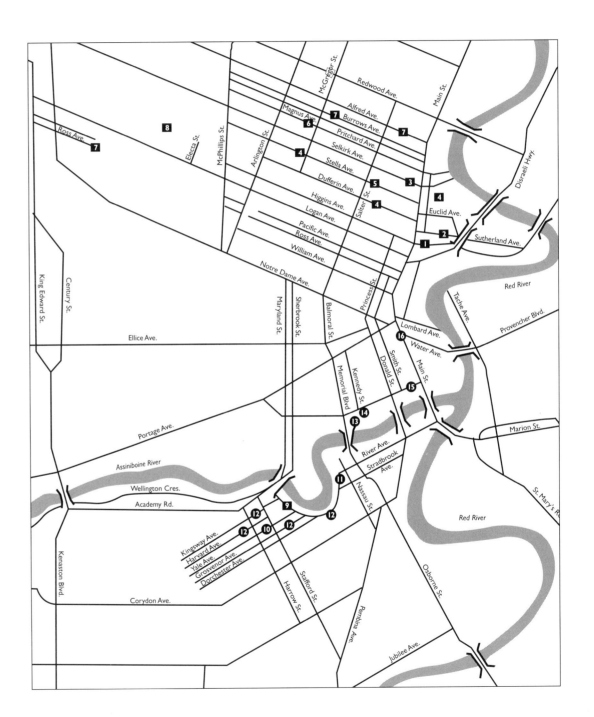

Officially the Winnipeg General Strike began at 11:00 a.m. on 15 May 1919, which was the time appointed by the Winnipeg Trades and Labor Council. But in the larger sense the General Strike was not an event that happened solely in isolation in Winnipeg or even in Western Canada in the spring of 1919. Its coming had been building for many years, and the responses of contemporaries must be understood in the context both of historical developments in Canada and in the world in 1919 and the years immediately preceding.

In order to appreciate adequately the background of the strike, we have to examine a number of intertwined sets of circumstances, ranging from international to local. One was the European situation. Here the Great War was only recently concluded and a revolution was still going on in Russia, where Canadian soldiers were helping to battle the insurgents. Another was the Canadian situation, where the Great War had produced a 'we-them' patriotism and the suppression by the state of many forms of dissent and criticism. A third involved the labour movement in Canada which, on top of a previous period of rapid immigration and industrialization, had been altered in a variety of ways by the wartime experience. Among the many developments of the war for labour was the politicization of a previously pragmatic working-class movement by the addition of radicals and reformers with other agendas. Last but not least, there was Winnipeg itself, a city almost perfectly divided geographically along class lines, which had experienced in 1918 a major general strike settled very much in favour of the strikers and was experiencing (with all of Canada) a rapid inflation of prices in 1919.

■ THE INTERNATIONAL SCENE:

The significance for Canada in 1919 of events in post-war Europe, particularly in Russia, cannot be over-empha-

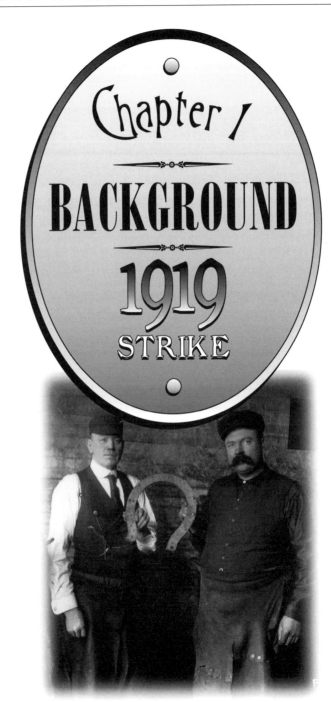

OPPOSITE PAGE:
COPPER SHEATHING THE ROOF OF THE FORT GARRY HOTEL, c. 1912-13.

THIS PAGE:
BLACKSMITH WITH GIANT HORSESHOE, 1912.

sized. The revolution in Russia had begun more than a year before the Armistice of 11 November 1918. A small cadre of well-organized and militant ideologues, claiming that they were the intellectual heirs of Karl Marx and Friedrich Engels, had managed in October of 1917 to seize control of a popular uprising begun earlier in the year against the Czarist regime. These 'Bolsheviki', led by Nicholai Lenin and Leon Trotsky, had employed workers' councils (or soviets) to achieve the 'dictatorship of the proletariat' and to work toward the elimination of capitalism in Russia. They also made a truce with Germany, which had freed more than seventy enemy divisions in the east. They had executed the Russian royal family, and attempted through 1918 to extend their authority against stubborn resistance from loyal forces of so-called 'White Russians' assisted by volunteers and soldiers from various Allied nations, including Canada.

The British War Cabinet had begun talking about intervention in Russia early in 1918, but little manpower was available. Nevertheless, the War Office on 14 January 1918 organized a British mission to the Caucasus region to recruit local volunteers. This mission included fifteen Canadian officers and twenty-six non-commissioned officers. It was disbanded a few months later without achieving its ultimate purpose. On 17 September 1918, ninety-two Canadian officers and non-commissioned officers sailed for Murmansk to join a special Allied force being formed there. A few days later, two Canadian artillery batteries, formed into the 16th brigade with eighteen officers and 469 other ranks, left Dundee for Archangel, on the White Sea. The soldiers sent to northern Russia would all see some action. The situation was a bit different in the East. When the Americans decided to send troops to Siberia in August of 1918, the Canadians soon agreed to join them. The force approved consisted of 5,000 men, not entirely volunteers. The first party of 680 from all ranks of the Canadian Expeditionary Force (Siberia) set sail from Vancouver on 11 October 1918. With the signing of the Armistice on 11 November, however, the Canadian government — under pressure from public opinion particularly critical of the involvement of conscripts for overseas military adventures — became less enthusiastic about Canadian adventurism in Russia. Much of the criticism, as we shall see, came from the ranks of Canadian labour.

The Communist takeover of Russia was a frightening occurrence to governments and their supporters everywhere in the western world, particularly when it was combined with information suggesting that the Bolsheviks were eager to export their revolutionary ideology around the world. The ideas of radical revolution ceased in 1917 to be the toys of an ineffective minority, but became both real and dangerous. Not only did the Bolsheviks continue to hold power in Russia, but a communist faction had risen to power in Hungary, and the Bolsheviks were threatening to capture control of postwar Germany. The Bolshevik victory probably had more impact around the world on those who feared them than on those who admired them. By 1919, the United States government, led by its Attorney-general A. Mitchell Palmer, had turned the Bolshevik threat into a paranoid search for Communist sympathizers everywhere within and without the labour movement. Nor did the witch-hunt stop with Communists. According to an advertisement in the Seattle *Post-Intelligencer* in early 1919, 'We must deport all "aliens", Socialists, Non-Partisan Leaguers, "closed shop unionists," syndicalists, "agitators," "malcontents" — all these must be outlawed by public opinion and hunted down and hounded until driven beyond the horizon of civic decency.' The year had begun in the United States with a five-day general strike in Seattle, the first general strike in American history, which had brought the city to a virtual halt.

■ THE GOVERNMENT, PATRIOTISM, AND THE WAR:

In Canada, the official reaction to the Russian revolution fit nicely into developments inherent in the mobilization of the nation for the Great War. Much of the population of Canada — particularly those of British origin — had entered the war in 1914 with considerable enthusiasm. An identification of Canadian patriotism with support for the British Empire and for the war effort had gradually coalesced. At the same time, the Canadian government had from the beginning of the war sought maximum power and freedom of action to pursue it. One of its first actions after the declaration of war was the passage of the War Measures Act, which gave almost unlimited power to the Governor in Council to 'make from time to time such orders and regulations, as he may by reason of the existence of real or apprehended war, invasion or insurrection deem necessary for the security, defence, peace, order, and welfare of Canada.' The Act included powers of censorship, as well as those of 'arrest, detention, exclusion, and deportation.' As the war went on, the list of 'non-patriots' expanded, while the government's suppression of dissent and criticism through incarceration, censorship, and deportation, grew. The internment operation of the Canadian government, from beginning to end, imprisoned 8,579 men, 81 women, and 156 children. The males included 2,009 Germans, 5,954 Austrians (mainly Ukrainians), 205 Turks, 99 Bulgarians, and 312 'miscellaneous.' Another 80,000 foreign-born Canadians were processed under registration and examination procedures. By August of 1918, nearly 200 non-Canadian publications were on the censor's proscribed list, not all of them in languages other than English or French.

At first only those Canadians born in enemy territory who were not Canadian citizens (the enemy aliens) were regarded as outside the patriotic circle, but the conscription crisis, beginning in 1916 with the efforts to introduce registration of all draft-age males, made clear that many French-Canadians and a number of Anglo-Canadians would have to be included as well. Individuals associated with organized labour were particularly critical of the introduction of registration and conscription. In Manitoba, Social Democratic Member of the Legislative Assembly Frederick Dixon declared at an anti-registration rally at the Strand Theatre on 7 January 1916, 'I am not afraid to die, but I want to know what I am going to die for. I am not going to die for a myth.' Dixon followed this up with a major speech to the Manitoba Legislature on 17 January 1916, announcing his non-compliance with registration, both because it invaded his British rights and because the war was being fought for bad aims and under bad principles, chiefly to assuage the predilections of the greedy. Dixon's speech was met with a chorus of hostile disapproval from those who, like *Free Press* editor J. W. Dafoe, saw him obstructing 'his fellow countrymen in pursuing the course imposed upon them by patriotic and democratic considerations as powerful and as conscientious as any that have aroused human hearts to the call of highest duty.' The Great War Veterans' Association went further than Dafoe, not only demanding Dixon's recall, but interrupting a meeting in Brandon at which he was speaking to demand that he sing 'God Save the King' as a demonstration of his patriotism. The veterans saw any opposition to or criticism of the war as an attack on their sacrifices. Government officials tended to see anti-conscriptionists as

FREDERICK JOHN DIXON, 1921.

JOHN WESLEY DAFOE, 1930.

troublemakers to be silenced at all costs. In July 1917, the commanding officer of Military District 10 (which included Winnipeg) wrote to his superior officers that a number of Winnipeg anti-conscriptionists — namely: R. A. Rigg, F. J. Dixon, John Queen, A. A. Heaps, and George Armstrong — ought to be dealt with summarily under the War Measures Act. Nothing was done in 1917, but four of these men (Dixon, Queen, Heaps, Armstrong) would be among the strike leaders arrested by the Canadian government in June 1919.

Not all Canadian or Winnipeg labour leaders were pacifists, of course, and attitudes toward the war did not always coincide with other ideologies. W. H. Hoop, organizer of the Winnipeg Retail Clerks, was an 'impossiblist' member of the Socialist Party (which meant that he believed that it was impossible to reform the existing capitalistic system), but he was also an ardent conscriptionist in 1916–1917. R. A. Rigg, Dixon's colleague in the Manitoba legislature, had originally agreed to support the government's registration programme upon assurances that it was not a prelude to conscription, later withdrew his support from registration — thus leading to his inclusion on the anti-conscriptionist list. But Rigg joined the army as a corporal late in 1917 (he was in his mid-40s and already had a son in uniform).

With the Russian Revolution, radicals (who had often been critical of the government in the past) were added to the unpatriotic list, regardless of their nation of origin. The year 1918 saw a considerable extension of censorship, for example, when PC 2381 of 25 September banned all publications in an 'enemy language', including Finnish and Russian, which were not enemy languages. The principal target was alien socialism. Ironically, of course, many of the most articulate radicals

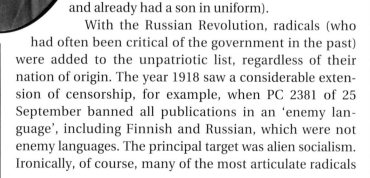

RICHARD A. RIGG,
C.1920.

in Canada critical of the war effort and the Siberian intervention were recent immigrants from the United Kingdom rather than enemy aliens. To some extent, the identification of true Canadian patriotism with both support for the war and with things British made it difficult for Canadian officials to conceive of the existence — much less legitimacy — of British radicals who might criticize the war effort or seek to overturn the government. That true British-Canadian workers might pay attention to these British radicals was completely unthinkable. The threatened spread of Bolshevism provided an explanation for the spread of radicalism in Canada which did not challenge cherished values. Radicalism was 'alien' and could be associated with the foreigner, who had long been an object of criticism. For many Canadian government officials, the elimination of alien radicalism would virtually remove any radical threat in Canada.

■ LABOUR AND THE WAR:

The Canadian labour movement was profoundly altered during the Great War in a number of ways. In the first place, the coming of war gradually brought about a period of full employment after some very lean years from 1911 to 1915. The prewar depression had reduced trade union membership substantially, as bad times always had a tendency to do. The coming of war, combined with a continued slow economy, had also greatly limited labour militancy. In 1912, there were 242 strikes across the nation, involving 43,104 workers and resulting in 1,136,345 striker days lost. By 1915, those figures had dropped to 86 strikes, 11,480 workers involved, and only 95,242 striker days lost. The transfer of millions of workers into the military, combined with the demands of war for increased production, had eventually improved the position of both the remaining workers and organized labour. The workers found steady employment, and labour found itself in a position where modest advances in wages and working conditions could be achieved. In the coal industry of Alberta, for example, war bonuses and wage increases, as well as other concessions, were won in a series of strikes from 1916–1918.

Labour had also won a number of concessions from provincial governments during the war, partly because it began to have some success at organizing politically and had become an interest group to be taken seriously. The legislature of Manitoba elected in late 1915, for example, contained two members from the Social Democratic Party of Manitoba, Robert Rigg and F. J. Dixon, both elected from predominately working-class districts of Winnipeg as 'labourites.' The Liberal government of T. C. Norris which came to power in this election introduced a number of reforms favourable to labour. Responding to blandishments from the Winnipeg Trades and Labor Council, the Norris government reorganized the provincial Bureau of Labour and made it responsible for enforcing the labour legislation already on the books. The government soon added more regulatory and social welfare legislation: the Fair Wage Act of 1916, the Workmen's Compensation Act of 1916, and the Minimum Wage Act of 1918 (which provided a minimum wage for female workers across the province). By the close of the war, Manitoba had some of the most progressive labour legislation in existence anywhere in North America. The presence of this legislation did not mean that the province enjoyed industrial tranquillity, for worker and employer fought bitterly and constantly over classic issues. But labour in Manitoba could fight its battles against employers with some encouragement about the attitude of the provincial government.

The period of the war had also seen a new radicalization of Canadian labour, particularly in the west. The labour movement in Canada before the war had been dominated by traditional trade unionists, organized into unions of skilled crafts devoted to improving conditions of work 'pure and simple'. The 'pure and simples' rejected the notion of the politicization of labour questions or the entry of labour leaders into the political arena. This attitude was often called 'Gomperism' after its leading international exponent, Samuel Gompers, the head of the American Federation of Labor. In the years after 1900, however, Canada experienced a substantial influx of immigrants from the industrial centres of the British Isles, who were familiar with new views of unionism and new ideologies of the class struggle. These men were militant and articulate. They were also far less committed to traditional trade unionism. It was not that the new leaders were necessarily more militant about labour issues, but that they sought new strategies for dealing with them.

Influenced by British labourism, which had organized its own political party, the emerging leaders were far more willing to form political parties sympathetic to or allied to labour, such as the Social Democratic Party or the Socialist Party of Canada. These parties did not necessarily agree with one another on ideology or strategy. The history of Canadian labour in politics during the wartime period is a complex and complicated one. But the membership criteria for political parties or omnibus unions were considerably different from that of skilled trades unions, and individuals who were not from the working class or who were interested in more than traditional working class issues were able to join the labour movement as it became more politicized. The greater range of membership helped add to the ideological confusion of these years. As well as the 'pure and simples', the labour movement now contained reformers of a variety of stripes (most of them Utopian in one way or another, many of them social gospel ministers). It also contained all manner of socialists, who ranged from inflexible supporters of the doctrines of Karl Marx to non-violent followers of British Labourism, from Bolsheviks to Fabians. By the close of the war, labour in Canada was involved in a major transition away from Gomperism, but how the new order was to be worked out in practice was not yet clear. The year 1919 would be a key one, and Winnipeg the site of the critical Canadian experiment.

■ WINNIPEG:

In 1919, with the Great War only recently concluded and the details of the peace still being worked out at the conference tables of Versailles, the city of Winnipeg was an ideal site for a Canadian experiment in industrial action involving a major confrontation between business and labour. This confrontation would have a number of nasty undertones, particularly racial ones, and it would result in a heavy-handed dose of government intervention. Winnipeg contained a business elite which had run the city since the beginning as an extension of its economic activity, and which had no intention of surrendering its control. It contained both a labour elite and a conscious working class, the former consisting mainly of recent immigrants from the British Isles thoroughly familiar with the ideologies and strategies of modern industrial unionism and eager to apply them to post-war conditions, and the latter made up of working people from Eastern Canada and Europe, as well as Great Britain. Winnipeg also contained a substantial population of recent immigrants from central and eastern Europe, many of whom had originated in parts of Germany and the Austro-Hungarian Empire, making them technically 'enemy aliens' in the eyes of the Canadian government.

Equally important was that Winnipeg's urban development had managed to segregate these three major groups into distinct residential districts, each with its own ethos. The central downtown core of the city (which contained the offices of business and government and would become the battlefield of the strike) was geographically the link between the otherwise separate territories of the business classes, the Anglo-Canadian working classes, and the immigrants. To some extent, all major cities in Canada shared these characteristics, but in few (if any) were they as pronounced as they were in Winnipeg.

THE BUSINESS ELITE: Winnipeg, since its incorporation in the early 1870s, had been dominated politically and socially by a business elite which saw growth as the city's major consideration. This group had come for the most part from central Canada, especially rural and small-town Ontario, migrating west either as youngsters with their parents or as young men starting a career. A large number of lawyers, whose livelihood depended upon business prosperity, were included in the latter category. Most had received apprenticeship training in law offices. Some of the business and professional leaders had been born in various parts of the British Isles, but most of them had also spent substantial portions of their careers in the city. Few of these leaders of the Winnipeg business community were native Winnipeggers (although their children were) or even native Manitobans, but they had worked in the city together for a long time. In 1919 the business community of Winnipeg was still almost without exception composed of self-made men, lacking in liberal education, who had risen to success by dint of their own often ruthless efforts at exploitation of both the environment and their employees.

Although the twentieth century had seen some of the business elite move

WINNIPEG GRAIN EXCHANGE, C.1920.

JAMES ASHDOWN, C.1915.

into industrial activities, especially metal fabrications associated with the railroads, the dominant ethos of the Winnipeg business community in 1919 was still commercial, strongly linked to the agricultural hinterland of the province. Supplying the farm community with goods and services and acting as middlemen in the marketing of its crops (through such institutions as the Winnipeg Grain Exchange) was good business in Winnipeg. So too were real estate development, construction, insurance, and banking, along with the inevitable legal paperwork required for such activities. Winnipeg's lawyers, like Canadian lawyers across the nation, were a highly conservative and parochial lot, whose training and legal experience included little exposure to wider international intellectual currents or to contemporary developments in a rapidly industrializing world. When free-thinker Marshall Gauvin came to the city a few years later, he was astounded to find the progressive intellectual community of the city among its labour leaders rather than its businessmen. The business leadership of Winnipeg was also its social elite, familiar with one another from membership in an overlapping and interlocking series of organizations ranging from the Board of Trade to the Manitoba Club to various curling clubs to the Historical and Scientific Society of Manitoba. Most were Protestants, many were Masons.

One example of the upper ranks of the business elite was the city's 'Merchant Prince', James Henry Ashdown. Although not a native-born Canadian, Ashdown had emigrated to Canada from London with his parents at age eight, spending his formative years in small-town Ontario. Apprenticed to a tinsmith, he worked in Chicago before coming to Winnipeg in 1868, just as the city was emerging out of the Red River Colony. Ashdown set up a hardware store which became a major wholesale supplier for the entire prairie region, and made millions in real estate speculation besides. In 1870 he had been one of John Christian Shultz's 'army' opposing Louis Riel's provisional govern-

ment, and he subsequently had a finger in everything, holding numerous directorships in banks and insurance companies as well as being a Mason, a Liberal, a Methodist, and a founder of Wesley College. In 1907 and 1908 he was elected mayor of Winnipeg, the second time by acclamation. No friend of insurrections, as he had shown in 1870, in 1908 he opposed a visit to Winnipeg by the Socialist agitator Emma Goldman. Both Ashdown's downtown warehouse on Bannatyne St and his mansion on Wellington Crescent still survive, the former recently developed as upmarket condominiums and the latter is a Shrine Temple.

Another examplar of the city's establishment was Thomas R. Deacon, in 1919 head of Manitoba Bridge and Iron Works and one of the city's leading industrialists. Deacon had been born in Perth, Ontario, working in the lumber camps of northern Ontario before obtaining an engineering degree at the University of Toronto. He began an engineering career in gold-mining around Kenora and Rainy River, the locals calling him 'Chief No-gold', before his arrival in Winnipeg in 1902. Deacon was in his own way public - spirited, leading the campaign for the development of Shoal Lake as the city's water supply. But he also hated trade unions. While mayor in 1914, he told the city's unemployed to 'hit the trail', at the same time opposing limitations on immigration on the grounds that millions of prairie acres were still available for settlement. In 1917 he had employed a private detective agency to supply strikebreakers from Montreal, and when this tactic failed he obtained an anti-picketing injunction and sued his striking unions for damages. He lived in Crescentwood at 194 Yale, and had a considerable private reputation for vulgar excess.

THOMAS R. DEACON, 1909.

The elite exemplified by Ashdown and Deacon — both recently mayors of Winnipeg — had controlled civic government since the beginning of the city, to the virtual exclusion of those from any other group. Their control occurred partly because they devoted a good deal of time and energy to maintaining their dominance, which was good for business in general and often their business in particular. In the years immediately before the Great War, for example, real estate agents, speculators, and financiers represented two-thirds of the membership of the influential Board of Control of the city. But dominance also resulted from a voting franchise that favoured property ownership and positively discriminated against the poor, particularly the immigrant poor. Property qualifications were sufficiently high, when combined with other requirements including British citizenship, to keep registered municipal voters in 1906 to 7,784 out of a total population in excess of 100,000. After 1890 the vote was further stacked by the introduction of plural voting, in which a citizen could vote in any ward 'in which he had been rated for the necessary property qualification.' The extension of the franchise to women of property would not alter the locus of control. Not surprisingly, the civic government resulting from such dominance was both cosily unimaginative and geared to material expansion at the expense of most other values. It was government in the interests of one class within the community.

By 1919, the business class and those other members

WELLINGTON CRESCENT, C.1914.

The Boulevard, Wellington Crescent, Winnipeg, Man., Canada.

of the middle class who supported its values (and often sought entrance into its ranks) had come to reside chiefly in certain districts of the southern and western sections of the city, mainly (although not exclusively) south of the Assiniboine River and west of the Red River. A few business leaders still lived downtown in mansions long since demolished or in luxury hotels. Dalnavert on Carlton St, the home of Sir Hugh John Macdonald, is one of the few surviving downtown mansions. More of the elite lived in Armstrong's Point, and still more along Wellington Crescent and adjacent Crescentwood, the sites of the city's largest and most exclusive mansions. Less affluent professionals and middle managers lived in River Heights, parts of Crescentwood, and in Wolseley, especially near and along the river. Some of the houses of the ruling group of Winnipeg in 1919 still survive. They are recognizable by their size and sometimes by the size of their lots. Many have been renovated as multiple-family dwellings, and — ironically enough — frequently turned into rooming houses or apartments for Winnipeg's less affluent residents.

THE LABOUR ELITE: By 1919 Winnipeg also had a rapidly-developing labour elite, consisting of men who had come into positions of prominence within various labour unions in the city. Almost without exception, such men had been born and educated (often on the job) in the industrial centres of the British Isles. They had grown up in both an urban and an industrial environment, developing both a working-class consciousness and strategies for articulating it. Many were members of the Labour Party of Britain, most were socialists of one sort or another, thoroughly conversant with the writings of men like Karl Marx, Friedrich Engels, George Bernard Shaw (the leading Fabian theorist), and Henry George, the American single tax reformer. This labour elite was hardly ideologically homogeneous; according to the later recollections of one of its principal members, the period of the Great War was one 'of the conflict of ideas, a war of ideologies and at times quite savage too.' Although often self-educated, they were far more aware of the contemporary world of ideas and ideology than were their counterparts in the Winnipeg commercial elite, and if they were more 'intellectual', they were correspondingly less parochial. Almost without exception these men had immigrated to Winnipeg as adults, as part of the massive migration of people from the British Isles to Canada in the first years of the twentieth century. Among the major local labour leaders in the 1919 general strike, for example, 55 per cent were English-born, 25 per cent Scots-born, 10 per cent Welsh-born, 5 per cent Irish- born, and only 5 per cent Canadian-born. Over ninety per cent had come to Winnipeg between 1900 and 1912 as adults straight from the 'Old Country.'

IMMIGRANT FAMILY, WINNIPEG, 1914.

Like the business elite, Winnipeg's labour leaders lived together in a relatively small number of districts of the city inhabited almost exclusively by highly skilled workers, mainly Canadians and recent immigrants from the British Isles. One of these districts — Fort Rouge — was technically on the southwest side of the city, located chiefly in a triangle between Osborne Street and the Canadian Pacific Railway's Pembina or Fort Rouge yards but spilling over into another triangle bounded by Pembina, Stafford, and Corydon. Another — St John's — was technically in the North End, located around St John's College and St John's Cathedral, with its centre at College St and Main St. Another — Weston — was on the border

MARTHA STREET, LOOKING NORTH- WEST FROM SOUTHEAST CORNER OF ALEXANDER AVENUE, 1918.

HENRY AVENUE, LOOKING EAST FROM MAIN STREET, 1918.

between the North End and the West End, located adjacent to the Canadian Pacific Railway's Weston yards and shops. Another district of skilled workers was to be found in the West End itself, stretching from Wolseley just south of Portage north to Wellington and even Notre Dame and west beyond Valour (which was renamed in honour of the three Victoria Cross winners of the Great War who had lived on the street). There was also another newly-emerging district of skilled workers by the Transcona yards, but it was not well integrated into the city. These districts were quite distinctive from those of the business and professional classes, as well as from those inhabited by recent immigrants from central and eastern Europe.

THE IMMIGRANTS:

Winnipeg was a city that grew on the backs of its immigrants, who had originally come chiefly from eastern Canada and the British Isles. Indeed, Winnipeg continued to be a 'British' city through the period of the 1919 strike, although as we have seen, a Canadian-born member of the business elite of British heritage did not necessary have much in common with a recent British-born worker from an urban-industrial background. The fact that the 'British' were the dominant ethnic group does not necessarily mean that this group was in fundamental ways homogeneous, except in reference to the later newcomers from central and eastern Europe. The so-called 'charter group' of British origins who established themselves in Winnipeg before 1890 may have had some common identity, but the city had experienced an enormous immigration between 1900 and 1913, growing from 42,000 people in the former year to 150,000 in the latter. The immigration of the early years of the century was about equally divided between industrial British and the so-called 'new' immigrants, mainly Slavs and Jews. A large portion of these new immigrants had come from regions officially part of Germany (such as Poland) and the Austro-Hungarian Empire (such as the Ukraine), which made them 'enemy aliens' when the Great War began.

The new immigrants lived almost exclusively in the North End of Winnipeg, variously known as the 'Foreign Quarter' and 'New Jerusalem'. The North End was once described as 'one gigantic melting pot north of the CPR tracks.' While it had initially been peopled chiefly by those of British origin, the percentage of British in the North End (80.8 per cent in 1886) constantly declined before 1919, reaching only 38.9 per cent in 1916 — and that mainly in certain selected districts. As late as 1905, two elementary schools in wards 5 and 6 (Aberdeen and Strathcona) had been attended almost exclusively by children of British origin, but by 1915 only 8 per cent of the schools' population was British, with 42 per cent Jewish, 20 per cent Slavic, and 22 per cent German.

The North End attracted the immigrants partly because of the presence of cheap housing, built on tiny narrow lots often lacking in amenities, which could be subdivided into small tenement apartments. J. S. Woodsworth described one of the poorest of these tenements in 1911:

Mike Bernecki was born in 1894 in the Ukraine and came to Canada with his brother Tony in 1910 or 1911. During the time of the strike he and Tony went to a place called Stella Park, which was a popular meeting spot. There were many people there and as Tony stood and watched the crowds, Mike sat on the grass speaking to a woman with a baby. Suddenly a large group of people known to many as 'scabs' came and started indiscriminately rounding up the people. Tony, who was just standing and watching was included in the rounding up of the people. My grandfather Mike was not picked up, perhaps because he was with the woman and child. Tony was locked up and despite numerous attempts by his brother and landlord, who spoke better English, was deported back to the Old Country. Tony's landlord was told that a payment of $200 was required to help get Tony out, but with no guarantees. This kind of money was unheard of back then.

Tony corresponded for a number of years with his brother and tried to get back into Canada, but was told that since he was deported the chances of getting back in were next to impossible. My grandfather married my grandmother a few months later in November. I feel very fortunate that my Grandfather Mike was not picked up also, as three generations of descendants or 24 people would not be here.

Don Barnicki
Winnipeg

Shack – one room and a lean-to. Furniture – two beds, a bunk, stove, bench, two chairs, table, barrel of sauerkraut. Everything was dirty. Two families live here. Women were dirty, unkempt, bare-footed, half-clothed. Children wore only print slips. The baby was lying in a cradle made of sacking suspended from the ceiling by ropes.

If cheap housing drew the newcomers, they were also attracted by the growth of familiar economic and cultural institutions. The stores along Selkirk Avenue and North Main Street were run by owners who spoke the languages of the newcomers, while they offered familiar goods, credit, and even haggled bazaar-fashion with their customers. The social and cultural life of the district literally throbbed with activity. There were at least five Ukrainian newspapers, two musical and dramatic societies, and several educational societies. Among the Jewish community, there were twelve synagogues, several newspapers, and even a Yiddish theatre on Selkirk Avenue. All the immigrant groups had their fraternal/political clubs; perhaps the most active was the Jewish Arbeiter Ring, formed in 1900 as an umbrella organization that included a number of radical political groups as well as a substantial fraternal component. The Arbeiter Ring had its own building, Liberty Temple. The North End 'ghetto' was alive and well in 1919. The North End immigrants could be denigrated because of their ghettoized living conditions and their minority status, but also because so many were considered 'unpatriotic' during the War.

THE GENERAL STRIKE OF 1918: Winnipeg had experienced a good deal of escalating labour unrest during the course of the Great War, particularly in its metal fabrication industry, which was allowed by the Imperial Munitions Board to manufacture shells for the war effort beginning in 1915. Munitions manufacture was both lucrative to the manufacturer and demanding of skilled workers, chiefly machinists. The leading independent shops of Winnipeg — Vulcan Iron Works, Manitoba Bridge and Iron Works, Dominion Bridge Company — were all owned by men extremely hostile to labour and manned by the best educated of the workers, a built-in recipe for trouble. There were a number of strikes and work stoppages in Winnipeg in 1917, and the situation only got worse in 1918.

One of the most serious disputes of 1918 arose between the City of Winnipeg and its civic employees. This labour dispute in a variety of ways served as a rehearsal for the 1919 general strike. The central issue in 1918 began as one of wages, but gradually changed to the right to strike. The workers initially wanted a substantial wage increase to reflect the increased cost of living, while the city's Board of Control suggested and the City Council approved instead a flat rate war bonus to its employees, which would not become part of a base pay when the war was over and which gave more money to lower paid employees. Various civic employee organizations rejected the bonus scheme, and the municipal Electrical Workers took the lead by going on strike on 1 May 1918. The strike gradually spread. The waterworks employees struck on 3 May, while the fire alarm workers joined the electrical workers. The city, for its part, threatened to fire the strikers, the *Tribune* insisting that 'IN ABNORMAL TIMES, in times of stress of war with the Huns pressing in countless hordes against our too thin line of defense, . . . no one must be permitted to clog the machinery of our production.' On 4 May, the City Council carried out its threat to dismiss the strikers. Instead of ending the disturbance, this action merely escalated it, with many unions objecting to it in principle.

On 7 May, the *Telegram* announced that the Winnipeg Trades and Labor Council had decided to call a 'general strike of organized labor throughout the city, by the gradual process of turning the thumbscrews and calling out one union at a time until all the civic employees' demands are met and all of the strikers taken back into the city's employ.' At the same time, the firemen were taking a strike vote shift-by-shift. Civic Teamsters joined the strike, and the Manitoba Government Telephone workers threatened to 'go the limit with the city employees' strike if necessary.' A projected meeting of the Street Railwaymen's Union led to a special meeting of City Council, spearheaded by labour members of that body, who met with over 500 adamant strikers at the Labour Temple on the eve of the council meeting. The mass meeting unanimously supported the striking unions, and the next day the firemen delivered an ultimatum to the council to settle the strike. The milk and bread wagon drivers also voted to strike. The result was a twelve-hour bargaining session between a special committee of council and leaders of the strikers, attended by the press. One of the strongest supporters of compromise was Controller Charles F. Gray, later mayor of Winnipeg in 1919.

(L TO R) COL. H.N. RUTTAN, J.A.M. AIKINS, ROBERT BORDEN AT C.N.R. STATION, 1911.

Unfortunately, the agreement hammered out on 10 May was not accepted by City Council on 13 May. The negotiating committee's report was amended by motion of alderman Frank Fowler and by vote of 9 to 8 to read that 'all persons employed by the City should express their willingness to execute an agreement, undertaking that they will not either collectively or individually at any time go on strike but will resort to arbitration as a means of settlement of all grievances and differences which may not be capable of amicable settlement', and referring the existing dispute to a Board of Conciliation. According to

Fowler, in a powerful speech, the issue was 'whether or not workers on a public utility have the right to go on strike, especially without submitting the matter in dispute to arbitration.' One of Fowler's strongest supporters was Controller Gray, who changed his vote because of his agreement that firemen and policemen should never have the power to strike.

In the wake of this council decision, labour's leaders and those of business began a process of confrontation. As the strike continued and threatened to spread, the Winnipeg Board of Trade began to raise a volunteer fire brigade, perhaps galvanized by a serious fire in the Richardson and Bishop building on 14 May. The volunteers were extremely successful, and their biggest difficulty was a spate of false alarms. To meet these, special constables were appointed to guard the fire alarm boxes; over 500 citizens, including Controller Charles Gray, volunteered for this obviously exciting task. Extreme statements were made by both sides. R. J. Johns told one mass meeting considering a resolution for a sympathy strike:

I am a Socialist and proud of it. You can call me a Bolsheviki if you want to. You must have nothing that flavors of compromise in this proposition. I say strike today, this has resolved itself into a question of right. You have the right to demand anything you have the power to enforce.

A dinner meeting of prominent businessmen at the Royal Alexandra Hotel passed resolutions emphasizing that during the war, all strikes and sympathetic strikes should be made illegal. Moreover, it should be a criminal offense for members of a police force to go on strike. A final resolution recommended the selection of a Committee of One Hundred 'to cooperate with the municipal and provincial authorities during the period of the strike and to promote in every way the resolutions passed at this meeting.' This committee was organized on 17 May 1918, and the names of exactly one hundred prominent citizen members were published in local newspapers the same day. The list included more than merely representatives of the Winnipeg business community. It also included prominent clergymen, including most of the Protestant clerical leadership of the city, as well as heads of a number of social service organizations. That such individuals were willing to associate themselves publicly with opposition to strikes suggests the strength of 'patriotic' feeling among the middle class of Winnipeg, as well as the extent of the gulf between Winnipeg's rising labour movement and the city's historic leadership. The typical member of the Committee of One Hundred, however, was not a bloated plutocrat living on Wellington Crescent in a huge mansion, but a middle manager or social service administrator residing in the less opulent parts of Crescentwood, Wolseley, or in the downtown district. Not only did the Citizens' Committee of 1918 publicize its membership, it also created a conciliation subcommittee to find a compromise solution to the labour dispute.

On 18 May, several hundred railway freight handlers joined the strike, raising the spectre of a national railroad tieup. For its part, the Trades and Labor Council offered conciliatory suggestions that City Council met in silence at about the same time that Prime Minister Borden had in a telegram appealed to the strikers for labour peace. Shortly after the Borden initiative, the federal government ordered Senator Gideon Robertson to Winnipeg to mediate the dispute, joining an envoy of the federal Labour Minister already on the scene. Premier T. C. Norris also began meetings with the contending parties. On 21 May, thousands of railway employees in Winnipeg walked off their jobs in support of the civic workers. Senator Robertson arrived in town late on the evening of 22 May, and went immediately to work. He met with labour and the next morning told City Council that they should agree to a strike settlement because of the war effort, adding, 'There are 200,000 union men in Canada today and none of them ever did sign away their birthright, for that's what you are asking them to do.'

At this point, the conciliation subcommittee of the Citizens' Committee of One Hundred made its report to Council, recommending acceptance of the agreement worked out on 10 May, with several compromise clauses regarding the firemen, which would have restored their right to strike provided they did not exercise it except under extreme provocation. This arrangement was finally accepted, and the strike was finally called off on 25 May when all employers agreed to reinstate their employees without prejudice. A later strike of Winnipeg metal workers in July of 1918 was met with a refusal to bargain by the independent ironmasters, which in turn was met with a vote taken for another general sympathy strike. Gideon Robertson again was instrumental in negotiating a solution which did increase wages. The general strike increasingly seemed a viable labour weapon. The *Western Labor News* would make no bones about it, subsequently exulting, 'We in Winnipeg . . . had the honour of pulling off the first general strike on this continent and through the swiftness and unexpectedness of our action we beat the capitalist class of this city handsomely.' Besides suggesting the value of the general strike as a labour strategy, the 1918 Winnipeg general strike in many other ways prepared the way for 1919. The organization of a general strike committee employed by labour in 1918 was repeated in 1919, and the Citizens' Committee of One Hundred of 1918 became the Citizens' Committee of One Thousand. Most of the city councillors of 1918 were still around a year later, and Controller Charles Gray was now mayor. For its part, labour was persuaded by 1918 that the strategy of the general strike had been a truly successful one, although the gradual escalation by 'turning the screws' of 1918 was different from the 'all at once' synchronization of 1919, and the 1918 goal — the reinstatement of dismissed workers — was much more defensive than in 1919.

The need for telling its own story led the labour radicals

to create the *Western Labor News* as an official organ of the Trades and Labor Council, replacing *The Voice*, privately owned and operated by Arthur Puttee for many years as a moderate labour newspaper. The jettisoning of Puttee's newspaper was one indication to some observers that moderates were losing ground in the Winnipeg labour movement. Another sign was a conflict in September 1918 between moderate F. G. Tipping, president of the Winnipeg Trades and Labor Council, and more radical critics over Tipping's behaviour as a member of the royal commission investigating conditions in the metal trades. The disagreement led to a 49 to 10 vote in the council for Tipping's suspension. Extremist statements by some labour leaders in 1918 — and by the *Western Labor News* — led various national security agencies, including the Royal North-West Mounted Police, to build up their files on suspected subversives. They also helped persuade some Winnipeg businessmen, who often required little persuasion, that — as J. B. Coyne put it in October of 1918 — the Winnipeg Trades and Labor Council was 'now largely dominated by labor leaders who are acknowledged Bolsheviki and whose desire I believe is to substitute a workmen's council with the Russian motto as the governing force in the municipality instead of the representative bodies now constituted by law.'

But 1918 was hardly 1919. The big difference, of course, was that the Great War still hung in the balance in 1918, and men could be persuaded to put aside their differences in the name of the war effort. These differences still prevailed in 1919, but the war no longer existed as a mediating influence. Moreover, the coming of peace meant that large numbers of demobilized soldiers were around Winnipeg in the spring of 1919, a volatile ingredient not present a year earlier. Other developments had occurred between 1918 and 1919 as well. One was a rapidly escalating inflation, which made labour even more anxious to win new wage concessions. Another was a very serious outbreak of Spanish influenza, which struck the city in the winter of 1918–1919 and killed hundreds. The flu epidemic, which had showed little sense of discrimination between rich and poor, helped provide an unmeasurable but very real edge to the public mood of Winnipeg in the first half of 1919.

On 22 December 1918, a mass meeting with an audience in excess of 1,700 was held in Winnipeg at one of the city's largest indoor venues, the Walker Theatre. The Walker, proudly described by its proprietors as 'Canada's finest theatre', had been built in 1907 on Smith Street. Its curtain boasted the motto, 'Finds tongues in trees, books in the running brooks, sermons in stones, and good in everything.' Cosponsored by the Winnipeg Trades and Labor Council and the Socialist Party of Canada — the exact billing was unclear — this December meeting was a perfect illustration of the new politicization of labour that had occurred in the later years of the Great War and would obviously carry over into the new period of peace.

Not only was a labour organization cooperating publicly with a radical political party, but the agenda of the meeting had little if anything to do with either traditional labour or industrial issues. Instead of 'lunchbucket' matters, it was concerned rather with controversial policy connected with the present Union government, still running the Dominion of Canada as if it were at war: orders-in-council under the War Measures Act, military intervention in Russia, and the incarceration of political prisoners. These issues and the question of censorship had been debated and protested at meetings of various organizations, including labour ones, right across the country. Perhaps the most outspoken protest had come from a convention of the International Association of Machinists of Ontario, meeting in Toronto, and reported in the *Western Labor News*. This convention had insisted that 'autocratic' government methods were 'a danger to social peace' in a world moving 'toward freedom and democracy' and in which 'Labour is asserting its right to rule.'

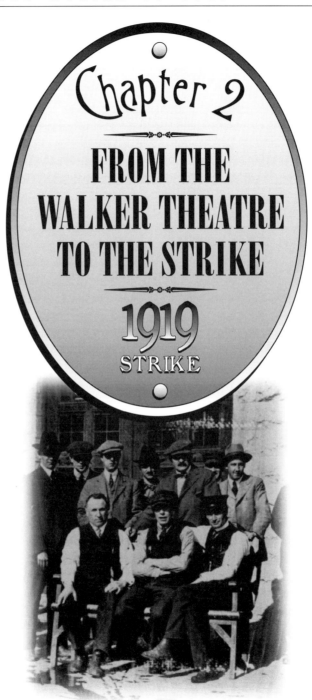

Chapter 2

FROM THE WALKER THEATRE TO THE STRIKE

1919 STRIKE

OPPOSITE PAGE:
CROWDS AT VICTORIA PARK, 1919.

THIS PAGE:
DETAIL FROM PHOTO OF FIREMEN,
20 MAY 1919

GEORGE ARMSTRONG, UNDATED.

JOHN QUEEN, 1921.

WILLIAM IVENS, C.1921.

The idea for a mass meeting in Winnipeg had been raised at an earlier meeting of the Trades and Labor Council by George Armstrong, one of the leading members of Winnipeg's Socialist Party and one of only a handful of Canadian-born labour leaders in Winnipeg. Armstrong had brought up the problems of the orders-in-council. He did not have to remind the gathering that matters had become more extreme in late 1918 with the passage of new regulations creating a ban on all 'enemy language' publications, including those in Russian, Ukrainian, and Finnish, and proscribing fourteen unlawful associations by name (mainly labour and left-wing groups in the Ukrainian community). Sam Blumenberg, another outspoken Socialist, advocated a general strike to force the Allies to withdraw from Siberia. Bob Russell, a third Socialist to speak at the meeting, added that it was useless to expect the Canadian Labor Congress officials in Ottawa (representing traditional trade unionism in Canada) to take any action against the orders-in-council, since 'They were in league with the powers that were suppressing the papers and magazines that stood for liberty.' John Queen reported that the military had refused him permission to hold a meeting to raise money for the new Labour Temple for the Ruthenians, one of the Ukrainian groups.

The result of a lengthy discussion was a decision 'that a mass meeting against Orders-in-Council and repression in general be held.' The 20 December issue of the *Western Labor News* thus advertised a forthcoming meeting under the auspices of the Trades and Labor Council and listed its principal participants: Alderman John Queen in the chair, and speakers F. J. Dixon, W. Hoop, R. B. Russell, George Armstrong, S. Blumenberg, and Rev. W. Ivens. This lineup of speakers was drawn from a variety of wings of Winnipeg radicalism at the close of the Great War. Not all were Socialists, although by the time John Queen opened the meeting at 2:30 on Sunday afternoon, the Socialist Party of Canada was described as a cosponsor. At the same time, Winnipeg's traditional union leadership, especially those men who had led the successful 1918 strike, were conspicuous by their absence from the podium that Sunday afternoon.

The Socialist Party of Canada in Winnipeg was a small cadre of no more than fifty individuals who insisted vehemently that they were Marxists. But as Gerald Friesen points out in his study of the Socialist Party of Canada, 'the nuances of socialist thought, like medieval philosophy, are many and subtle.' While most Canadian members of the Socialist Party of Canada employed the rhetoric of revolutionary Marxism, they were not active revolutionaries. At the same time, although the Socialist Party of Canada drew its membership heavily from the ranks of labour, most of its leading lights were not important figures in their unions. Moreover, the party itself had historically been hostile to trade unionism because it 'diverted working men from the true cause of revolution', achievable only through political activism.

Alderman Queen opened the Walker Theatre meeting by explaining its genesis as a means of protesting three aspects of government policy. He pointed out that the government had justified orders-in-council, the incarceration of political prisoners, and military intervention in Russia in terms of the wartime emergency. But the recent signing of the Armistice, Queen insisted, had eliminated the 'alleged reason' for such measures, and protest meetings in various parts of the country were being held to urge the Government 'to restore to the people the freedom they used to have.' This declaration was met with cheers by the packed house in the Walker Theatre, and was carefully noted — as were the entire proceedings — by Royal North-West Mounted Police intelligence agents scattered in the audience. Their evidence would subsequently become a critical part of the government's legal case of seditious conspiracy against the leaders of the Winnipeg strike.

W. H. (Bill) Hoop opened the proceedings proper by moving a resolution describing government by order-in-council as a 'distinct violation of the principles of democracy' and demanding 'the repeal of all such orders, and a return to a democratic form of Government.' Hoop had been born in Durham, England, had worked as a steel-worker in London, and had immigrated to Winnipeg in 1893. He was an organizer of the Retail Clerks' Union and a member of the Socialist party. In his accompanying speech, he described the order-in-council as 'the sum total and reflex of the doctrine of property — property is the corner-stone of all capitalistic constitution.' He noted that Charles the First had lost his head employing orders-in-council 'against the liberties of the British constitution', maintaining that there would be repetitions of this form of government so long as there was capitalism. Hoop was highly critical of the government for its lack of preparation for the coming period of reconstruction. George Armstrong seconded the Hoop resolution, defending the Socialist Party of Canada from charges of being 'enemies of authority.' He stressed instead that the Party opposed particular authority maintained by physical force, and he insisted on the established rights of minorities under the British constitution. At this point Mr Charitinoff, the editor of *Robotchny Narod* (Working People), made his appearance in the hall. His newspaper was a Ukrainian socialist one, which had printed a good deal of Bolshevik material in recent years and had been suppressed by the government in 1918. Charitinoff himself was presently under indictment for the possession of seditious literature. According to the report of this meeting, he 'made no statement.' But he did not have to speak. His mere presence produced a round of applause from the audience, and effectively made its point.

The attention of the audience then turned to the Reverend William (Bill) Ivens, who introduced a second resolution, this one about the liberation of political prisoners. Ivens was the recently-appointed editor of the *Western Labor News*, the Winnipeg Trades and Labor Council's weekly newspaper. Born in Batford in Warwickshire, he had come to Winnipeg in 1896 and worked as a gardener. He had also attended the University of Manitoba as a Methodist ministerial candidate and become pastor of McDougal Methodist Church. One of a number of ministers affiliated with the Methodists with social gospel leanings, Ivens believed that Christianity was a social religion through which men and women found meaning for their lives by attempting to realize the Kingdom of God on earth. A pacifist, Ivens had fought with the Methodist Church over its support of the Canadian war effort and had been expelled from the ministry for his refusal to accept church authority. His resolution urged the Government to liberate all political prisoners now that the Armistice had been signed and any justification for their imprisonment had been removed. In his supporting speech, Ivens maintained that he was not asking for the release of criminals, but for the release of crimeless prisoners. He was particularly impassioned in his discussion of those who had conscientiously objected to war on 'religious and socialistic grounds.' He insisted there was an authority, Divine Command, higher than that of the state.

The Ivens' resolution was seconded by Frederick J. Dixon, who had earlier been such a prominent opponent of registration and conscription. Like Ivens, Dixon had been born in England and trained as a gardener, coming to Winnipeg in 1903. He was a radical social reformer and civil libertarian, but was not an exponent of socialism, which he continually criticized for its ultimate tyranny over the rights of the individual through ownership of the rights of production. In his seconding speech, Dixon characterized the true criminal of the war effort not as the individual who followed 'the dictates of own conscience', but the 'unscrupulous men who stifle the voice of their own conscience while they suck the life-blood of the nation.' He continued, 'Personally, I think those responsible for the

ROBERT BOYD RUSSELL, UNDATED.

Ross rifle, defective shells, shoddy clothes, paper boots, and the whole black record of profiteering and graft gave ten thousand times more aid and comfort to the enemy than all the Socialists and conscientious objectors put together, but the malefactors of great wealth are not sent to jail.' He complained that the nation rewarded 'its hypocritical knaves with titles and its honest men with shackles.'

R. B. Russell then took the floor to move a resolution protesting against sending further military forces to Russia and demanding that those allied troops already there be withdrawn, 'thus allowing Russia to work out her own political freedom without outside interference.' Russell was a Clydeside Scot who had come to Canada in 1911. A member of the Socialist Party of Canada, he had taken no part in opposition to the war or to conscription. The resolution he was presenting, he insisted, was 'the most important resolution confronting the audience.' It was also arguably the most controversial, since as Russell pointed out, 'there is good reason for suspicion that there is a concerted attempt to overthrow the Proletarian Republic of Russia', which he claimed was being willfully misunderstood and misrepresented in the western press. The capitalists were protecting their investments by intervening in Russia, said Russell, and he concluded by prophesying that capitalism must disappear.

Russell's resolution was seconded by Sam Blumenberg, whose sporting of a red tie was regarded as significant by the police intelligence agents in the audience. Blumenberg was a Jew, a prominent member of the Socialist Party in Winnipeg, and proprietor of a local dry-cleaning shop. He saw the Russian experiment as the first example of a proletarian dictatorship, and defended Bolsheviks from being seen as something like the 'flu', a reference to the

influenza epidemic currently spreading around the western world with the return of the troops to their homes. Insisting that distrust of Bolshevism was caused by fears that American or Canadian workers would follow the Russian example, Blumenberg added, 'Bolshevism is the only thing that will emancipate the working class. . . . There are thousands of men coming back who went over to fight. They will say, We have fought for this country and by the gods, we are going to own it.' He then called for Canadian workers to send greetings to the Russian Soviet Republic and wish them success. Chairman Queen called for three cheers for the Russian Revolution. The meeting then, according to the report in the *Western Labor News*, 'ended with deafening cries of Long live the Russian Soviet Republic! Long live Karl Liebknecht! [a radical German socialist recently killed in postwar violence] Long live the working class!' Bill Ivens would subsequently declare in the next issue of the *Western Labor News* that meetings of this sort were 'a great opportunity to blow off steam', and if held regularly, might help avert 'a bloody revolution.' Many in the Canadian government would not be so capable of seeing these gatherings in such a light, however. Nor would everyone in the local Winnipeg community.

Pleased with the Walker Theatre meeting, the Socialist Party of Canada called for a repeat performance on 10 January 1919 in the Majestic Theatre at 363 Portage. The Winnipeg Trades and Labor Council refused to co-sponsor this follow-up meeting, probably because its leadership had come to appreciate that the agenda was blatantly political. At least, so charged the socialists in a stormy meeting of the Trades and Labor Council on 23 January. One commented in the course of the heated debate, 'In Winnipeg tonight we are fighting with ideas, but we shall soon be fighting with rifles.' In any event, John Queen was replaced in the chair this day by W. Breeze, the secretary of the local Socialist Party of Canada. Speakers included Bob Russell, George Armstrong, and Sam Blumenberg, who had been prominent on the Walker Theatre platform, as well as Dick Johns, an English-born toolmaker who had come to Canada in 1912. Johns was a member of the Manitoba branch of the Social Democratic Party, which in 1917 had offered to unite with the Socialist Party of Canada on the basis of the Bolshevik programme in Russia.

Armstrong lectured his audience on 'the nature of wealth in present-day society', emphasizing that any plans for postwar reconstruction advanced by 'capitalist or semi-capitalist parties' had to be based upon the ownership and protection of private property. He called on workers to support only reconstruction schemes that would abolish the exploitation of the working class. Johns spoke critically of the reconstruction schemes of the Canadian Manufacturers' Association, and insisted that only an educated working class could avoid impending bloodshed. Russell attacked the capitalistic system and parties attempting to reconstruct it, doubting that a capitalism which could with one third of the labour force (the other two-thirds in armies and munitions work) supply the world during wartime with food and shelter could possibly deal with postwar demobilization and unemployment. According to the later testimony of one of the undercover agents attending this meeting, Russell also 'went severely after the press and pulpit and censorship and said the truth had not been told about Russia.' Russell concluded by calling for a new system in which the working class would have control. The notion of 'workers' control' would be a prominent theme in 1919, and not only among socialists. Blumenberg insisted that 'capitalist prosperity means poverty for the working class.'

This Majestic Theatre meeting concluded with an announcement of another gathering the following Sunday to 'discuss the causes of the German revolution', an uprising in postwar Germany led by radical Marxists commonly called the 'Spartacists' and at this time receiving much negative publicity in the press. The management of the theatre successfully encouraged the Socialist Party of Canada to cancel this proposed meeting, on the grounds that it had heard that such a gathering would be broken up by returned soldiers. The Party claimed that the subsequent announcement of an outdoor meeting for Market Square in downtown Winnipeg on 26 January was made without authorization by several of its members. This Market Square meeting never really got under way, because several hundred returned soldiers arrived looking for trouble and successfully broke it up. While the soldiers were aimlessly milling about, an unidentified voice called for a march against Socialist Party headquarters on Smith Street.

Demobilized soldiers had been returning to Winnipeg since before the Armistice, and their reabsorption into society, and the labour force, posed a real problem for governments in 1919.

As Bob Russell had pointed out at the Majestic Theatre, wartime economies had succeeded in supplying civilian needs with more than half the work force in the military or producing wartime goods. Many of the veterans had returned from overseas in an ugly mood, a combination of disillusionment at the seeming futility of the war, the stresses of years of suffering and the threats of injury or death in the trenches, and widespread unemployment at home. Many of the returned veterans were ready to search for scapegoats and immediately turned to enemy aliens who had worked during the war as an obvious target. They were inherently unsympathetic to critics of the war or the wartime Canadian government, most feeling that such criticisms denigrated their sacrifices. They were also prepared to employ tactics of violence (how could it have been otherwise, given their recent training and experience?). When asked a few months later how the soldiers would get their way, a veterans' leader answered, 'We will enforce democracy here in the same way we did in France.' The returned soldiers were a highly volatile and explosive force in the Winnipeg of 1919, a force not present a few months earlier when labour had 'won' its general strike.

The soldiers invaded the Socialist Party's hall opposite the Marlborough Hotel, pushed a piano out a window and onto the street, then began tossing out the window books and other literature from the Party's library. Both piano and books were then burnt in a ceremony of unofficial censorship. For several days after this Smith

Street attack, soldiers roamed the streets searching for 'aliens' to intimidate; those they found were required to perform various humiliating acts signifying their loyalty to Canada. Sam Blumenberg's shop on Portage Avenue was devastated. On 28 January, a band of veterans visited the Swift meat packing plant, which had employed many alien workers, demanding that they be fired. Mayor Charles Gray persuaded the soldiers to disperse, perhaps by hinting at the prospective establishment of the province's Alien Investigation Board, which was in the process of being formed to certify the loyalty of enemy aliens, thus placating fears of soldiers that they had lost or were losing their jobs to men and women who were neither Canadian nor loyal to Canada. But the January riots clearly demonstrated that the soldiers were a force to be reckoned with in current Winnipeg affairs, as well as suggesting the ways in which hostility to aliens could be manifested. Curiously enough, given their recent performance at Socialist headquarters in Winnipeg, many observers feared most that the veterans would become easy dupes of 'radical labour agitators' and 'Bolsheviks.'

As for those radical labour agitators, many of the ones active in western Canada found their way to Calgary in early March of 1919 for a major convention. Calgary had been recently in the news because a meeting of returned soldiers held there on 23 February had called for 'full re-establishment' to civilian conditions by the payment of a bonus of $2,000 to every Canadian soldier who had served overseas. This 'Calgary Resolution' was summarily rejected by the Borden government because of its enormous cost. The Calgary labour convention was a consequence of the disdain in which the western labour group had long regarded eastern trade unionists, mired as they still were in Gomperism. The more radical western leaders had some idea of what they wanted, although not of all its implications. A resolution for a referendum taken at the Winnipeg Trades and Labor Council on the eve of the Calgary meeting succinctly defined the question: 'Are you in favour of scientifically reorganizing the workers of Canada upon the basis of industrial organization instead of craft unionism?'

The concept of industrial unionism, which had its origins in Europe and the United States at the turn of the century, was simultaneously quite simple and very complex. In its basic form it called for the organization of one single union of all workers rather than limiting union membership to particular skills within an industry. But there were other implications as well. Virtually the only principle upon which a great variety of workers could be unified in a single union was 'working class solidarity', which in turn depended upon a view of society as divided into only two classes — the workers and the capitalists — as well as some implicit notion of the ultimate overthrow of the capitalist system by the workers. In both Europe and the United States (where the main industrial union was the International Workers of the World, the Wobblies), industrial unionism was heavily freighted with the syndicalism theory, in which unions directly and consciously employed their power, including strikes, to take over the state. In Great Britain, the source of most western Canadian thinking on the subject, industrial unionism, like socialism, was more gradualist and less comprehensive. But the rhetoric and vocabulary of industrial unionism was universal. It tended to sound syndicalistic and revolutionary.

The meeting at Calgary which began on 13 March was well covered in the press, and equally well reported to the Canadian authorities by undercover intelligence agents, some of whom would subsequently testify against the leaders of the Winnipeg Strike who had attended the convention. A full verbatim transcript of the meeting was prepared by a stenographer brought in from Fernie. This transcript, covering ten newspaper pages, was published in the Winnipeg *Tribune* on 5 April. One of the early items of business was the public unmasking of a police spy, William Gosden, alias Smith, alias Brown. Denunciations of Gosden were led by Royal North-West Mounted Police constable F. W. Zaneth, posing as Harry Blask, an American International Workers of the World leader who was a delegate at the convention. Other agents burrowed even deeper than Zaneth/Blask, however. One was known even to his superiors only as 'Agent No. 10.' Another early item of business was a motion that smoking be discontinued in the hall. It was easily defeated.

The first policy resolution, which was 'carried without a dissenting voice, amid prolonged cheers,' defined the 'aims of Labour as represented by this Convention' as 'the abolition of the present system of production for profit and the substitute therefore of production for use, and that a system of propaganda to this end be carried out.' The convention hereby called for the end to capitalism, which was to be replaced by what most contemporaries understood as 'producerism', the concept that those who actually produced the goods deserved the profits. Producerism went well back in North American reform ideology, and it would retain a long credibility. Among its ancestors was Henry George's 'single tax' proposal, among its descendants was Major C. H. Douglas's social credit scheme. Much of western populism was infused with the urge to return profits to the producer rather than have them siphoned off by the capitalist, and most farmers were in this sense 'producerists.' Indeed, the language of producerism was rampant among agrarian protest and populist reform right across western North America. Capitalism was to be replaced, but the Calgary resolution did not specify how or when. Its main suggestion for action was 'propaganda', by which men of the time meant the circulation of material designed to persuade; the term did not yet necessarily have negative connotations of falsehood and deceit.

The convention then turned to a debate over the organization of 'an Industrial Organization of all workers.' Not surprisingly, agreement on details was not easy here, and a policy committee was sent away to prepare a document. Dick Johns was Manitoba's representative on this committee. When the policy committee made its report on the morning of 15 March, the spelling out of precise organization continued to be vague at best. The committee did agree on the name of the proposed organization — 'The One Big Union.' It also recommended a steering committee to carry out a referendum, the drafting of which was to be left to it. Dick Johns was elected to the steering committee, and among the five men chosen in absentia 'to carry out the propaganda' for Manitoba were Bob Russell, W. D. Lovatt, and Andrew Scoble (who refused to have anything to do with the One Big Union).

The organizational business of the convention having been completed, the resolutions committee of the convention reported a number of resolutions, which were coupled in an omnibus fashion. The convention decided to wire Ottawa demanding the immediate release of all political prisoners and the repeal of orders-in-council, and then moved on to the resolutions. These were far more politically inflammatory than those dealing with the One Big Union, although critics would insist that they indicated the kinds of thinking that propelled the convention. Four resolutions dealt with theoretical matters. The first insisted that current parliamentary machinery was corrupted by its capitalistic nature, and expressed a preference for 'the system of Industrial Soviet Control by selecting of representatives from industries.' The next expressed accord with and sympathy for the 'aims and purposes of the Russian Bolshevik and German Spartacan Revolutions.' It added an insistence for immediate withdrawal of all Allied troops from Russia, and threatened a general strike on 1 June, should the Allies persist in their policies. The third declared 'full acceptance of the principle of "Proletariat Dictatorship" as being absolute and efficient for the transformation of capitalistic private property to communal wealth', and the fourth insisted that since the interests of all members of the working class were identical, there could be no 'alien' but the capitalist, at the same time opposing wholesale immigration of workers at the instance of the ruling class.

The meeting then turned back to labour matters. It adopted by acclamation a resolution of the Convention of the British Columbia Federation of Labour demanding a six-hour day and five-day work week by 1 June 1919. It then resolved no longer to plead for legislation to improve the lot of labour — what it described as 'the passing of legal palliatives which do not palliate' — but rather to build up 'an organization of workers on industrial lines for the purpose of enforcing, by virtue of their industrial strength, such demands as such organizations may at any time consider necessary for their continued maintenance and well-being.' One delegate from Vancouver insisted that the vote was useless. 'So far as taking the franchise off let it go so long as we line up conditions alongside the workers and fight.' The gathering concluded by condemning Samuel Gompers and calling for joint councils of soldiers and labour.

What would the intelligence community and its masters, the Dominion government, make of this performance? Those participating would subsequently insist that they were merely behaving as labour people always did. 'It was a gathering of trades unionists . . . dominated by the spirit of working class solidarity', reported *The Strikers' Own History of the Winnipeg General Strike*, written by Winnipeg strike leaders later in 1919 while awaiting trial on federal charges of seditious conspiracy and seditious libel. 'Resolutions similar in spirit and content have been passed in every part of the empire', continued this defence, but only the Canadian government took them seriously. To have employed such charged language in the context of 1919 was, if intended as mere rhetoric, fairly naive. On the other hand, according to Agent No. 10, who had infiltrated the meeting, the radical Socialists had taken

During the first World War my father was in the Reserve Army (due to his age), and worked as an engineer with the Dominion Bridge Co., which at that time was making munitions.

With so many men fighting overseas there was a shortage of trained mechanics and labourers, and the company began to employ the occasional American who came to them looking for work.

One day, one of the foremen came to my father and told him that a number of these Americans were getting together and holding secret meetings that none of the other workers were allowed to attend. The foreman was convinced that these men were members of the Industrial Workers of the World which sympathized with the Bolsheviks (who in 1917 overthrew the Russian government).

The company investigated with the help of an undercover man (Royal North-West Mounted Police?). He found that what the foreman had suspected was true. They were International Workers of the World men. Twenty-five by now had infiltrated the plant, and more were coming over the border and moving into Winnipeg industries and utilities. Remember, this was during the first World War.

My father said that the undercover man gradually won the confidence of the International Workers of the World group and was finally allowed to attend meetings. Eventually he was made their secretary.

With the end of the war the high cost of living compared to the low wages of the average workman made things ripe for the International Workers of the World to move in and stir up the labourers. Next step was the General Strike of 1919 when all the public utilities were affected. My father was called by the army and was ordered to defend the Bank of Montreal building at Portage and Main when the strikers tried to storm the bank.

Recently, I read the account in the book, The Royal Canadian Mounted Police by Nora and William Kelly, and what my father told us was confirmed in the reports.

(Mrs.) E.C. Hodgson
Winnipeg

over the conference and sought the overthrow of the existing order. They planned to use the One Big Union and a general strike to achieve their ends. These leaders — namely J. Knight, Victor Midgely, J. Kavanagh, William Pritchard, Joseph Naylor, and R. J. Johns — made public declarations of non-revolutionary intentions, reported Agent No. 10, but privately they hoped to precipitate a breakdown of civil order which they could exploit. His superior officer argued that this assessment was 'over drawn' and talk of revolution was merely 'far fetched dreams.'

Number 10's report was not forwarded to Ottawa. Instead, Number 10's superior merely sent the document to Royal North-West Mounted Police Commissioner A. B. Perry in Regina. Perry himself subsequently met with Midgeley, Pritchard, and Kavanagh sometime just after the Calgary meeting. In his report, which did go to Ottawa, he characterized these men as 'Revolutionary Socialists' who wanted extreme change but were 'opposed to force or violence.' While Perry was 'not prepared to say that they are aiming at a revolution', there was always the possibility of one if strikes led to civil disorder which extremists could exploit. He identified British Columbia, chiefly Vancouver and Victoria, as the likely trouble spots, rather than Winnipeg. The Royal North-West Mounted Police Commissioner warned against attempting to suppress these leaders, however, on the grounds that more moderate people in the labour movement took their civil liberties seriously. And he insisted that employment must be found for the returning veterans.

A harder line was taken on the question of potential revolution by the assistant comptroller of the Royal North-West Mounted Police, C. F. Hamilton, who prepared a 'Memorandum on Revolutionary Tendencies in Western Canada', which circulated widely in the corridors of power in Ottawa early in April. A former journalist and military historian, Hamilton had spent the war as deputy chief censor for Canada. He thought there was an underground organization being managed by a 'central directing body somewhere in Canada.' Hamilton had no hard evidence

for such an observation, but deduced it from the actions of the radicals over the preceding months. Their ultimate aim, of course, was the overthrow of the existing system in favour of 'Soviet Government' through the 'Dictatorship of the proletariat.' Even an armed revolution was 'conceivable under existing conditions.' Not surprisingly, acting prime minister Sir Thomas White on 16 April cabled Sir Robert Borden in France (Borden was attending the Paris Peace Conference) of cabinet concern over a possible 'revolutionary movement' in British Columbia. The dominion government's attention soon turned from British Columbia to Winnipeg, however, as another major labour confrontation began building up in that prairie city.

The Winnipeg labour movement over the spring of 1919 was feeling fairly rambunctious, partly because of the times and partly because of its 1918 successes. It insisted on distancing itself from 'legal palliatives which do not palliate', as the Calgary convention had put it in March. The Winnipeg Trades and Labor Council did not support the Manitoba government's proposed Industrial Disputes Commission (which was established in March with sweeping powers to deal with labour disputes and related matters such as the cost of living, unemployment, and excessive profit-taking). By refusing to nominate labour members to the five-man board, labour organizations rendered it useless, doubtless aggravating Premier Norris and his progressive government in the process. The Winnipeg Trades and Labor Council would also refuse to testify before the federal government's fact-finding royal commission on industrial relations in Canada being chaired by Chief Justice T. G. Mathers, on the grounds that it was appointed by a government that was a large part of the problem it was trying to investigate and rectify. It was true that by the time the Mather commissioners got to Winnipeg to hear testimony, on 10 May 1919, the city was on the verge of a general strike, not the atmosphere for fact-finding. The Winnipeg Trades and Labor Council had also rudely refused to hear a speech by the president of the Canadian Trades and Labor Congress when he came to Winnipeg in early May.

Winnipeg's new labour troubles, as might have been expected, had begun in the metal trades industry and spread to the building industry as well. The problems of the two industries were quite different. The metal trades industry needed to adjust to peacetime conditions without weapons' contracts, while the construction sector was gearing up for a building boom deferred for many years by the war. The Manitoba Fair Wage Board decided in early April to let the two opposing sides in the metal trades dispute settle matters privately, something not likely to occur. The ironmasters continued to refuse to bargain with the Metal Trades Council, the central body to which all nineteen craft unions (including railway unions) of the metal trades belonged. This issue of recognition had not been decided in 1918, but rather avoided. The employers insisted that they were not rejecting collective bargaining, but merely the Metal Trades Council's definition of it. Management was quite prepared to deal with particular craft unions, but not with an industrial umbrella organization that included 'outsiders' (the railway unions). It insisted that its understanding of collective bargaining was the commonly accepted one, and this claim was at least arguable. What the metal workers quite legitimately wanted was to move to a new form of collective bargaining, one

which had been recognized in Vancouver in 1918, albeit under wartime conditions, and was being advocated in many places in the United States. At the same time, the Metal Trades Council had in its 1918 opening offer suggested leaving the issue of Council recognition in abeyance, but had simply been ignored by the major shops. The members of the unions comprising the Metal Trades Council met at the Labour Temple on 30 April, voting unanimously to give the ironmasters one more chance

L-R: PREMIER T.C. NORRIS & R.S. THORTON, C. 5 JUNE 1919.

before beginning their strike on 2 May.

In the building trades, the Winnipeg Building Trades Council was attempting in 1919 to assert for the first time a similar industry-wide responsibility for negotiations with the Builders' Exchange. The builders themselves admitted they liked the idea of being able to settle with everybody at once, but insisted they simply could not afford the wage demands of the Building Trades Council. According to the Building Trades Council, however, union recognition had become involved in the negotiations, the Builders' Exchange threatening to withdraw it unless their wage offer of 10 cents an hour across-the-board (the union had wanted twenty) was accepted. The Building Trades Council itself acknowledged that it was an industrial union that had passed well beyond the acceptable bounds of tolerance of the international unions of its members. It warned that the internationals would not provide strike benefits. But its members went on strike anyway on 1 May, and were joined by the Metal Trades Council on 2 May.

Labour unrest in Winnipeg was hardly confined to the metal trades and building industries. All unions desperately sought wage increases, since the cost of living had inflated much more rapidly than wages during the war and especially immediately after the armistice. A number of other local unions, including the telephone operators and the policemen's union, had managed to settle with employers in April. Many others had not, and even those who had reached accords were not entirely happy. The street railway employees were one large union that had not been able to agree to a new contract, voting 912 to 79 to strike, although they agreed to conciliation under the Industrial Disputes Investigation Act of the province of Manitoba.

By the time the Winnipeg Trades and Labor Council met on 6 May on the second floor of the Labour Temple, the city's labour movement was feeling quite confrontational. The delegates became excited when word arrived that a striking metal worker had been arrested, and tension mounted while a committee sought after him. It finally returned with the striker in tow. The general strike was

LABOUR TEMPLE, JAMES AVENUE, c.1904.

then discussed. An impassioned speech by Bob Russell fired the delegates even more. 'Winnipeg must stand firm', insisted Russell, 'for the sake of labour elsewhere.' Others advised caution, but nobody this day wanted to listen. The delegates voted to distribute general strike ballots to every Winnipeg local, with the results to be returned before a special meeting on 13 May. A simple majority of all union members would be sufficient. The ballot sent out included a second question, on the One Big Union, as well as the strike vote. This coupling of the two issues was probably a mistake.

Although the threat of a general strike was duly publicized in the local newspapers, it somehow got buried in other news, such as the impending homecoming of the 16th battalion, the Canadian Scottish, which had arrived in Montreal aboard *The Empress of Britain*. The developing story many Winnipeggers probably most closely followed during the period between 6 May and 13 May, however, was not the strike but the growing confrontation between returning soldiers and the enemy aliens. This tale arguably began on 1 May when an eastern Member of Parliament alleged in the Commons that the Manitoba government was exempting enemy aliens from deportation. The next day, the Great War Veterans began proceedings as common nuisances in County Court against those aliens labelled by the Alien Investigation Board as 'undesirable citizens', demanding their deportation and the confiscation of all but $75 of their property for the benefit of soldiers' orphans and widows. The prosecutions had been suggested by Premier Norris in a meeting with veterans,

since he claimed the Alien Investigation Board had no authority to deport without due cause. A few days later, veterans were reported to be tracking down a newspaper called *The Socialist Bulletin*, which allegedly had been spreading Bolshevik and 'red socialist' propaganda.

On Saturday 10 May at 3:00 p.m. in Market Square, a mass meeting of returned soldiers was held to 'discuss the alien question', the precursor of many such soldier meetings which would be held in the ensuing weeks. The gathering was not under the auspices of any of the veterans' associations, although surviving photographs indicate that a very large crowd was present. This meeting drew up resolutions demanding that the provincial government take steps within 7 days for interning and deporting aliens, or resign and appeal to the people for power to deport them. The speakers charged Lieutenant-Governor James Aikins with employing alien labour as household servants, and issued thinly-veiled threats of the use of force if necessary. The *Tribune*, which was most active in promoting the alien question, subsequently on 13 May reported a dominion-wide veterans' campaign against radical bolshevik newspapers which it was claimed the soldiers held responsible for industrial unrest and upheaval. Here was the one linkup of the impending strike, the returned soldier, and the enemy alien that was being developed in the press, and it was obviously a tenuous one at best.

Not until 12 May did the local authorities take any serious action to head off a general walkout. On that date Mayor Charles Gray called an emergency conference on the strike in the Builders' Exchange offices. The conference was attended by Premier Norris. Talk of last-minute negotiations by the politicians were just that. Nobody could be found interested in negotiating. The ironmasters firmly refused to deal with the metal trades council, and this point was regarded by the labour side as the critical question to be determined by strike action. Although the authorities and the media were a bit slow off the mark, the people of Winnipeg, especially the women, were better prepared. Stores had been quickly emptied of flour, potatoes, carrots, and other staples.

The final strike vote was announced at the Winnipeg Trades and Labor Council meeting of 13 May. 'Never before in the history of Winnipeg has there been such a Trades Council session', wrote the *Western Labor News*. 'It was tense, electric and determined, yet seized with a wonderful gravity. Every inch was jammed with a seething mass of trades unionists, men and women.' Ernest Robinson rose to announce the results of the referendum. Returns were incomplete, but over 11,000 had voted in favour and only 500 against. The meeting 'unanimously and enthusiastically' voted to begin the strike at 11:00 a.m. on Thursday 15 May. Ernest Robinson, secretary of the Winnipeg Trades and Labor Council, issued a press statement: 'Every organization but one has voted in favour of the general strike, and the biggest strike in the history of Winnipeg will take place as above stated [on Thursday 15 May, at 11:00 a.m.]. No exceptions are anticipated in this strike. All public utilities will be tied up in order to enforce the principle of collective bargaining.' Robinson's statement about total tie-ups and no exceptions proved a slight exaggeration. Although the Winnipeg police had voted 149 to 11 for the strike, they were almost immediately requested by the strike committee to remain on duty, so that the city would not be placed under martial law. Further exceptions would soon follow. The strike did have a specific goal, the recognition of 'collective bargaining' in the construction and metal industries. There is no evidence that the announcement of a limited time-span — a procedure advocated by moderates in Seattle to ward off fears of revolution — was ever considered in Winnipeg.

LOOKING WEST DOWN BROADWAY AVENUE FROM MAIN STREET DURING THE WINNIPEG GENERAL STRIKE, 1919.

The 14th of May was a busy day. Helen Armstrong announced that more than 500 bakery and confectionery workers, most of them women, had failed to show up at work and were now on strike. The remainder would join the general walkout on 15 May. The wife of George Armstrong, Helen, was a major labour figure in her own right, head of the local chapter of the Women's Labor League and often referred to as the 'business manager for the Women's Unions.' The Young Women's Christian Association offered to provide emergency accommodation during the strike for women with long distances to travel. The Winnipeg *Tribune* reported that railway workers were threatening to refuse to handle trains carrying scab labour from outside the city, especially for T. Eaton & Company (which the newspaper also noted intended to remain open during the strike). The 1918 Committee of One Hundred called a public meeting, out of which emerged the Citizens' Committee of One Thousand. Less publicly visible than its 1918 equivalent, the Committee of One Thousand never produced a complete membership list. Its first step toward meeting the emergency was the formation of a volunteer fire brigade to man the pumps.

Ominously for the strikers, Brigadier-general H.D.B. Ketchen, military commandant of district 10 (which included Winnipeg), telegraphed the secretary of the military council in Ottawa. Ketchen informed the government that he had been notified by Mayor Gray of an intention to ask military authorities to protect property in the event of a

L-R: SIR J.A.M. AIKINS & GENERAL H.B.D. KETCHEN, 1926.

LT. COL. H.B.D. KETCHEN, C.1915.

strike. Perhaps equally ominously, hospital authorities at Winnipeg General Hospital requested of the strike committee, and were granted, a special dispensation to keep essential services at the hospital in operation. Further concessions would be made by the strike committee over the next few days. These concessions would lead to much criticism from the opponents of the strikers.

On Thursday 15 May 1919, the first workers off the job were the telephone operators, who punched off work at 7:00 a.m. and were not replaced. But most workers observed the 11:00 a.m. time punctiliously. Almost in orchestration the trams ceased running, the post office shut down, restaurants were abandoned by their employees, even the elevators stopped. Somewhere between 25,000 and 30,000 workers in both the public and private sectors walked off their jobs. As one of the Winnipeg strike's pioneer historians, Donald C. Masters, put it: 'This meant for Winnipeg in general no mail, street-cars, taxis, newspapers, telegrams, telephones, janitor service, elevators, barbers, or express, freight or baggage service. For a time it meant no gasoline, milk, or bread, very little meat, and much reduced restaurant service.' In addition, other basic services such as water and fire-fighting were hardly certainties. The waterworks employees remained at work courtesy of the strike committee and produced a reduced pressure. An offer from the firemen to supply emergency services when life was threatened was ignored by the city council.

On Thursday evening a meeting was called by the executives of the major veterans' organizations for Convention Hall of the Board of Trade Building. It was attended by three thousand returned soldiers. According to the *Western Labor News* the meeting passed a resolution of sympathy with the strike, calling for labour and the returned soldier to get together after the strike to 'discuss the deportation of the enemy alien.' The Great War Veterans' Association would subsequently deny that its membership had done anything more than endorse the principles of collective bargaining. According to other reports, the meeting defeated a lengthy executive resolution which in its preamble talked sympathetically about labour but evinced unhappiness at the 'spreading propaganda of the most virulent and disloyal type with the avowed object of causing unrest and instigating a revolution', arguing the soldiers had fought to maintain 'the ideals of true democracy, British justice and fair play, all of which are now threatened by revolutionary doctrines and propaganda mentioned as well as by the undesirables, enemy aliens and others, permitted to remain at large in our midst and in many cases to debase the labor unions and obtain the employment to which we are justly entitled.' This resolution wanted the soldiers to endorse strict neutrality and place themselves at the disposal of the agents of law and order. The failure of the opponents of the strike to win over the soldiers at the outset was an important victory for labour, and the first day of the strike ended with many pro-labour Winnipeggers in a distinctly holiday mood. Meanwhile, in Ottawa, instructions were issued for a squadron of Royal North-West Mounted Police returning from service in Russia to be demobilized in Winnipeg. The federal government had begun to reinforce its military position in the city.

WINNIPEG GENERAL HOSPITAL FROM ALEXANDRA PARK, C. 1920.

The first two-plus weeks, from 15 May to 30 May, constituted a distinct period of the Winnipeg General Strike, one of experimentation and improvisation on all sides. The strikers had not worked out all the implications of the strategy they were employing, and the prospective opponents of the strike, both the various levels of government and the Citizens' Committee of One Thousand, were simultaneously hardening their opposition and inventing their responses as events developed. There was a definite sense of fluidity to the developments of this period, which was also marked by a relatively low level of mass involvement and activity. The appearance of the first mass march and assembly of soldiers on 31 May came right at the point where the city's regular police force was in process of being locked out, and a few days before the strike committee on 4 June decided to 'turn up the heat' by withdrawing many services previously permitted.

By noon on 16 May, the stereotypers and webb pressmen had joined the strike. This meant that there would be no regular daily newspapers for five days. In their place the strikers began publishing their own newspaper, and were quickly answered with one brought out by the Citizens' Committee of One Thousand. William Ivens, the editor of the strikers' newspaper, insisted in the second special strike edition that since the dailies continually misrepresented the workers, it was 'a case of simple justice to muzzle for a few days the enemies of freedom and truth.' This was at best another illustration of Ivens' tendency to overstatement, and neither the action he was defending nor the defence itself made very much sense. The strikers did not need to be labelled as opponents of freedom of the press, and careful readers would note a new virulence to the strike in the dailies, especially the *Free Press*, when they reappeared. In Regina, a

PERMITTED BY

AUTHORITY OF

STRIKE COMMITTEE

Chapter 3

FROM 16 MAY TO 30 MAY

1919 STRIKE

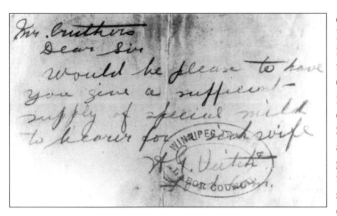

'PERMISSION LETTER' ISSUED
DURING STRIKE.

detachment of twenty Royal North-West Mounted Police were instructed to leave for Winnipeg on the earliest train possible. The Commissioner A. B. Perry, in informing the Winnipeg Mounted Police commander Colonel Cortlandt Starnes of these reinforcements, also advised Starnes that the federal government would be amending the laws regarding treason and seditious libel, and would be exercising the power to deport undesirable aliens whether naturalized or not. Revisions to the Immigration Act had been in preparation in Ottawa for some time, and were not a particular response to the Winnipeg situation. They were intended to deal with the perception of many in the federal government, however, that most radicalism in Canada was being generated by people who were not of either Canadian or British origin.

The first issue of the strikers' own newspaper, the *Strike Bulletin* of the *Western Labor News* appeared on the streets on Saturday 17 May. Editor William Ivens attempted to explain 'WHY SOME INDUSTRIES ARE RUNNING.' He wrote:

Theatres and Picture Shows are running under strike permit so that the worker can keep off the streets. Milk and bread concerns are running under permits to feed the people. Hospitals are given permits so that the sick may not suffer. Water is kept at low pressure rather than cut off so that the workers shall be able to get it. Light is supplied for the same reason. The police were ordered to stay on the job so that there should be no excuse for martial law. So it is with all the industries that work under permit of the Strike Committee. They are supplying the prime necessities of life to the workers so that the fight may be carried on until it is won. All these concerns are organized fully, and could be stopped at a minute's notice, but for the present the Strike Committee believes that it is better to let them run; hence its order for them to stay on the job under permit.

This explanation would do nothing to assuage the conviction of both the authorities and the non-striking middle classes that the strikers intended a revolution. Indeed, in its assumption of the power to 'permit' whatever activities it saw fit, the Strike Committee only evoked a paroxysm of hostility from many in the city. Methodist missionary John MacLean wrote in his diary on this day, 'The labour men have the upper hand, and so far as they can are showing Bolshevik methods.' He added, 'Mounted Police have come to the city, several thousand men are drilling and in readiness for any riots.' MacLean's mention of the Mounted Police was a reference to the arrival of the detachment from Regina. As for men drilling, there were thousands of men still in uniform being barracked in Winnipeg, many at the Fort Osborne barracks to the immediate north of the legislative building, and their officers had them out in preparation for any call to service.

The Strike Committee was of necessity playing things pretty much by ear. It must be remembered that nobody in Canada had any experience at operating a general strike as big as the one in Winnipeg. The whole business of what to do about essential services, which were as necessary to the workers as to the non-strikers, is an excellent illustration of the unforeseen difficulties of administering a total shutdown of the city, and a total shutdown was what was aimed for. It is probably true that the Strike Committee, as its members always claimed, had no intention to overthrow duly established government by violent means. There is much evidence that the Strike

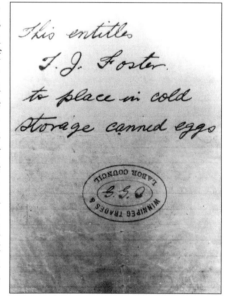

Committee did its utmost, with considerable success, to avoid and prevent violence. At the same time, this was an unprecedented situation, and the strike's leaders certainly all believed in the need for extreme social and economic change, particularly the elimination of capitalism. What the Strike Committee seemed to be feeling its way toward through this general strike was a way of achieving ultimate revolutionary ends, outside the normal political channels, through non-violent and non-syndicalistic means. Whether or not the Metal Trades Council and its demands were modelled along industrial lines is only part of the picture, and to define 'the strike' in terms solely of the metal workers (or construction workers) who began it is essentially a very narrow approach. The remainder of the picture was the general strike, sympathetic or otherwise.

In short, the strike leaders hoped to introduce into Canada a new conception of industrial unionism, not so much through the collective bargaining definitions of the Metal Trades Council as through the general strike tactics of the Strike Committee. As Ernest Robinson, secretary of the Winnipeg Trades and Labor Council, explained to a strikers' meeting on 18 May, 'We have withdrawn labour from all industry, and it will stay withdrawn until the bosses realize that they cannot stand against the masses of labour. If we can control industrial production now, at this time, we can control it for all time to come, and we can control the Government of this country too.' And so they could, were they to be successful. The overall concept owed far less to the Russian Revolution than to the British labour movement, adapted to suit Canadian conditions. But if the strike was not revolutionary in a Russian or Bolshevik sense, if it eschewed violence, it was nevertheless potentially quite transformational. The strikers' history of the Seattle strike well captured this distinction, insisting, 'If by revolution is meant violence, forcible taking over of property, the killing or maiming of men, surely no group of workers dreamed of such action. But if by revolution is meant that a Great Change is coming over the face of the world, which will transform our method of carrying on industry then we do believe in such a Great Change and

that our General Strike was one very definite step towards it.' In mounting an opposition, government authorities and private citizens were not overreacting to the possible danger that the Winnipeg strike represented to the status quo and to their interests. But if the strikers were not violent revolutionaries, neither were their adversaries necessarily conspiratorially agreed on a strategy of opposition, as the strikers often suggested and later historians have implied.

The strike opposition was itself playing things by ear. Both the authorities and the middle classes well understood the potential threat, but there was at the beginning little concerted orchestration of opposition, either among the three levels of government or between those levels and private bodies like the Citizens' Committee of One Thousand. Initially, the government's chief concern was with violence — something the Strike Committee was doing its best to avoid. On 19 May Brigadier-General Ketchen wired military headquarters at Ottawa, 'At the request of the mayor and on his written statement that he anticipated disturbances beyond the

> *Somehow I missed the happenings outside the City Hall the day of the trouble because I was walking around town or in Eaton's. I found out later that the people I boarded with on Simcoe Street had phoned hospitals for news of me. Of course, they got no report. I had finished the afternoon in the quiet of Wardlaw Avenue. In April 1919 I was delivering groceries at the P & B Store (Patterson & Black), at the corner of Portage Avenue and Toronto Street with a horse and wagon. There were, I think, about eight stores around town. A movement was made to join the Teamsters' Union, Local 119, so that is what we did. The result of our activities was that P & B quit delivering and we had no job. We took the horses to the farm at Headingley on the south side of the river, crossing by ferry as there was no bridge there then.*
>
> *I was sent by the Union to picket at Spiers, Parnell Bakery on Elgin Avenue. While outside, Mr Parnell came along and asked what I was doing there. He told be I should be at school. I told him I had to work for a living. Later on I got a job on the route in Crescentwood. I remember there was a wooden club under the seat which had been supplied by the Citizens' Committee. Not for me. When the strike was on, the bread wagons and the milk wagons were supplied with a sign saying deliveries were being made 'Courtesy or permission of the Strike Committee.' This bothered a lot of people, but on the whole my thinking is that things went pretty quiet considering the times.*
>
> *A. E. Sturney*
> *Winnipeg*

powers of civil authorities to deal with, a percentage of the active militia has been called out.' Eleven battalions were involved. On that same day, the first issue of the *Winnipeg Citizen*, the newspaper of the Citizens' Committee of One Thousand, appeared on the streets. Both Mayor Gray and Premier Norris were extremely unhappy with the famous (or infamous) placards issued by the Strike Committee that made possible deliveries of essential goods like bread, milk and ice, as well as the continuation of some services such as the movie theatres, in the early days of the strike. The provincial government ordered theatre owners to remove signs that read 'by authority of the strike committee' on threat of licence cancellation, and Gray complained that the placards suggested to the outside world that the Strike Committee had usurped the authority of the city government. As indeed it had. In some areas, such as the telegraph, management refused to accept offers from the strikers to continue emergency service, presumably because of unwillingness to surrender power to the Strike Committee. The Citizens' Committee of One Thousand insisted that the placards were 'probably the first official act of what the Citizens of Winnipeg now recognize was not an industrial strike but an attempt at Soviet Government, a challenge to constituted authority.'

Fears of violence were natural and endemic in the sort of unprecedented situation that prevailed in Winnipeg at this time. Thousands of workers were on strike, which meant that normal activity in the city had been cut off and curtailed. With the daily newspapers not being printed (and with radio in its infancy) there was virtually no way of assuring the general public that the social fabric had not indeed broken down into a Hobbesian war of all against all. John MacLean entered in his diary on 20 May, 'We are under the sway of Bolshevism in the city. Everything is quiet, but there are some ugly rumours floating around, and the Home Defence Guards are all ready for action at a given signal. In his unpublished autobiography, J. W. Wilton referred to this home guard as 'rather corpulent gentlemen handling rifles as if they were sticks of dynamite.' As indeed the rifles were. Fortunately no one was killed by one. Mayor Charles Gray tried to be reassuring. He told a delegation of large property owners who waited upon him with pleas for action: 'Law and order have been maintained. Law and order will be maintained at all costs. If any radical element attempts to interfere with enforcement of law and order, we are prepared to smash it immediately. The mayor is directing affairs from his office in the City Hall, and the British flag is flying over the building.'

The Citizens' Committee of One Thousand operated in these early days on several fronts. Its principal efforts appear to have been devoted to providing volunteers to keep some essential services open. In this sense it was merely acting out in a more politicized context the sort of volunteer activities that had always been, and still are, characteristic of the Winnipeg middle classes. The Committee provided volunteers to man the fire department as it had in 1918. But simply providing firemen was not enough. The reduced water pressure being produced under orders of the Strike Committee was inadequate to reach above the second floor of buildings or to fight almost any serious fire. The Citizens' Committee therefore took over the pressure pumps, as well as the auxiliary steam

WOMEN VOLUNTEERS AT GAS STATION DURING WINNIPEG GENERAL STRIKE, MAY 1919.

MEMBERS OF THE CITIZENS' COMMITTEE AT A BANQUET AFTER THE STRIKE, 1919.

plant necessary to generate the electric power to run them. Volunteer staff worked these facilities in eight-hour shifts. Moreover, the volunteer firemen could be exhausted by false alarms rung by strikers or pranksters, and so a patrol organization was formed to guard more than 350 fire alarm boxes, as well as to walk the city streets at night. The Citizens' Committee also provided volunteers (mainly female) to pump gasoline at service stations and eventually to keep the telephone lines open with the outside world.

On another level, individual members of the Citizens' Committee lobbied with government leaders for action to end the strike. It is not at all clear whether they did so with any authorization, since the Citizens' Committee maintained no formal records and kept its deliberations shrouded in secrecy throughout the crisis. One of the many curious questions remaining about the strike is the one about the reasons for all the furtiveness by the Citizens' Committee. Presumably the executive committee of the Citizens' Committee directed its activities, but to what extent and how is not clear. On 21 May, for example, a delegation of lawyers headed by Arthur J. Andrews met acting Dominion Minister of Justice Arthur Meighen and Labour Minister Gideon Robertson in a railway car outside Thunder Bay. The Winnipeggers told the federal ministers that the strike was a revolution and that strong action was necessary. Most histories of the strike have always described this meeting as one between the Dominion government and the Citizens' Committee of One Thousand. But there is little contemporary evidence about this event, and it is quite likely that the Winnipeg delegation, while all

ARTHUR G. MEIGHEN, C. 1920.

members of the Citizens' Committee, were acting on their own behalf. Those few acknowledged members of the Citizens' Committee certainly subsequently denied any involvement in the labour question. J. E. Botterell would later testify in the preliminary hearing of William Ivens, 'We did not take any part between employer and employee.' When Messrs Sweatman and Andrews participated in Mayor Gray's special Round Table Conference on 23 May, they did so 'acting for themselves' rather than as representatives of the Citizens' Committee, although their preemptory attitude might have suggested that they had been empowered by somebody.

The discussion, or rather non-discussion, at the Round Table Conference called by Mayor Gray for 23 May plainly exposed the extent of the conceptual gulf between the strikers and their opponents. Meeting on Friday evening, the gathering consisted of: His Worship in the chair; two pro-labour aldermen (Fisher and Simpson); Messrs Winning and Russell of the Strike Committee; Messrs Carroll and English of the Running Trades railway unions; D. J. Scott; R. B. Graham, Crown Prosecutor for the eastern judicial district; and Messrs Andrews and Sweatman. Andrews insisted that the strike had gone well beyond the issue of collective bargaining. There could be no negotiations, he insisted, until postal workers, firemen, waterworks employees and telephone operators were back at work. Were that yielded, the principle of collective bargaining could be recognized. Bob Russell asked for assurances on this point, and Andrews quite legitimately responded that none could be given.

The two strike leaders insisted that they were not try-

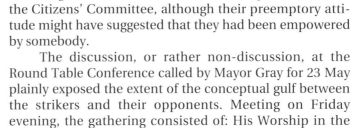
VOLUNTEER FIREMEN POSE WITH ONE OF THE CITY OF WINNIPEG FIRE DEPARTMENT TRUCKS DURING THE WINNIPEG GENERAL STRIKE OF 1919.

ing to overthrow the government, and were acting within the Anglo-Canadian constitution. Said James Winning, 'Give us a guarantee that collective bargaining will be recognized and we will all be back at work in 48 hours.' A. J. Andrews might have responded by asking whose definition of collective bargaining would have to be recognized. Instead, he answered, 'We say you've done a wrong. You now have a chance to retire gracefully. If you do not do this, we will line up against you the Dominion, Provincial, and Civic Governments', adding, 'If your attitude is that the causes must be removed, we shall have to wait for the millennium.' Moreover, he said, 'the provincial government could pass legislation guaranteeing the right of collective bargaining, while the dominion one could make it a crime for unions to violate agreements.' R. B. Russell brought up a resolution passed by the Strike Committee on 21 May favouring legislation making recognition of collective bargaining compulsory on all employers. Andrews insisted, 'I will not negotiate until the men on the public utilities are back. I will not bargain.' Thus labour continued to insist that both its means and ends were legitimate, while the opposition refused to negotiate under duress. Labour was indeed trying to introduce one innovation (industry-wide collective bargaining) through the coercion of another innovation (the general strike).

WINNIPEG BOARD OF TRADE BUILDING WHICH WAS THE HEAD-QUARTERS OF THE CITIZENS' COMMITTEE, JUNE 1919.

Mr Carroll of the railway unions observed that Andrews' position itself constituted a threat, resolving itself 'into a question of who should yield first. The employers must yield some. Our employers frequently yield points. Why can't the Ironmen do the same?' Andrews shot back, 'This is not a case between employers and employees.' And indeed, the problem with the general strike (sympathetic or syndicalistic) has always been that it holds uninvolved third parties hostage to an industrial dispute, thus changing the nature and dynamic of that initial disagreement. It was presumably the damage done innocent third parties that allowed Sweatman and Andrews (on their behalf) to participate in the discussion in the first place. Not surprisingly, the committee rose at midnight with nothing settled.

In its edition dated 23 May, the *Toronto Star* saw the strike as a legitimate labour action over wages and collective bargaining, rather than Bolshevism. 'There is no soviet. There is little or no terrorism', wrote the *Star*. Thanks to volunteers from the Citizens' Committee, Winnipeggers no longer had to get their daily news — and views — from Toronto, however. The *Manitoba Free Press*, which had resumed publication under a management staff, was once again being sold on the streets, and the other dailies would soon follow. Not surprisingly, the Winnipeg newspapers after their reappearance had a new virulence to their hostility to the strike. The Reverend John MacLean reported in his diary, 'The *Free Press* has installed a wireless on the roof of its building so now we are all right, and the strike is practically broken, as the working folks have no money and they are sick of the strike.' Acting prime minister Sir Thomas White assured the House of Commons that the militia units 'are completely filled up with volunteers, with plenty of reserves available in case of trouble. In addition to that, the Royal North-West Mounted Police are on duty in Winnipeg.'

The rhetorical war continued unabated in the city. On the same day as the Round Table Conference, the Metal Trades industry released a statement in the *Winnipeg Citizen* (the Committee of One Thousand's free newspaper) that 'We want you to know that we recognized the principle of "collective bargaining" with our employees long before this strike was declared.' On the other hand, the special strike edition of the *Western Labor News* reprinted a letter from L. R. Barrett, general manager of Vulcan Iron Works, to his employees. This letter declared that Vulcan ran an open shop, but would meet with any employees who had a grievance. The *WLN* also declared in this issue, 'The fight is on. It overthrew the government in Russia, Austria, Germany, etc. It has compelled drastic innovations in Britain. Now it has Winnipeg in its grip.' Bill Ivens was certainly correct about the increasingly combative nature of the conflict. Brigadier-General F. W. Hill, who had been ordered to Montreal to report on the Winnipeg situation, was advised that on the 24th at 3:30 a.m. he could pick up eight Lewis guns at the Turcotte Yards in Montreal. The guns would be packed in ordinary packing boxes and marked 'regimental baggage, 27th Battalion.' They were to be placed on the first train carrying the 27th to Winnipeg and delivered upon arrival to General Ketchen. The message added, 'An officer will deliver twelve Lewis guns similar packed and addressed at Smiths Falls on arrival of the first train. It is desired that these guns reach Winnipeg without anyone being the wiser.'

On 24 May the Canadian ministers, Meighen and Robertson, issued a statement in Winnipeg outlining their views on the strike. The two saw the strike as 'a cloak for something far deeper, an effort to "overturn" the proper authority.' They added, 'there was absolutely no justification for the strike.' Labour was particularly disappointed in Senator Robertson's position, since he had not only been particularly supportive of the labour side in the 1918 strike, but in the Vancouver shipyards dispute of that year had encouraged the sort of collective bargaining by an industrial council that the Metal Trades wished to extend to Winnipeg. Labour found at least part of the explanation for the *volte face* in the conferences that members of the Citizens' Committee of One Thousand had with the ministers outside Thunder Bay. According to *The Strikers' Own History*, the 'minds of these two ministers[,] already poisoned by the highly coloured reports from the West, were well prepared for the reception of the plausible stories poured into their ears by the spokesmen of reaction. . . .' The two ministers had been in town since 21 May. They

had met with various parties opposing the strike, but had refused to speak formally to the Strike Committee and thus never held any discussions whatever with the strikers. On 23 May the government had informed the striking postal workers to return to work by noon on 26 May or face dismissal, and the post office was authorized to use volunteer labour provided by the Citizens' Committee of One Thousand to get the mail moving.

On the same day as the ministerial pronouncements, a women's dining room organized by Helen Armstrong of the Women's Labor League was opened at the Strathcona Hotel. The initiative was designed to provide free meals for women strikers, of whom there were several thousand in the city. The kitchen would serve between 1,200 and 1,500 free meals daily. Despite the large number of female strikers and volunteer replacements, the role of women in the strike received very little attention in the contemporary press. There were at least two women on the large Strike Committee of the Winnipeg Trades and Labor Council, and perhaps others (as in 1918) on the Citizens' Committee of One Thousand. The public part played by women was far better documented, however, than was the quietly supportive nature of most of their activities in keeping families fed and together during extremely difficult times. One of the few glimpses into the home and family life of a 1919 striker is provided by James Gray in his autobiographical *A Boy from Winnipeg*. Gray's father was a municipal worker out in sympathy with the metal trades and construction workers. His mother did not approve of the strike, however, since she was totally unable to understand why a low-paid worker like Harry Gray should be sacrificing his family's income in sympathetic support of highly-paid skilled workers in the metal trades and construction industries. Gray's portrait must be set against James Winning's contemporary characterization of supportive mothers, who 'went to the corner store and returned without milk, and have gone home and said, "Stay with it John. The women will do without milk and we will make some shift for the kiddies, but you must win."'

On Sunday 25 May, Senator Robertson called a meeting of postal employees at the post office. The main reason Robertson was in Winnipeg was because of the postal problems. Unlike most other services being disrupted by the sympathetic strike, the post office was a federal responsibility. Few postal workers showed up to hear Robertson. Most were diverted by the Strike Committee to the Labour Temple to discuss the government's ultimatum, which was a harsh one. Not only did the posties have to return to work by 10:00 a.m. on Monday 26 May, but they also had to sign an agreement never to take part again in a sympathetic strike and to sever their connection with the Winnipeg Trades and Labor Council. If they failed to return, they would be discharged, losing their rights to pension and forfeiting any rights of employment by the Dominion. This ultimatum was so unconciliatory that it could only have been intended to provoke the strikers. Robertson telegraphed Ottawa that he could not make a

declaration in favour of the principle of collective bargaining 'as it would be grasped at as an excuse by strikers to claim they have forced the government and thereby provoked success of sympathetic strike.'

On Sunday evening, 25 May, a Labour Church meeting was held at Victoria Park, one of the first of many gatherings (mainly pro-strike) to be assembled in that facility two blocks from City Hall over the ensuing weeks. For the first week or more of the strike, most Winnipeggers had accepted the instructions of the Strike Committee to stay at home and avoid trouble. But the weather was warm, and people soon looked for excuses to get out. They apparently viewed such meetings as outings, and in photographs of the time they were dressed, as they usually were when they visited parks or the zoo, in their formal best. It was claimed that 5,000 people were present at this Labour Church gathering. The Labour Church had been organized in late June 1918 by William Ivens as 'an independent and creedless Church based on the Fatherhood of God and the Brotherhood of Man.' Its platform was open, and instead of sermons, those attending heard discussions of the fundamental problems of the day. On this Sunday evening, F. J. Dixon, Laurence Pickup (from the postal workers), and Bill Ivens spoke to the enormous crowd. Ivens concluded by calling out, 'The Citizens' Committee say you must call off the sympathetic strikes. What is your answer?' With one voice the crowd responded, 'No!' At 5:00 on Monday morning, 26 May, only a few hours after the end of the Labour Church meeting, Helen Armstrong began her campaign against smaller stores in the city where women were still working. The *Tribune* complained, 'employees going into the business places are accosted and efforts are made to persuade them to join the general strike.' Only sixteen postal workers showed up for work on Monday morning. The three levels of government (federal, provincial, and municipal) all began issuing ultimatums to their striking employees at the same time that they began recruiting replacements. The *Citizen* advertised for volunteers to resume the telephone services. At an impromptu press conference before the City Council meeting in the evening,

CROWDS AT VICTORIA PARK DURING WINNIPEG GENERAL STRIKE, 1919.

Mayor Gray told reporters that he could no longer remain neutral in the strike, for he believed that the strikers were wrong. Gray thus effectively disqualified himself from any further attempts as a mediator.

The federal government initiated a new tactic of opposition on 26 May. Arthur Meighen wrote A. J. Andrews that the goals of the strike leaders were 'of a most sinister character and far different from those that the ordinary sympathetic striker has in view.' He thereupon appointed Andrews as special representative of the Justice Department in Winnipeg, assigned to examine evidence against the leadership of the strike to ascertain 'whether or not the activities of these men is of a seditious or treasonable character and to advise as to what should be done.' For his part, Labour Minister Robertson declared, 'the kind of collective bargaining through centralized control like trade councils or like the One Big Union demanded by the Trades Council is utterly unjustified.' General Ketchen was able to report the arrival of the 27th battalion and the Lewis guns 'in serviceable condition.' According to John MacLean's diary, 'There is a battalion for every district of the city, soldiers are sleeping at Post Office and public buildings, and military ready for anything at a given signal.' As MacLean suggested, the city had taken on more than a bit of the appearance of an armed camp, with thousands of soldiers and militia standing about waiting for something to happen. Actual incidents of violence were still almost non-existent, however.

A. J. Andrews, the Department of Justice representative, looked over the Royal North-West Mounted Police files on 'Bolsheviks and Agitators' on 27 May with a view to seeing whether prosecutions could be started. The files of a number of strike leaders who had come to government attention during and after the war were doubtless examined, but Andrews decided that convictions could not be

A.J. ANDREWS, C.1899.

obtained on charges of sedition, and that 'the publicity and stir resulting from a trial would do more harm than good.' While Andrews was combing the Mounted Police files, Gideon Robertson wrote his deputy minister in Ottawa that the 'motive behind this strike undoubtedly was the overthrow of constitutional government.' The Winnipeg *Telegram* began running advertisements for 'Telephone Operators and Experienced Telephone Men', listing a new schedule of wages higher than the old one. In Ottawa, Prime Minister Robert Borden told the Commons that 'the government has taken no sides' in the Winnipeg strike. But, he added, 'if the needs of the people as a whole are to be regarded we cannot have in this country a complete dislocation of public services founded upon such reasons as have been put forward by the postal employees of Winnipeg.'

The federal government got the post office working. The province's major responsibility was the telephones. By 28 May, George Watson of Manitoba Telephones had the provincial system back up and running. He now had more than 600 women and girls operating telephone exchanges. 'We will not use strike breakers', he was reported as saying. 'We are giving permanent employment to young women who show aptitude for this work.' But many of the new 'Hello Girls' were temporary volunteers. Telephone workers operated under considerable tension at the best of times, and the new replacements found the work very difficult, partly because of petty harassment by those sympathetic to the strike. According to a later story in the Winnipeg *Tribune*, 'This is the way it usually happens. "Are you a volunteer?" he coos disarmingly. "Yes", the unsuspecting phone girl responds. "Well, I don't care to talk to a ------- scab", the man responds. "Suit yourself", the girl says and unscrews the little electric globe which registers a call from that line and puts in a small piece of cork.' Nearly 600 cheques would eventually be sent 'as a mark of appreciation for the service which the volunteers have rendered during the strike'.

For its part, the municipal government concentrated on the police force. Notice was given officially to members of the Winnipeg Police on 29 May that they would be required on threat of dismissal to sign a contract eschewing sympathy strikes and revoking membership in any association affiliated with an authority beyond that of the municipal government. Some opponents of the strike were persuaded that the police were entirely too sympathetic to the strikers. The *Tribune* on the eve of the strike had carried a story in which Police Chief Donald McPherson had praised the metal workers for their decorum. He had declared, 'The men have been out two weeks and we have yet to receive a complaint from an employer of an interference.' General Ketchen insisted the police were 'hand in hand with the strikers.' But there was no concerted opposition campaign against the policemen. Indeed, Arthur J. Andrews wrote Arthur Meighen that the city's ultimatum to the police was ill-conceived and impractical, adding 'it would never do to have the Mounted Police take the place of striking Policemen, it would prejudicially affect our situation throughout Canada.' As a result of subsequent refusals by the dominion authorities to allow the Royal North-West Mounted Police to police Winnipeg during the emergency, the civic authorities would be forced to recruit special police.

As the city edged toward a police lockout, a meeting was held that prepared the ground for a real test of whoever would replace the city police. A gathering of returned soldiers sympathetic to the strike was held at the request of

ex-sergeant A. E. Moore, a member of the Alien Investigation Board of the provincial government (and later head of the Canadian Legion). It began at 8:00 p.m. and continued until 11:00 p.m., deciding to send a delegation to wait on the premier and his cabinet to insist that the government settle the strike by special legislation making collective bargaining compulsory. Moore and Roger Bray, a British-born former Methodist lay preacher and socialist, led the campaign for veteran support of the strikers. Their action was quite independent of the strike committee, although it would have a profound impact on the Winnipeg situation.

The next day, 30 May, manoeuvring continued over the policemen, while a delegation of returned soldiers confronted Premier Norris in the legislative building. Having

ROGER BRAY AT VICTORIA PARK, 13 JUNE 1919.

presented their demands, the veterans promised to return the following morning to hear the premier's answer. The policemen's union met in the Police courtroom to respond to the ultimatum that its members return to work. It asked for another twenty-four hours to consider the agreement. Meanwhile, a delegation from the Canadian Problems Club, consisting of R. A. Rigg, F. M. Black, R. F. McWilliams,and Professor Chester Martin, waited on the city council to urge some modification of the pledge the city was asking its employees to sign. McWilliams, who had been a member of the Citizens' Committee of One Hundred in 1918, on this occasion argued that the council, in endeavouring to ban sympathetic strikes, was interfering in man's fundamental right to associate with others for mutual benefit. The Club got nowhere with council in its pleas, however, Alderman Frank Fowler being the most vehement in his categorical insistence, 'No chance.'

The entire nature of events in Winnipeg would change dramatically on 31 May, when thousands of returned veterans marched for the first time since the strike had begun. Marches and huge public gatherings meant the need for crowd control and the constant threat of the eruption of violence. These were not matters to be left in the hands of an amateur police force. After 30 May, the strike would enter a new and more menacing phase.

The Winnipeg General Strike moved into a new — and potentially more violent — phase on 31 May, with the introduction of public demonstrations organized by the demobilized veterans. As had been promised, the returned soldiers lined up on 31 May in Market Square and marched to the Legislative Building on Kennedy Street. Thousands of former soldiers confronted Premier Norris that Friday morning demanding the immediate settlement of the strike by the introduction of compulsory collective bargaining. Perhaps 2,000 managed to enter the legislative chamber, while up to another 10,000 waited outside in the drizzling rain. Premier Norris was backed by his provincial treasurer, attorney-general, and minister of education. Spokesman Roger Bray told his compatriots, 'Boys, you have signified confidence in your committee and its ability to handle the case. Please don't interrupt the speakers. If anyone tells lies there are enough of us here who know the facts to confound them without you butting in.' Bray demanded the immediate withdrawal of the ultimatum to provincial employees or the resignation of the government.

Norris replied that there was a constitutional means for getting rid of a government. For a government to make such a decision without consulting the people 'would be entirely unconstitutional.' Such an argument was totally disingenuous, of course, as Norris doubtless knew. A law passed by his government allowing for provincial referendums on important issues had been struck down in the courts only a few years earlier. In the British parliamentary system, parliaments governed, and Norris had the power to pass any legislation he desired — if he and his government also had the will. He and it probably did not. The Norris government in 1919 was heavily dependent on rural support in the legislature, and Norris was caught between his own progressive instincts and other forces. Innovative labour legislation was not high on the list of priorities of most rural Members of the Legislature, and the strikers

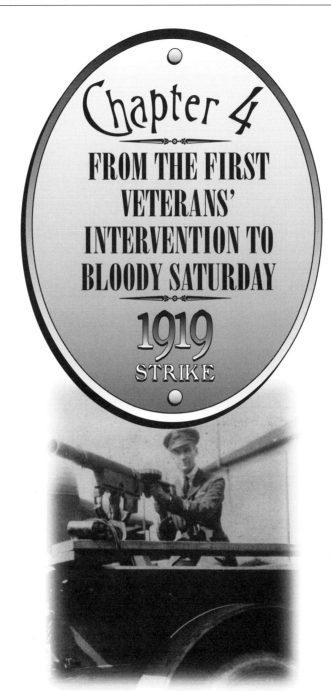

Chapter 4

FROM THE FIRST VETERANS' INTERVENTION TO BLOODY SATURDAY

1919 STRIKE

OPPOSITE PAGE:
WINNIPEG STRIKE, 21 JUNE 1919.

THIS PAGE:
R.P. DENNISTOREN, FORT OSBORNE BARRACK, 21 JUNE 1919.

had made no effort to present their case outside the city of Winnipeg. What Manitoba farmers saw was the shutting down of Winnipeg as a market for their products and a disruption in the wheat trade. Editorial opinion in Manitoba newspapers outside Winnipeg ran heavily against the strike. When urged by J. L. Wilton to announce legislation

PREMIER NORRIS ADDRESSING ANTI-STRIKE LOYALISTS VETERANS' ASSOCIATION, 4 JUNE 1919.

to enforce collective bargaining, Norris had replied, 'No, I can't see my way clear to do that. I think we'd better keep out of the fight.'

Instead of promising action, the premier appealed for fairness and moderation. He claimed to be in favour of collective bargaining, although he was opposed to sympathetic strikes – especially on public utilities. 'The great majority of people of the Province outside the city are not aware of the issue and have to be considered', he argued. 'Just as soon as the people say I should retire I will step down cheerfully.' The delegation wondered if the premier would call them 'Bolsheviks' or 'aliens.' He said absolutely not. The soldiers also complained about terms like 'English and Scotch anarchists' being applied to the strike leaders. Roger Bray pointed out to Norris, 'In 1914 and 1915 we came to your support, and thousands of us voted for you as a strong-minded and straightforward man. Those we represent are men. Those supporting the Committee of One Thousand are not men. That committee represents the same bunch of boodlers who plundered this Province to the verge of bankruptcy.' The crowd booed the profiteers, and particularly munitions supremo Joseph Flavelle. A voice called out, 'there are 349 millionaires in Canada.' Bray quickly responded, 'They have purchased real estate to the extent of thousands of dollars and have made money out of the innocent, while we were over there defending the land we love.' Spokesmen for the delegation declared the Running Trades committee of the railroads, which was proposing a major conciliation effort, were the 'old Tories of the labour movement.'

The soldiers marched from the Legislative Building to City Hall to meet with Mayor Gray. Their spokesmen entered the council room while City Council was in session; it adjourned. Gray met the soldiers on the steps of City Hall. The soldiers then marched by the Industrial Bureau to St Boniface, where they met with its mayor. They ended up at Victoria Park, having allegedly overturned a Coca-Cola wagon at Eaton's warehouse. The march had been executed smartly and peacefully, but it unquestionably injected a new element into an already inflammatory situation. The veterans not only were a potentially volatile group, but, even among those soldiers who were pro-labour, had quite different concerns and goals from those of the Strike Committee. Most soldiers, whatever their politics, were hostile to enemy aliens, thus encouraging efforts to find a connection between the strike and the aliens. Moreover, the addition of the soldiers into the strike situation helped provide a link between the recently-completed war effort and what was currently happening in Winnipeg. How that link could be exploited by opponents of the strike was demonstrated by R. J. Cromie, publisher of the *Vancouver Daily Sun.* In Toronto after a visit to Winnipeg, Cromie on the same day as the veterans' march characterized the strike as 'not a battle between employer and employee, but . . . a battle between the constitutional reform and the Soviet method.' He continued, 'it makes my blood boil to see five men, none of whom is Canadian born, or who has served overseas, run Winnipeg as they are at the present time.'

By 1 June, Arthur J. Andrews had decided that 'the law as it now stands seems to me to be very ineffective in copying with the Bolshevik movement.' His legal reference was apparently to the difficulty of obtaining convictions for sedition in jury trials. Andrews therefore wrote Arthur Meighen, 'Some legislation, either by Order in Council or by Act of Parliament, should be passed at once to deal with the situation.' The next day Parliament held its first open debate on the strike. Dr M. R. Blake (M.P. for North Winnipeg) argued that most workers had not voted for the strike. Major G. W. Andrews (Centre Winnipeg) defended the strikers, insisting that the issues were the right to organize and to have a living wage. For his part, Arthur Meighen told the Commons, 'a general strike to succeed or, indeed, to continue, must result in the usurpation of governmental authority on the part of those controlling the strike. It did so result in Winnipeg; it must ever so result.' From Meighen's perspective, the logic of the general strike was that it had to be revolutionary. Were the Winnipeg strike to succeed, he continued with a mixture of logic and extrapolation, it would produce 'a combination

MAYOR GRAY ADDRESSING ANTI-STRIKE LOYALIST VETERANS' ASSOCIATION, 4 JUNE 1919.

of all organizations of labour in the Dominion taking part in and determining the event of every dispute as to labour conditions and wages here, there, and at any other point, why then you have the perfection of Bolshevism.' Whether or not industrial unionism was the perfection of Bolshevism, the argument that Bolshevism was the enemy in Winnipeg achieved greater currency. At a meeting with a deputation of returned servicemen, Mayor Gray asserted that he had information about a Bolshevik takeover of the city, presumably given him in the course of his daily conferences with General Ketchen, Commissioner Perry of the Royal North-West Mounted Police, Premier Norris, and the

ANTI-STRIKE LOYALIST VETERANS,
4 JUNE 1919.

But not all veterans supported the strike. Other self-styled leaders, such as F. G. Thompson, who subsequently insisted that he was not connected with the Citizens' Committee of One Thousand, were already organizing counter-parades and demonstrations in support of the authorities. According to Thompson's later testimony, 'I went out, and knowing a lot of returned men, around town, I put my views to them — that something had to be done, and I got an auto and chased around to other places . . . and preached the word from mouth to mouth that we would have to parade as a counter to this other parade and set a time and place.'

On 4 June, as Thompson's efforts came to fruition, the Strike Committee escalated the strike. It ordered restaurants and theatres again closed, and discontinued the delivery of bread and milk under its auspices. But the opposition was also increasing the pressure. Volunteers, possibly at the instigation of the Citizens' Committee of One Thousand, lined up on Broadway outside the old buildings of the University of Manitoba. They joined the veterans in a 'Loyalist' parade to the Manitoba legislative buildings. One of the organizers of this event later recalled, 'We formed an army . . . We formed infantry units . . . We had some men on horses . . . The parades of the other side quit. We scared the hell out of them.' One banner of the counter-parade read, 'We will maintain constituted authority, law & order. Down with the High cost of Living. To Hell with the alien enemy. God save the King.' The strikers would claim that this counter-parade was composed largely of 'lawyers, insurance, and real estate clerks', and insisted that 'if you saw the moving picture film of the two parades you could tell the real veterans.' F. G. Thompson, on the other hand, maintained that many of his veterans were still in their khakis, so recently

Attorney-General of Manitoba. The soldiers offered him 2,000 volunteers to serve without pay to maintain order if the police force was locked out.

Representatives of the Citizens' Committee of One Thousand met with Commissioner Perry and officials of the provincial government on 3 June to lobby for the arrest and prosecution of the strike leaders on charges of sedition. No action was taken, however. In the evening, 2,000 members of the Great War Veterans' Association jammed into a meeting at Manitoba Hall. A resolution was passed supporting the strike by a two-thirds majority despite the protests of chairman J. O. Newton that the resolution was out of order, given the association's policy of neutrality.

demobilized they had no time to obtain civilian clothes.

The counter-paraders visited Premier Norris and Mayor Gray, who welcomed them effusively. They tendered resolutions about 'law and order' and 'constituted authority.' Shortly afterwards, the first arrest of the parades was made — of a marcher carrying a gun. Four other gunmen were subsequently arrested and released. While the 'Loyal' veterans were marching around the downtown area, soldier strikers 4,000 strong marched through the wealthy residential districts of South Winnipeg, the stronghold of the opposition to the strike. They sang old favourites or whistled as they marched. American labour leader James Duncan of Seattle later addressed an enthusiastic audience of over 10,000 in Victoria Park. Meanwhile, A. J. Andrews wrote Meighen that Commissioner Perry was preparing to deport 'one hundred dangerous aliens', and a meeting was held of the premier, A. B. Perry, Colonel Cortlandt Starnes, General H. B. D. Ketchen, and T. J. Johnson, to consider whether the strike leadership could be detained under existing laws. Ketchen, Starnes, and Perry all argued that such action would be counter-productive, merely producing sympathetic strikes across the west.

On 5 June, 'The Act to Amend the Immigration Act', long on the order paper in Ottawa, was finally passed. It excluded from Canada persons who believed in or advocated the overthrow of constituted government by force or violence or who advocated the unlawful destruction of property. It also removed immigrants in prohibited or undesirables classes from the provision that any immigrant domiciled in the country for five years could not be deported after a special hearing before an immigration department panel. When the text of the new legislation was wired by Arthur Meighen to A. J. Andrews, the

DEMONSTRATION AT WINNIPEG BOARD OF TRADE BUILDING, 4 JUNE 1919.

Winnipeg lawyer was gravely disappointed because the act did not include 'the dangerous class not born in Canada', the British radicals. The amended immigration act, answered Andrews, would not 'meet the situation or satisfy citizens who if I inform them of the real facts will be greatly disheartened and disgusted.' Meighen responded that when he perused the Act himself on the evening of 5 June he immediately saw its inadequacies, and he had prepared a further amendment 'sufficiently wide to cover all except those born or naturalized in Canada.' This new amendment would be passed

RETURNED SOLDIERS, ATTENTION

To those of you who do not wish to be represented by the parades—supposedly of Returned Soldiers—which took place on Friday, Saturday and Monday:

Assemble at Corner of Main and Broadway
By 11 o'clock on Wednesday (This Morning)

for the purpose of demonstrating that you do not approve of intimidation of those in authority and that you believe in personal liberty and our constitutional form of government.

within twenty-four hours. Also in Ottawa, Labour Minister Robertson authorized 44 railway porters to be brought from the United States to replace Canadian Pacific Railway men on strike. In Winnipeg, eleven persons were arrested on Main Street near Market Square and charged with inciting violence. And in yet another

SWEARING IN 'SPECIAL' CONSTABLES, 5 JUNE 1919.

WINNIPEG, FRIDAY, JUNE 6, 1919

PROCLAMATION

By virtue of the authority vested in me I do hereby order that all persons do refrain from forming or taking part in any parades or congregating in crowds in or upon any of the streets of the City of Winnipeg, and do hereby request of all law abiding citizens the full compliance with this proclamation.

Dated at the City of Winnipeg, this 5th day of June, A.D. 1919.

CHARLES F. GRAY, Mayor.

GOD SAVE THE KING.

development, police chief Donald McPherson, who had resisted a restructuring of the police department and the organization of a special police force, was replaced by his former deputy chief Chris Newton.

The following day, what labour labelled the '40-minute legislation' was passed in Ottawa. Minister of Immigration J. A. Calder explained to the House of Commons that yesterday's amendment 'had been looked into further and the law officers of the Crown have advised that the section as it stands does not really cover all that was intended.' The new amendment defined Canadian citizen by the phrase 'either by reason of birth in Canada, or by reason of naturalization in Canada.' It passed three readings in both the House and Senate within less than an hour. Thus the vast bulk of the leaders of the Winnipeg strike, previously Canadian citizens by virtue of their British birth, suddenly became aliens subject to summary deportation under the Immigration Act. This was a blatant example of inequitable harassment by a government that ought to have known better. The special committee of the House appointed on 1 May 1919 to review the Criminal Code now reported on criminal laws relating to sedition and seditious propaganda. Such legislation was voted to be given force on 1 October 1919.

In Winnipeg, the Loyalist Returned Soldier Association (organized by F. G. Thompson) met in the Amphitheatre. The soldiers were later addressed by

Brigadier-General Ketchen in the Auditorium Rink, where Sarah Bernhardt had once performed 'Camille' in French to an adoring audience. Ketchen told his listeners that all undesirables, alien and otherwise, would be dealt with. He continued, 'I think that when the time comes for this information to be given to you officially, you will realize that I have told you only a part of it. Right now it is our duty to support civic authority, and I would ask you to do your best in backing up the Mayor in whatever he puts before you.' Mayor Gray appealed for special constables, concluding with the ringing declaration, 'when this thing is over the British flag will still be on the City Hall and not the red flag.' Hundreds of men were sworn in as special constables after the meeting. The men accepted Gray's proclamation banning parades in good spirits and without opposition. He explained that the reason for banning parades was an instruction from the Attorney-General for the Dominion, Arthur Meighen.

Outside the Auditorium, a big pro-striker parade headed by a pipers' band with the Transcona brass band was forced to march back to Victoria Park after police said they would have to stop it. In the Auditorium, Ketchen stood on the platform with his hand raised in salute while the gathering of returned soldiers roared out three cheers and a 'tiger'.* The soldiers were told that posters would be placed around the city reading, 'Neutrality means Bolshevism, says the G.W.V.A.' In another development, A. J. Andrews wired Gideon Robertson to come to Winnipeg at once, because conciliation efforts in the general strike by the railway running trades appeared to be heading toward a railway walkout that would totally disrupt the country's rail transportation.

With street marches forbidden, the pro-strike veterans turned to holding mass meetings in Victoria Park, which came to be known as the 'Soldiers' Parliament.' The

---

* A 'tiger' was an additional cheer called for after the usual three cheers! Hurrah! Hurrah! Hurrah! — and a tiger — Hurrah!

continued success of the strikers at tying up the city meant that there was not much to do, either for those who had walked off their jobs or for those returned soldiers who did not have jobs to attend. The Victoria Park gatherings filled a considerable void, as James Gray testified in his memoir *The Boy from Winnipeg*. On 7 June Mayor Gray addressed the soldiers reportedly to some effect. On Sunday evening, 8 June, J. S. Woodsworth — who had only just returned from Vancouver — spoke at the Labour Church service in Victoria Park. Some 10,000 people listened for three hours to a learned address on the economic situation of the day. F. J. Dixon and Ernest Robinson also spoke. A collection of $1540 was taken to help the strikers. At its meeting, the City Council voted a special appropriation of $150,000 for the organization of a special police force to replace the regular one about to be dismissed.

On Monday 9 June, the strikers produced letters that had been sent to businessmen from the Citizens' Committee of One Thousand appealing for financial assistance for a special compensation fund, intended to reimburse volunteer workers for their efforts. The solicitations had been sent to most business associations in the city and province. They claimed that over $800,000 had already been raised, and that $1,000,000 was in prospect. That morning, General Ketchen and Canon F. G. Scott addressed the Soldiers' Parliament at Victoria Park. Ketchen complimented the veterans 'on the orderliness and discipline of your parades.' 'Padre' Scott, the popular chaplain of the

My father, Fleming Parrott, was a returned soldier, living in Grandview, Man. He was called in 'Returned Soldiers Group'. He spent the night with friends. They had breakfast together and went to their respective posts. (Sorry I don't remember their name). The woman worked in a bakery, was marching with the strikers. The man was a policeman, was upholding law and order. My dad was posted behind a machine gun, on the corner of Portage and Main, in front of the Royal Bank building, at about the same spot the statue of the soldier stands. The bakery worker said, 'Fleming, if you see me, don't shoot'. I asked my dad what he would have done, were he ordered to shoot, and we both knew he wouldn't have done it.

Bernice (Parrott) Fanning
Winnipeg

SPECIAL CONSTABLES ARMED WITH
WOODEN CLUBS MARCH ALONG
PORTAGE AVENUE, 10 JUNE 1919.

Canadian Expeditionary Force's first division in France, had come to Winnipeg to 'help his boys.' He spoke sympathetically if generally to the audience about the strike. Meanwhile, A. J. Andrews wrote Arthur Meighen that if patience were observed, the strikers might depose the strike leadership, 'a splendid lesson if the strike fails without any hatred or rancour being engendered and the sober workers feel that they have made a mistake.' The big danger, added Andrews, was that the Running Trades Conciliation Committee would make a report that could be endorsed by the strike leadership. 'What we want to avoid if possible', argued Andrews, 'is a definite finding by this Committee against the Metal Trades and in favor of the strike Committee as this is bound to have an injurious effect. If on the other hand, this Committee can be persuaded to make no finding at all or a finding that the employers have offered what appears to them to be a fair settlement, no bad results will follow their negotiations.' While Andrews hoped to win cleanly, he was obviously pre-

pared to do anything necessary to beat the strikers.

On the evening of 9 June, the city dismissed its regular police force, replacing it with special police hired at $6 per day. The head of the special police, Major Hilliard Lyle, who had been appointed on 5 June to organize the 'specials', met privately with the strike committee that night to warn them that the authorities were prepared to shoot if necessary. Little is known about Lyle, who was soon dismissed and disappeared from Winnipeg. According to the strike leaders, Lyle admitted at their meeting — called at his initiative — that many of his police force were 'thugs' he would have difficulty controlling. He also insisted that he had seen enough bloodshed in Europe, and intimated that he would order his men to withdraw rather than confront the strikers.

The new specials appeared the next day on the streets armed with wagon neck-yokes sawed in two, about the shape of a baseball bat. It was a lovely summer strike-bound day in Winnipeg, and the streets were crowded with automobiles cruising and people promenading. By 1:00 p.m., traffic control had broken down, and a crowd at Portage and

10 JUNE 1919 - PORTAGE AND MAIN

Main surrounded a handful of specials there. Within a few minutes, mounted specials (supposedly on animals the property of the large department stores) rode down Main Street from Notre Dame Avenue, attempting to disperse the crowd. Some of the riders had trouble controlling their mounts, and the crowd responded with flying missiles, chiefly sticks and stones, mixed with a few bottles. While the strikers always maintained an air of injured innocence about this confrontation, someone had done some advance planning, since there were normally precious few sticks, stones, and bottles lying about the corner of Portage and Main. Fortunately, no one was killed. One special policeman, a Victoria Cross winner named Coppins, was injured. The newspapers claimed he had been beaten by foreigners — the *Tribune* said 'enemy ruffians', while the *Citizen* blamed 'three Austrians.' Coppins later testified

SPECIAL POLICE RIDING WEST ON PORTAGE AVENUE, 10 JUNE 1919.

that he had been hit by missiles, but could not say who had thrown them. Mayor Gray was able to persuade (with threats) the organizer of a parade being formed in Victoria Park not to march up Main Street. Two hundred specials on foot finally succeeded in dispersing the crowd in the late afternoon.

There were mutterings that Major Lyle had not

demonstrated sufficient firmness with his forces, and he was quickly dismissed. A. J. Andrews was beside himself with rage over this confrontation, chiefly because of what he regarded as the incompetence of the special force. It was, he wrote to Meighen, 'wholly inadequate and the net result is that they have been chased off the streets, a number of them hurt, some badly wounded and the crowd in possession of a number of their clubs.' The 10 June 'riot' was important because it was the first serious sign of the impending breakdown of the sense of order and decorum in Winnipeg that up to this point had been maintained by all sides — strikers, strike opponents, returned soldiers, and police. A shooting incident the next day at the corner of Higgins and Main further distressed the authorities. Andrews reported to Ottawa that loyal returned soldiers would follow General Ketchen's orders, and advised, 'the time has arrived to act.'

Thursday 12 June was 'Ladies Day' at the Soldier's Parliament in Victoria Park. Large numbers of women and girl strikers occupied the seats of honour near the central platform, while returned men and strikers stood at the rear. Speakers included Roger Bray, F. J. Dixon, and J. S. Woodsworth. At the conclusion of Woodsworth's address, which called for the emancipation of women and the equality of the sexes, the women and girls shouted together, 'We'll fight to the end.' W. A. Pritchard of Vancouver also addressed the Victoria Park mass meeting that day. Head of the Vancouver Longshoremen's Union, Pritchard was a member of the Socialist Party of Canada and a principal organizer of the One Big Union. He had been born in England of Welsh descent, and he was regarded as one of Canada's most brilliant orators. His speech, which noted that the government now opposing collective bargaining was the same government that had given it to the Metal Trades employees of Vancouver in 1918, received more than the regular three cheers and a tiger. Speakers at the Labour Church meeting in Victoria Park in the evening included Woodsworth, Pritchard, and the Reverend A. E. Smith of Brandon. A band opened the services, and familiar hymns were rendered with great enthusiasm. Woodsworth told the crowd that the old forms of religion were now inapplicable. Smith, an ex-president of the Manitoba Methodist Conference, claimed that it was next to impossible for a preacher to preach the genuine gospel of Christ in the traditional churches. The Bankers' Association and the Committee of One Thousand were themselves 'One Big Union', he maintained. Smith called the sympathetic strike 'as religious a movement as a Church revival.' This gathering provided substantial evidence of the contributions of the social gospel into the general atmosphere of the strike.

While crowds gathered and promenaded in the warm air of a Canadian prairie summer, others met behind closed doors. The conciliation efforts of the railway Running Trades was reaching a critical juncture, with some unions actually preparing to join the strike because of their sense of the intransigence of the Metal Trades employers. The executive officers of the international unions blamed this defection on 'the Red element.' Gideon Robertson reported to Ottawa that he, A. J. Andrews, the military, and the Citizens' Committee had agreed that immediate steps were required 'to remove the cause of the whole trouble.' The plan again discussed involved moving a number of troublemakers immediately to Camp Kapuskasing. As many as one hundred immigrants may have been incarcerated as a result of this initiative. None of those arrested here were active strike leaders, however,

since the strike leadership was without exception composed of people of British origin.

At this point Robertson succeeded in persuading the ironmasters to make concessions, to be publicized on 16 June, to prevent the general walkout of the railway conciliators. The metal trades proprietors agreed to a system of collective bargaining similar to that between the railways and the railways running trades union. This concession fell short of recognizing the Metal Trades Council as a collective bargaining agent, but it was regarded in many quarters as a 'master stroke.' The *Toronto Star* editorialized that with the 'persuading of the ironmasters to suddenly concede collective bargaining and getting the railway brotherhoods and other railway managers to endorse it as being safe in effect and principle', the running trades were prevented 'from going out in sympathy and tying up transportation throughout Canada.' At this point, on the evening of 14 June, a violent thunderstorm did substantial damage in Winnipeg. It ripped off part of the roof of the Children's Hospital and demolished several other buildings. Some took the storm as an omen of things to come.

On 16 June the press published a statement containing conditional acceptance of collective bargaining by the ironmasters. The employers agreed to recognize unions and bargain with them — but not with the Metal Trades Council. The press statement was accompanied by three affidavits — one by Gideon Robertson, one by the railway managers, one by the mediation committee. All agreed that this position represented

LEFT: ALBERT EDWARD SMITH C.1921.

AFTER THE SUMMER STORM 14 JUNE 1919.

an acceptance of collective bargaining as practised on the railroads. The members of the mediation committee wrote, 'The undersigned representatives of the train service organizations, being familiar with collective bargaining as practised by the organizations we represent, endorse the policy of collective bargaining as outlined by the metal trade employers . . . being in principle and effect the same as that enjoyed by these organizations.' In theory these declarations could provide strikers who were wavering with an excuse for returning to work. More than one observer thought that the ordinary worker was getting tired of the strike and only needed a bit of a push to return to the job. Had these concessions been made much earlier and under different circumstances they might have had more effect, however. At a meeting of the General Strike Committee on the evening of 16 June, the running trades proposals and concession of the ironmasters was summarily rejected, because it did not concede the principle which the strike leaders insisted had been the cause of the strike: recognition of the Metal Trades Council as bargaining agent with the employers.

Not long after the vote of the General Strike Committee, indeed, shortly after midnight on the morning of 17 June, a frantic woman raced from her Winnipeg home to the nearest police station. From the station she placed a telephone call to the recently-appointed Chief of Police, Chris Newton. 'They have a warrant to arrest George', she told Newton. 'They' were constables of the Royal North-West Mounted Police, and 'George' was her husband George Armstrong, one of the leaders of the strike. The 'warrant', sworn by a Royal North-West Mounted Police sergeant named A. E. Reames, charged Armstrong with conspiracy 'to excite divers liege subjects of the King, to resist laws and resist persons, some being part of the police force in the city of Winnipeg. . . and to procure unlawful meetings, and to cause divers liege subjects of the King to believe that the laws of the dominion

were unduly administered.' Learning of the warrant, Newton replied, 'I guess it's all right, then'. So Helen Armstrong calmly returned to her home and allowed the arresting officers, who had waited patiently while she made her telephone call, to take her husband into custody. Helen was, of course, more than capable of putting up a fight. She had been arrested herself several times during the preceding month in the course of labour demonstrations. But she was fully prepared to allow 'British justice' to take its course.

George Armstrong was one of a number of strike leaders and 'foreign agitators' arrested and taken by automobile to Stony Mountain Penitentiary that June morning under instructions from A. J. Andrews and Gideon Robertson. Also arrested were William Ivens, R. B. Russell, John Queen, A. A. Heaps, R. E. Bray, Moses Almazoff, Mike Verenchuck, O. Choppelrei, and M. Charitonoff. Russell, Queen, Heaps, and Armstrong had all been on the 1917 government list of dangerous critics, as was Dickie Johns, who was not immediately arrested but would be picked up in Montreal. Almazoff, Choppelrei, and Charitonoff were all well-known foreign-born 'agitators', although none of the three had played any significant role in the strike itself. Verenchuck was arrested totally in error, and without a warrant, at the home of one Davieatkin, who was away in the country. A war veteran who had been wounded several times, he was hardly a typical alien agitator, although he would be held for some time without charges and had great difficulty in gaining his freedom. The homes of all those arrested had been searched for seditious literature, as were the Labour Temple, the Ukrainian Church, and Liberty Temple (the home of the Arbeiter Ring). Much material had been confiscated. For the strike leaders, at least, as well as for most of Winnipeg, the arrests came as an unexpected bolt from the blue. From Ottawa, Arthur Meighen in a telegram expressed doubts 'as to technical legality of arrests', but felt that 'rapid deportation is best course now that arrests are made and later can consider ratification.' Retroactive authorization for the arrests of those taken under section 42 of the Immigration Act was subsequently given by Immigration minister Calder.

News of the arrests 'electrified' a meeting of returned soldiers 'vibrant with emotion' at Victoria Park on the morning of 17 June. But there is little doubt that this controversial action effectively broke the back of the strike. Whether the arrests and the subsequent prosecutions of those arrested, plus William Pritchard, Dick Johns, J. S. Woodsworth, and F. J. Dixon, who were taken later, were appropriate policy is another matter entirely. The arrests themselves were not universally applauded, even by opponents of the strike. John Dafoe, in a *Free Press* editorial on 17 June, opposed 'the Strong Arm policy of breaking the strike', and a day later argued that arrests 'at this time may do the extremists an actual service. They were in the position of leaders of a senseless criminal strike which was nearly at the point of collapse. . . Their arrest will enable them to pose as martyrs in the cause of the working-man and will also supply them with a plausible excuse for failure.' Canadian Trades and Labor Congress President Tom Moore, no friend of the Winnipeg strike, warned government that organized labour would not 'stand for strong arm methods for the suppression of legitimate labour demonstrations, and if the proof is not sufficient to show the Winnipeg labour leaders were plotting danger to the state, the government will be held strictly accountable.'

Andrews and Robertson had waited to see the results of the ironmasters' concessions, but apparently had then decided on decisive action to end a strike that showed no signs of ending in a negotiated settlement and many indications of spreading into other cities, which were already mounting sympathy strikes. Not surprisingly, Andrews and Robertson chose to concentrate on those strike leaders who had long been critical of the government and who had reputations (and police files) as 'radicals' and 'socialists.'

The action was certainly applauded by Prime Minister Robert Borden, who wired Robertson on 19 June with 'warmest congratulations upon your masterly handling of a very difficult and complicated situation.'

The initial intention of A. J. Andrews was 'to deport all that are deportable and to try the balance on whatever charges we think will warrant their conviction.' He was opposed to bail for the strike leaders, which he saw as 'a fatal error . . . interpreted as weakness although the accused have all promised to refrain from taking part in the strike . . . if we allow them liberty.' By 20 June the government changed its mind. Bail was arranged for all the strike leaders on the condition that they took no further part in the strike. A large deputation from the Strike Committee assured Andrews that 'the offer of the Metal Trades Employers was satisfactory to them and that they were prepared to recommend the calling off of the sympathetic strike.'

Neither Andrews nor the government ever gave a reason for the change of policy. Andrews would concede in a letter to Meighen of 25 June that it might be more difficult to deport native-born Canadians among those arrested (George Armstrong) under immigration regulations than to try them all in court. General Ketchen opposed release on bail, as did the Citizens' Committee of One Thousand. But the decision to release on bail meant that the federal government would have to meet Tom Moore's challenge by convincing a jury, under the rules of 'British justice', that those arrested were plotting to overturn the government.

Before the dominion could either present or prove its case, the authorities in Winnipeg had to deal with a final challenge. If we think of the Winnipeg Strike as merely a general labour walkout, the events of 21 June were distinctly anti-climactic, since the strikers had already agreed in principle to return to work. But 21 June suggests that the strike was more than merely a labour event, for the final challenge came not from the chastened Strike Committee, but from the less cowed returned soldiers, who met in Market Square on the evening of 20 June and decided to have a silent parade of veterans march to the Royal Alexandra Hotel the next day to speak to Senator Robertson about the arrests. Estimates of the crowd ranged from 5,000 to 6,000. Three soldier leaders, Martin, Grant, and Farnell, would be indicted (but not convicted) for speeches made here. Farnell had assumed the leadership of the pro-strike soldiers after the arrest of Roger Bray, announcing that 'if the Government won't settle the strike, returned soldiers will.' He blamed the Citizens' Committee for the thwarting of the strike, calling for nightly meetings in Market Square until the strike was ended. J. A. Martin referred to Saturday's proposed parade as 'the only weapon we have left.' For his part, Mayor Gray renewed the ban on parades, saying that civic authorities have 'absolutely committed themselves to the breaking up any . . . demonstrations.' He warned that 'any women taking part in a parade do so at their own risk', a caution difficult to misinterpret.

Early Saturday morning Ivens, Russell, Queen, Heaps, Armstrong and Bray were initially released on bail. Pritchard and Johns had not yet arrived in Winnipeg after their out-of-town arrests, and F. J. Dixon and J. S. Woodsworth had not yet been charged with seditious libel for taking over editorship of the *Western Labor News* from William Ivens. 'J. S., you act as editor and I'll act as

21 JUNE 1919 - ABOUT `1:45 PM. NO ATTEMPT WAS MADE TO USE THE SPECIAL CONSTABLES TO PREVENT THE PARADE.

reporter', Dixon had said on hearing of Ivens' arrest. The four 'foreigners' were all kept in custody. They were not intended to appear in a common-law courtroom, but before an Immigration tribunal. Hence they were not able to take advantage of habeas corpus. Later, on Saturday morning, a last-minute meeting between the authorities (Gideon Robertson, Commissioner Perry, A. J. Andrews, and Mayor Gray) and the soldier leaders failed to produce a cancellation of the demonstration, planned to start at 2:30 p.m. Mayor Gray finally stomped out of the meeting at nearly 1:45 p.m., having been informed on the telephone by Chief Newton that crowds were forming along Main Street between City Hall and Portage Avenue. As the numbers of people grew and grew, Newton became increasingly panicked about the specials' ability to manage the affair. He urged Gray to call out the Royal North-West Mounted Police, and in the presence of the provincial attorney-general, Gray requested emergency Mounted Police assistance from Colonel Perry. A mixture of red and khaki coats on horseback (the khaki representing Mounted Policemen who had just returned from army duty in Russia) soon appeared on Portage Avenue and turned on Main Street. 'Bloody Saturday' had begun.

What happened next depends to some extent on which eyewitness account one chooses to emphasize. The accounts were not necessarily inconsistent, for there was clearly a confusing melee, and few in the crowd had an unobstructed view. There can be no doubt about the which ran between Market and James Avenues. Here in ten minutes of conflict near 4:00 in the afternoon, twenty-seven casualties were produced. Soldiers patrolled the streets of the downtown area in the evening. Before the fighting was over, however, there had been ninety-four arrests (including four women) and countless small injuries, most never reported. Should the Mounted Police have ridden

FIFTY-FOUR MOUNTED POLICE RIDE NORTH FROM PORTAGE AND MAIN TO CLEAR THE STREET, 21 JUNE 1919.

INSPECTOR PROBY'S MOUNTED POLICE APPROACHING THE CORNER OF PORTAGE AND MAIN, 21 JUNE 1919.

Mounted Police charge. The mounted men galloped into the crowd on Main Street swinging baseball bats. On the steps of City Hall, Mayor Gray read the riot act at 2:35 p.m. The Police continued past City Hall to McDermot Ave. and swung around, transferring bats into the left hands and drawing their guns. They apparently fired three volleys, the second at a crowd surrounding a tram, partially overturned and on fire. The photograph of this tram at this moment has become one of the icons of the strike. Whether the police fired first or were fired upon first remained in dispute. What was not in question was that several spectators had been hit by the volleys. Mike Sokolowiski, a tinsmith, died instantly. Steve Schezerbanowes would die later of gangrene as a result of gunshot wounds suffered in the melee. The crowd dispersed only gradually, as the specials, wearing white armbands and carrying batons, took over. The most intense fighting between crowd and specials took place in 'Hell's Alley',

into the crowd? Was Mayor Gray justified in reading the Riot Act? Who fired the first shot? Definitive answers to these sorts of questions are, of course, quite impossible.

'Bloody Saturday' was seen by many opponents of the strike as the logical consequence of both its challenge to authority and the government's decision to release the strikers on bail. A. J. Andrews disagreed on the second point, writing to Arthur Meighen: 'Those who falsely suggest that my leniency was the cause of the riot on Saturday

CANADIAN ARMY SERVICE CORPS TRUCKS AND SPECIAL CONSTABLES ON MAIN STREET, 21 JUNE 1919.

know very little of the situation. Meetings had been called to protest against keeping these men in gaol without bail and all the strikers were demanding bail. When the men were released on bail the Strike Committee, and this has been proven by reports from our secret agent, did all in their power to prevent the parades which on this account were confined to a much smaller number than if they had been swelled by the strikers demanding the release of these men on bail. There is no question in the world the riot would have been much worse if I had taken any other course.' Furthermore, insisted Andrews, if the riot had occurred over denying men bail, 'people throughout Canada. . . would have blamed the Government for their action in furnishing provocation for the riot.' In the wake of the riot, the dominion government sent more aliens to Kapuskasing internment camp, and prepared warrants for the arrests of J. S. Woodsworth and F. J. Dixon.

The Winnipeg General Strike was officially called off on 26 June at 11:00 a.m. The provincial government agreed to establish a royal commission to investigate the origin and nature of the strike. This was the only concrete concession made to the Strike Committee. The metal workers received a reduction in their work week from 55 to 50 hours, but no pay rise. At that, they did better than the telephone operators, who had to reapply for jobs without

seniority protection and only after pledging that they would never again participate in a sympathy strike. Not everyone was rehired. In the end, reinstatement of any kind was denied not only to 119 telephone workers, but to 403 postal employees and 53 firemen. Who in Winnipeg in future, particularly in low-paying jobs, would ever want to walk out in sympathy? James Gray's mother had been right. 'There never was in history', commented one contemporary labour organizer, 'a strike in which the workers answered the call so spontaneously, and there never was a strike in which the workers were so badly trimmed.' The opponents of the strike, led by the federal government, appeared to have won a great victory. Or had they?

Although the Winnipeg General Strike ended on 26 June 1919, some of its many tangled threads and repercussions took much time to work out. Almost immediately came the organization of the One Big Union and the hearings of the Robson Royal Commission, as well as the beginning of the trials of the arrested strike leaders. These last took several years to work completely through the appeals process. Even before the trials were completed, there had been revisions to the Criminal Code to prevent a reccurrence of the General Strike. In the autumn of 1919, the first civic elections since the strike indicated that one of its enduring legacies would be a polarized city of Winnipeg, with municipal politics organized according to class lines inherited from the strike. At about the same time, as a direct result of the Winnipeg strike, the Royal North-West Mounted Police and the Dominion Police were amalgamated into one agency, renamed the Royal Canadian Mounted Police. Finally, of course, there is the matter of the verdict of history. The historical assessment of the strike has been an unending process, certain to be expanded at the 75th anniversary.

■ **THE ONE BIG UNION:** The question of the organization of the One Big Union had lurked as a presence over the course of the strike. As many historians have pointed out, the One Big Union had not yet been organized at the time of the strike, although the referendum approving it in principle was forwarded to members of Winnipeg Trades and Labor Council unions in the same package as their general strike ballot , and therefore could not have been a concrete factor in the strike. At the same time, the spectre of industrial unionism represented by the One Big Union frightened government and business leaders. It was the One Big Union which immediately came to the mind of opponents of the strike when they labelled the strike as revolutionary. It was the One Big Union that seemed to the

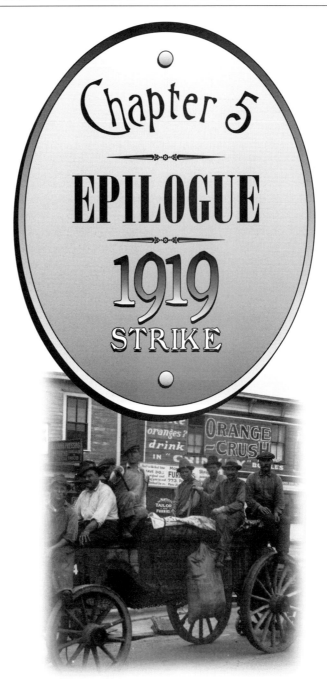

Chapter 5
EPILOGUE
1919
STRIKE

OPPOSITE PAGE:
LORD BYNG, J.A.M. AIKINS AND GROUP AT GOVERNMENT HOUSE, 18 JUNE 1922.

THIS PAGE:
STREET ASPHALT CREW AT PORTAGE AVE. AND TORONTO STREET, 14 JUNE 1922.

opposition to embody the 'Bolshevism' which had to be fought at all costs.

The defeat of the Winnipeg General Strike probably helped limit the immediate success of the One Big Union in western Canada. The situation in Winnipeg made clear the lengths to which the government and the business opposition would go to suppress radical industrial unionism. Nevertheless, the One Big Union grew rapidly across the Canadian West in 1919, and achieved its greatest success in Winnipeg. In that city, alienation from traditional trade unionism only grew in the wake of the strike. The Strike Committee wanted the Canadian Trades and Labor Congress to call a general strike in support of the arrested strike leaders. They were turned down on the grounds that the general strike was contrary to Trades and Labor Congress policy, and that calling a general strike would admit that the policies pursued by the Winnipeg strikers had been a correct one. In view of the ongoing antagonism between the national Trades and Labor Congress and the Winnipeg Trades and Labor Council, it was not surprising that the latter heard on 15 July that the referendum on adoption of the One Big Union constitution had resulted in a 8,841 to 705 victory in favour of secession from the Canadian Trades and Labor Congress. Only R. A. Rigg spoke in opposition to the plan, and the Council voted to prepare a new constitution consonant with the One Big Union. That constitution was adopted at a special council meeting on 29 July, and the council was newly constituted as the Winnipeg Central Labor Council of the One Big Union. It then elected temporary officers. R. A. Rigg refused to allow this transition to occur without a fight, and gaining control of the Canadian Trades and Labor Congress charter and seal of the Winnipeg Trades and Labor Council, he called a meeting of loyalists who kept the Winnipeg Trades and Labor Council in operation.

The two Winnipeg councils engaged in a struggle over union assets. One issue was control of the *Western Labor News* and William Ivens, who had initially kept his job as editor on condition that he observe Trades and Labor Council authority, was sacked when the next issue of the *News* indicated that it was now published by the One Big Union. It took an injunction to get him out of the office of the paper. The One Big Union was forced to issue its own journal, the *One Big Union Bulletin*, which would publish a large number of articles by William Cooper setting forth a distinctive One Big Union ideology.

With considerable financial and moral assistance from the traditional international and national trades union movement, the American Federation of Labor and the Canadian Trades and Labor Congress, the Winnipeg Trades and Labor Council fought an uphill but ultimately successful battle with the One Big Union over membership. Initially, the One Big Union did extremely well in Winnipeg on the membership front, even gaining the large street railway employee union in August of 1920. Nationally, the One Big Union at the time of its first convention in Winnipeg early in 1920 was able to claim over 40,000 members. But except in Winnipeg, the One Big Union failed to control a sufficient percentage of local workers to dominate any region. It soon became a victim of internal disagreement and financial woes, having difficulty collecting its dues from local unions. The One Big Union voted late in 1920 to move its central headquarters from Vancouver to Winnipeg. By 1921 the One Big Union treasury was in serious trouble, and was salvaged only when the *Bulletin* began to run a weekly pool based on the English football results. By April 1922, the pool was attracting 150,000 entries a week. When the Manitoba Court of Appeal ruled the pool as constituted illegal, the Winnipeg council shifted to allowing readers of the *Bulletin* to enter free on a coupon to be found in the newspaper. The result was a circulation, at its height, of nearly half a million copies. The Crown continued to oppose the lotteries, but the One Big Union continued with them in various forms throughout the 1920s. It could probably legitimately claim to be the grandfather of the lottery systems which various Canadian governments began to use in the 1970s to supplement their coffers. As for the union, its memberships continued to decline to the point where it was forced in 1927 to merge with the All Canadian Congress of Labor, thus disappearing as an independent force from the labour scene.

■ **THE ROBSON COMMISSION:** The 'Royal Commission to Enquire into and report upon the causes and effects of the general strike which recently existed in the City of Winnipeg for a period of six weeks, including the methods of calling and carrying on such strike' was created on 4 July 1919, when H. A. Robson was appointed commissioner by letters patent from the Manitoba lieutenant-governor. Robson was a level-headed judge who was a favourite choice to head provincial investigative commissions. The conclusions of this fact-finding commission are often cited and quoted by historians. According to one team of scholars, Robson's report 'has been widely respected as an objective and accurate assessment of the strike, free of the rancour and extremism that marked other interpretations that appeared at the time.' But it must be remembered that Robson's operations were hardly on the sort of level of the later Warren Commission which exhaustively investigated the assassination of John F. Kennedy (although its findings have never been completed accepted) or of subsequent landmark Canadian royal commissions such as those headed by Rowell-Sirois or Vincent Massey. H.A. Robson was the sole commissioner, assisted by C. P. Wilson, K.C., and C. H. Locke.

Surviving documentary material on the Robson Commission, beyond its published report, is sparse, consisting mainly of correspondence in national archives advocating a much broader, and federal, inquiry into the dispute. A number of Winnipeg businessmen, and the Citizens' Committee of One Thousand, all pressed hard for a Dominion-level inquiry beginning on 24 June, when the provincial government announced that it would appoint a royal commission. The critics maintained that a provincial investigation would be inadequate, partly because there would be insufficient financial commitment to do the job properly and because its scope was quite limited. Most of the critics, it must be added, saw a federal royal commission as another opportunity to expose the political dangers of the strike, as a public 'show trial.' Lawyer Edward Anderson insisted that much of the collateral evidence seized by the authorities in various raids, while inadmissible as evidence in a criminal trial, could be used before a Dominion commission. As it turned out, much of this evidence was allowed in the criminal court trials. Arthur Meighen considered giving the Robson commission a federal status, but in the end nothing was done. The dominion government appeared ultimately satisfied that its trials of the strike leaders were sufficient public exposure of its position.

HUGH AMOS ROBSON, C. 1915.

The provincial commission had virtually no staff, and its major research consisted of eleven days of hearings, held in open sessions in Winnipeg between 16 July and 10 September 1919. The hearings were supplemented by a questionnaire on the costs of the strike, distributed to larger industries and businesses in Winnipeg. To this questionnaire 602 replies were received, but little serious analysis of them was undertaken, and the originals have apparently not survived the ravages of time. About all the questionnaires disclosed was that the strike had been expensive to everybody in lost income and wages. At the hearings, T. J. Murray appeared on behalf of labour, and Jules Preudhomme held a watching brief for the City of Winnipeg. W. J. Moran appeared on behalf of Manitoba Bridge and Iron Works. No other employers except Moran testified. No representatives of the Citizens' Committee of One Thousand appeared before the commission, although the Committee did file a statement, not reproduced in extenso in the final report. Indeed, the Commission's report reprinted at length only the testimony of labour moderate James Winning, who had been pushed to one side by the radicals earlier in 1919. At the time of his testimony he was involved as president of the Winnipeg Trades and Labor Council in a fierce struggle with the One Big Union for control of Winnipeg's labour movement. Winning testified that the workers had not intended to overthrow the government, and were only seeking to achieve traditional economic goals.

The Robson commission's report maintained that there was a high level of discontent among workers in Winnipeg, with particular concerns focussing upon unemployment and the cost of living. It also insisted on the existence of an aggressive Socialism in Winnipeg, often within the ranks of people of Russian and Austrian origin, although it had made some headway among British subjects. Robson denied that these radical Socialists were serious labour leaders, although 'genuine labour was given the appearance of being linked up with the movements of these men.' Nevertheless, the commissioner insisted that 'the general discontent among labour has been fomented by the Socialist leaders.' Making a careful distinction between leaders and the bulk of workers, he further denied that workers of British or Canadian origin would ever intend to elevate labour to a state of dictatorship or to endorse the course that would lead to the Russian condition, however readily they responded to a strike call. The commissioner offered no evidence for this assertion beyond the testimony of James Winning and an apparent unwillingness to believe that workers of British origin would ever be truly radical.

The strike was in Robson's view a protest against existing living conditions and a demand for general relief. Much of the credit (or blame) in preparing the way for the strike, Robson maintained, went to William Ivens's *Western Labor News*. The commission report discussed at some length the shift from the moderate tone of the trade unionism of *The Voice* to the socialism of the *Western Labor News*, which 'played a large part in fanning the discontent of the working class, and bringing this discontent to such a pitch that, as a class, the working people of Winnipeg were in an extremely receptive mood when the proposal of the General Strike was brought before them.'

Robson insisted that the question of the cause of the strike, which for him was rooted in basic economic concerns, was not identical with the issues of sedition being tried in the courts. He added, 'it should be said that the leaders who had brought about the General Strike were not responsible for the parades or riots which took place, and, in fact, tried to prevent them. In his view, 'turbulent persons affected by this extraordinary condition broke loose.' This careful distinction between the strike proper and the

---

My father, Albert L. Crossin, did not talk much about the Winnipeg General Strike. He seemed to feel that he had done what needed to be done at the time and had put it all behind him.

As the years went by he did seem rather surprised by the continuing interest in the strike, especially as it was focused entirely on the labour side of the story.

The most significant result of the strike was, in his opinion, the defeat of the general strike as an effective tool for settling labour disputes in Canada. 'Since 1919 there has not been another general strike in this country.' As far as I know this statement is still correct.

He was proud of the good job that volunteers did in keeping essential services operating in the city. He said the Citizens' Committee was pleasantly surprised by the ease with which engineering students from the University of Manitoba were able to keep the hydro electric power stations along the Winnipeg River in operation. 'Fortunately there were no equipment failures or we would have been in trouble.'

Alan L. Crossin
Winnipeg

surrounding activities of others was not discussed in detail in the report, nor did Robson attempt to deal with the related question of whether responsibility for the turbulence rested with those who had brought about the 'extraordinary condition.' With this balanced approach contemporaries would have to be content.

■ **THE SEDITION TRIALS:** Until very recently, the post-strike sedition trials of the arrested strike leaders were a relatively unexplored dimension of the Winnipeg General Strike. The trials were important in several respects. In the first place, they were some of the most important (and, at least at the time, most public) sedition trials in modern Canadian history. Secondly, most of the arrested leaders were actually tried and convicted by a jury of their peers on charges of seditious conspiracy; conspiracy cases are normally avoided by the prosecution like the plague, because conspiracy is so hard to prove and so much can go wrong, and seditious conspiracy is just that little bit harder to demonstrate. Thirdly, in gaining convictions, the government was forced to put its case and prove 'intent' to the satisfaction of a jury, the only point in the entire historical record of the strike where the question of the nature of the behaviour of some of its leaders was subjected to the rigours of the adversarial system of the courts, whatever advantages the Crown may have enjoyed in presenting its case. Finally, the trials provided through the evidence introduced and the testimony given a rich tapestry of information about many aspects of the strike available nowhere else.

As we have already seen, the government's initial inclination was to deal with the arrested strike leaders under the provisions of the recently amended Immigration Act, which excluded from its provisions only Canadian-born and naturalized citizens. Of the strike leaders initially arrested, only George Armstrong was a native Canadian. The remaining figures were all British-born and not natu-

ralized, which meant they could in theory be deported using summary proceedings completely outside the well-known safeguards of the common law, including habeas corpus and trial by jury. The 'aliens' arrested at the same time as the strike leaders were handled through the Immigration tribunals. Three of the four were subsequently freed by this procedure, Moses Almazoff being eventually allowed to leave voluntarily for the United States. Only Oscar Choppelrei was deported, technically not for strike activities but because of irregularities in his papers. Almazoff's case had clearly demonstrated the limited legal protection for those facing Immigration Boards of Inquiry. His application for bail pending a decision of the Inquiry Board was denied by Mr Justice Mathers, who held that his court had jurisdiction to grant habeas corpus only in criminal proceedings. Almazoff's case also demonstrated something of a double standard among subsequent chronicles of the strike, for his impassioned speech of defence before a special deportation commission, fully reported in the Jewish press (in Yiddish), was quickly forgotten, while the defending speeches of others arrested at the same time, such as Frederick Dixon and William Pritchard, received much broader coverage.

While the reasons for the government decision to prosecute the strike leaders in the criminal courts rather than using Immigration tribunals remain uncertain, the likelihood is that public pressure for 'British Justice' was fairly irresistible. On 24 June, for example, a petition from the Soldiers' and Sailors' Labor Party was forwarded to Arthur Meighen with 356 signatures. It complained that the government had acted contrary to 'those principles of Liberty and Democracy for which we volunteered to fight.' To some extent the Union government found itself bound by its own wartime rhetoric of British Patriotism, particularly when labour (and other elements of Canadian society) insisted on holding the government to it. 'British Fair Play', cabled 400 members of Winnipeg Machinists Lodge

189 to the federal minister of justice on 2 July, 'consisting of a trial by Jury,' should be granted to all the political prisoners.

On 3 July, six of the prisoners (Ivens, Russell, Heaps, Queen, Bray, and Armstrong) appeared initially in police court before magistrate Sir Hugh J. Macdonald. They had all given notice to A. J. Andrews that they would not recognize the agreement they had signed, calling for their non-participation in labour affairs, as a condition for release on bail. The reason given was that given the way the men had been tried in the press and found guilty, they would not be able to receive fair trials. Thus there was a further legal scuffle over bail, which was set at $8,000 each. At this point the government read the names of the other prisoners who had been taken to Immigration Hall for hearings. When Mike Verenchuck's name was read, A. J. Andrews acknowledged that there was no evidence upon which to hold him under the criminal code, a necessary expedient in his case since Verenchuck was a naturalized Canadian citizen. Instead, Verenchuck, whose sanity was being questioned, was turned over to the military authorities before being finally released.

The subsequent preliminary hearing in magistrates' court before R. M. Noble lasted four weeks, its principal task was to set the terms of the indictments. The Crown introduced large amounts of what it claimed was evidence, the defense objected on the grounds that it was not relevant, and the trial judge usually ruled in favour of the Crown. What was therefore admitted was evidence not directly connected with the accused themselves, such as that of the events of 21 March. According to Magistrate Noble, since the accused were 'ringleaders during the strike', therefore 'evidence of what others did, sympathisers or cooperators in that strike, what they said and did is admissible.' Both in this court and subsequent ones, the defence insisted that this interpretation

SIR HUGH JOHN MACDONALD, 1921.

of admissibility of evidence presumed a fact that the Crown still needed to prove, namely, that the accused had led the strike. The resultant 'true bill', consisting of seven complicated charges of seditious conspiracy, took 52 minutes to read to the eight men accused (the six mentioned above, plus Johns and Pritchard). What needs emphasizing is that the accused were not simply charged with seditious conspiracy in terms of their behaviour in the general strike, but in terms of other 'overt acts' before the strike, some involving the One Big Union. Dick Johns was indicted despite having been physically in Montreal throughout virtually the entire strike period. In addition to the eight charged with seditious conspiracy, Dixon and Woodsworth were charged with seditious libel, and three soldier strikers (Martin, Farnell, Grant) were indicted for 'seditious utterances' at the veterans' meeting on 20 June in Market Square.

A protest parade was held in Winnipeg on 2 September 1919 to object to the proceedings against the eight strike leaders. An estimated 7,000 people took part. The women's section was headed by the Women's Labor League, which contributed two floats, one portraying the figures of Liberty, Equality, and Fraternity. Despite a heavy rain, the parade was followed by a large protest meeting. Helen Armstrong, who had been active in organizing the woman's section of the parade, told a mass protest meeting a few days later that 'Women's vote had given us the club. Now we wanted women to use it.' She visited Ontario frequently in the autumn of 1919 to plead for assistance for the arrested strike leaders. A number of meetings within and without Winnipeg were held to protest the trials, and many resolutions supporting the arrested strike leaders were sent to Ottawa.

On 25 November 1919, the trial of R. B. Russell for seditious conspiracy began in the Court of King's Bench before Mr Justice Thomas Metcalfe. The Crown recognized the dangers of proceeding against multiple defendants simultaneously (as the Americans would in the later and not totally dissimilar 'Chicago Seven' trials), and chose instead to move first against Russell alone. This trial would establish the pattern for those which followed, and so it was generally regarded as the crucial one, followed closely in the press. The selection of a jury of non-Winnipeggers took considerable time. The choice of Robert Cassidy to lead the defence may have been a mistake. Although he had earlier practised in Manitoba, he had been in British Columbia for over twenty years and was regarded as a 'hot-shot' outside criminal lawyer. He repeatedly annoyed Judge Metcalfe throughout the trial, particularly by raising the question of who was paying for the prosecution, which he insisted should be the responsibility of the province and not the federal government. Russell might well have been better advised to defend himself, since he could then have requested more leeway from the court than his defence actually received from Judge Metcalfe.

The performance of Mr Justice Metcalfe, particularly his charge to the jury, clearly played a crucial role in the Russell case, as was probably inevitable given its complexity and high political context. Metcalfe insisted that it was his duty (and not that of the lawyers) to instruct the jury in matters of law, 'and in such matters you ought to follow my directions', although 'in all matters of fact you are the sole judge.' This distinction between fact and law could not genuinely be sustained, however, since much of the evidence introduced into the trial was admitted upon the factual presumption that the accused had led the strike. The defence complained continually that Metcalfe's legal constructs enlarged the area in which fact could be presumed. Metcalfe's trial notes survive, demonstrating that he had done considerable advance research on the law of sedition and related matters before stepping to the bench in this case. Since there was no specific Canadian law of sedition, Metcalfe was forced to rely on the common law for his definitions, which to his mind showed 'how wide

the legal notion of seditious conspiracy is.'

Sedition was defined by Metcalfe through a quote from the English legal authority Archbold: 'It embraced all those practices, whether by word, deed or writing, which fall short of high treason, but directly tend to have for their object to excite discontent or dissatisfaction; to excite ill-will between different classes or the King's subjects; to create public disturbances, or lead to civil war, to bring into hatred or contempt the Sovereign or the government, the laws or constitution of the realm . . . to incite people to unlawful associations, assemblies, insurrections, breaches of the peace.' This broad definition, said Mr. Justice Metcalfe, did not stand in the way of free discussion provided that discussion did not take place '*under circumstances likely to incite tumult.*' He insisted, 'a torch applied to a green field may not be likely to cause a fire, yet when the grass is ripe and dry a spark may cause a conflagration.' Metcalfe also pointed out on more than one occasion that there must be seditious intent: 'When a man is charged with a crime, the essence of the crime is the guilty mind; that is not peculiar to sedition.' At the same time, he added, 'How can a general sympathetic strike, the object of which is to tie up all industry, to make it so inconvenient for others that they will cause force to be brought about, to stop the delivery of food, to call off the bread, to call off the milk, to tie up the wheels of transportation — can such a strike be carried on successfully' without a breach of laws relating to restraint of trade or the breaking of contracts? The judge also gave a broad interpretation to conspiracy, which, he said, 'consists in the agreement of two or more persons to do an unlawful act or to do a lawful act by unlawful means.' Perhaps still more controversially, Metcalfe insisted that while in conspiracy cases the parties must be shown to be pursuing one common intention, it was not necessary that evidence be presented that the individuals accused had actually joined in concert or had met the others charged. 'The usual evidence in a conspiracy case is that the parties are shown to have pursued a line of conduct arising in the estimation of the jury from a common intention.' In short, conspiracy could be implicit as well as explicit. This point was repeatedly denied by the defence, which insisted that the accused had little in common and often fought among themselves.

Whether Metcalfe had operated within the accepted limits of his judicial authority is a matter that will be debated by legal historians for years to come. Certainly the appeal court found nothing untoward in his actions, although Metcalfe had opened the law on sedition and conspiracy about as far as it could be taken and assumed for himself a leading role in interpreting that law. On 23 December the jury delivered a verdict of guilty in the Russell trial, and on 28 December Russell was sentenced to two years in Stony Mountain. A disturbance among the spectators led to the arrest by the bailiffs of one of those present for calling for a 'tiger.' Russell would appeal his conviction unsuccessfully on questions of law to the Manitoba Court of Appeal and then to the Judicial Committee of the Privy Council, which refused to hear the appeal on the grounds that appeals from Canadian criminal courts should remain in Canada.

Before the trials of the remaining seven leaders began, the Crown in January opened the trial of Frederick J. Dixon for seditious libel, with Mr Justice A. C. Galt on the bench. Dixon had been arrested a few days after taking over (with J. S. Woodsworth) the *Western Labor News* following the detention of William Ivens. He elected to defend himself, as had famous Canadian editors Joseph Howe and William Lyon Mackenzie when charged with seditious libel nearly a hundred years earlier. Like his illustrious predecessors, he undertook a crash reading course in the law and visited Lewis St. George Stubbs, one of the province's more radical lawyers, at his home in Birtle over the Christmas holidays. The charges against Dixon were both less extensive and less general. Conviction would

have to rely on whether what Dixon had actually said and written was seditious, and not on what other people had said, written, and done. Dixon approached his defence as a vital matter of freedom of speech and press. In his final speech to the jury, Dixon insisted that his intention had always been to seek peaceful reform. 'Liberty of speech and press have been secured by the fearless action of British juries and Canadian juries, and they can be preserved by the same method,' he maintained. In his peroration, he told the jury, 'You are the last hope so far as the liberty of the subject is concerned. . . In your hands is placed the question of liberty of speech. Whether a man has a right to criticize government officials or not.' The judge did not offer a sympathetic summation to the jury, but Dixon was acquitted on 16 February 1920 after forty hours of jury deliberation. His speech was quickly published by the Winnipeg Defence Committee, set up to raise money to support the costs of defending the strikers. The acquittal of Dixon led to similar charges against J. S. Woodsworth being dropped by the Crown through a *nolle prosequi* plea. (An entry made on the record of a court when the prosecutor or plaintiff is unwilling to continue the suit against the defendent). This action avoided the potential absurdity of the government attempting to prove that two passages from the Old Testament of the Bible quoted by Woodsworth — Isaiah X, 1, and LXV, 21-2 — were indeed 'seditious libel.'

The Russell appeal was dismissed by the Manitoba Court of Appeal on 19 January 1920, and three days later, the trial of the 'Winnipeg Seven' began. Having established a variety of precedents with Russell, the Crown tried the remaining seven defendants together in an omnibus action. Four of those accused (Queen, Heaps, Pritchard, and Ivens) chose to defend themselves. Given the Russell experience, this was probably good strategy. The defence got nowhere attempting to challenge the composition of either the court or the jury, the latter on the grounds that potential jurors had been investigated in advance for their political opinions by the Crown. The defence was unable to prove its allegations before an independent investigation undertaken by the foreman of the Grand Jury. The two sides used the full panel of 110 jurors to select a jury of twelve, all from rural Manitoba.

The evidence introduced was much the same as in the Russell case, as was Metcalfe's charge to the jury. The closing speeches, four of them by the accused defending themselves, were lengthy efforts. William Pritchard's speech, later published, ran to 216 pages. William Ivens spoke for fourteen hours. All the defendants insisted that they had not conspired together, that much of the evidence had been collected by professional spies and informers, and that their rhetoric was not to be taken literally. Pritchard at one point insisted that the term 'revolution', when used among Canadian radicals, usually meant change rather then violence. However, only Abe Heaps managed to persuade the jury that he was not part of the conspiracy. He was acquitted on all seven counts. Roger Bray, who had led the returned soldiers, was convicted only on charge 7, which dealt with conspiracy to commit a common nuisance under sections 221 and 222 of the criminal code. The remaining five were convicted as charged. They were sentenced to a year in prison each, while Bray got six months. Some of the prisoners (including Russell) were subsequently released early, apparently in response to pressure from various labour quarters.

The government had apparently proven its case. Two juries, which were capable of some discrimination, as the acquittal of Heaps and

ALDERMAN A.A. HEAPS, 1924.

the conviction on only one charge to Bray indicate, had been convinced that a seditious conspiracy had indeed fomented the 1919 Winnipeg General Strike. The government had by swift action prevented what it regarded as an incipient revolution, what would in a later context be called an 'apprehended insurrection.'

■ **WINNIPEG POLITICS AFTER THE STRIKE:** While the strike itself had been broken, the spirit of labour in the city of Winnipeg was not. Indeed, the emergence of labour as a force in municipal politics, which had begun before and especially during the Great War, after the strike took on new meaning. For many years after 1919, Winnipeg municipal politics continued the class warfare of the strike itself, with the Citizens' League (an apparent successor to the Citizens' Committee of One Thousand) being systematically opposed by labour. As in most Canadian cities of the time, the Citizens' League was theoretically non-partisan. At the mayoral and aldermanic level, particularly, the political confrontation was very much between the Canadian-dominated business establishment claiming to be politically non-aligned and British-born labour interests. Other ethnic groups seldom had a look-in, even in the immigrant-dominated North End. The only successful ethnic politicians were Jews of British birth, at least until the Citizens' League began endorsing North End ethnic candidates in the 1940s. For twenty-five years after 1919, however, the businessmen never once lost control of the Winnipeg City Council.

STRIKE LEADERS AT STONY MOUNTAIN
L-R, BACK ROW: R. E. BRAY, GEORGE ARMSTRONG, JOHN QUEEN, R. B. RUSSELL, R. J. JOHNS, W. A. PRITCHARD.
L-R, FRONT ROW: W. A. IVENS, A. A. HEAPS, C. 1920.

Establishing a direct connection between the Citizens' Committee of One Thousand and the Citizens' League (variously renamed over the ensuing years) is rendered impossible by the non-existence of membership lists for the former. But the same patterns of personnel as had existed before 1919 prevailed afterwards. The Citizens' League candidates were almost exclusively Protestant (with Anglicans the largest single component and on the increase over time), Canadian-born (the percentage of native-born Manitobans increased greatly over time), and exclusively from a small number of business and professional occupations (including the law). They resided in single-family dwellings, assessed at a minimum of $2,000 and with nearly half assessed at over $5,000, and did best electorally in the wealthier districts of the city. Citizens' Leaguers claimed their non-partisanship partly because they could belong to either of the major national or provincial political parties. Labour continuity was easier to establish, although it was no less coherent than the Citizens' League. Labour politicians were more likely to be Jewish, but equally unlikely as Citizens' Leaguers to be Roman Catholic. Not one labour alderman was Winnipeg-born, and only one Manitoba-born. Labour politicians came almost exclusively from Great Britain, and like the strike leaders of 1919 had been educated in British industrial politics of the turn of the century. Occupationally, they divided about equally into skilled craftsmen and white collar workers. In terms of housing, most labour aldermen lived in homes assessed between $1,000 and $2,000, and none resided in a house assessed for over $5,000. Labour politicians also belonged to two national and provincial political parties, in their case the Independent Labor Party (later the Co-operative Commonwealth Federation) and the Communist Party of Canada. As might be expected, labour support was strongest in the less wealthy and more ethnically mixed districts of the city.

While the two 'parties' did not divide cohesively on every issue debated by City Council, on the key issues with important economic or ideological overtones, such as social welfare, working conditions, or levels of taxation, the polarity was almost perfect throughout the period. For an entire generation after the Winnipeg strike, the two establishments which had fought one another in 1919 continued to do battle on the municipal hustings and in City Council. If anything, the labour group changed even less than the Citizens' League over the subsequent quarter-century after 1919.

■ **CHANGES IN LAW AND LAW ENFORCEMENT:** One of the most demonstrable results of the Winnipeg General Strike was the reorganization of Canada's national police force and the creation of the Royal Canadian Mounted Police. Throughout the Great War, Canada's national police forces, the Royal North-West Mounted Police and the Dominion Police, had assumed an increasing role in the protection of national security. The head of the wartime Canadian secret service was Colonel A. P. Sherwood, Chief Commissioner of the Dominion Police, who was from 1910–1918 also Chief Commissioner of the Boy Scouts' Association of Canada. During the war, the Mounties had spent much of their time under Sherwood's direction investigating rumours of spying and enforcing the War Measures Act among the enemy alien population of the west. As the war came to an end, they, like the government they served, became increasingly interested in radical labour, which seemed most active in western Canada. On 12 December 1918 the Mounties were given responsibility for national security west of the Lakehead, with a force augmented to twelve hundred.

The Royal North-West Mounted Police had played a role in both the events leading up to the Winnipeg General Strike and in the strike itself. Mounted Police undercover agents had infiltrated labour organizations and filed reports as part of a major covert intelligence network. The police had also been publicly present in large numbers in Winnipeg during the period of the strike, although they had not played an active role in law enforcement in the city. They were employed, however, to carry out the arrests and searches for evidence of sedition of 17 June and later, and of course they had performed their famous mounted charge on Black Saturday. The strike itself appears to have demonstrated to the federal authorities the need for a better security and intelligence force in Canada, and the prime minister held discussions on this subject with Royal North-West Mounted Police Commissioner A. B. Perry in early August of 1919. This meeting led to a lengthy memorandum from Perry advocating the creation of a new federal police force.

Perry complained that, under existing arrangements, the Mounted Police were responsible to the president of the Privy Council, the Dominion Police to the minister of justice. The best way to resolve this problem was by amalgamation. Perry understandably preferred to see his own force as the model for the merged organization, and he pointed out that the Royal North-West Mounted Police was a paramilitary operation with a respected reputation which could serve as the basis for a national agency. He recommended that the Mounted Police be given jurisdiction over all of Canada. The federal government's response was swift. On 10 November 1919 there were amendments to the Royal North-West Mounted Police Act which absorbed the Dominion Police, headquartered the new agency in Ottawa, and renamed it the Royal Canadian Mounted Police. The legislation took effect on 1 February 1920, and Commissioner Perry became the first head of the Royal Canadian Mounted Police. Its immediate task was to be the preservation of government authority against what the government perceived to be incipient revolutionary activities such as had occurred in Winnipeg.

In order to strengthen its hand against the revolutionaries, the federal government also made a number of changes to the Criminal Code and to the Immigration Act. The amendments of 6 June 1919 to Section 41 of the Immigration Act, which limited immunity from deportation to those native-born or specifically naturalized and thus legalized the deportation of a large group of Canadian citizens, remained in force for ten years despite a number of attempts to eliminate them. Criminal Code amendments were also added by order-in-council in July of 1919, particularly through the introduction of sections 97A and 97B, later known as Section 98. The former defined as an 'unlawful association' any organization that sought by acts or threats of force, violence, or injury to 'bring about any government, industrial, or economic change' in Canada. Anyone associated with such an organization, if there was no proof to the contrary, was regarded as a member. This 'guilt by association' principle would be at the heart of later Communist witch-hunting, particularly in the United States. Section 97B provided for heavy prison sentences for anyone involved with publication, literature and advertising for such organizations, and made it a duty for public officials to seize such materials wherever found. At the same time, Section 133 of the Criminal Code, which had stated that criticism of the government or His Majesty was not seditious if such criticism was intended to point out what were sincerely believed to be mistakes for the purpose of lawfully changing them, was repealed by Parliament. In this process of Criminal Code reform, a positive provision for the guaranteed right of free speech had been lost, replaced by guilt by association. Section 98 itself was itself not repealed until 1936.

■ **THE VERDICT OF HISTORY:** In 1919, there were two competing extremist interpretations of the Winnipeg General Strike. The conspiratorial one propounded by its opponents was, as the *Citizen* put it on 27 May, 'the so-called general strike is in reality revolution, or a daring attempt to overthrow the present industrial and governmental system.' The other view, maintained by the strike leaders and expressed in *The Strikers' Own History of the Winnipeg General Strike*, was that the strike was nothing other than a legitimate peaceful effort on the part of labour to demand 'the recognition of the right to organize, and the establishment of a living wage.' A more mediated interpretation was in 1919 offered by the Robson Commission, which saw the strike rooted in legitimate labour complaints and demands, but also acknowledged the presence in Winnipeg of radical Socialists who might have sought something else.

While none of these conflicting interpretations gained immediate dominance in 1919, *Free Press* editor John W. Dafoe was certainly correct in his assertion immediately after the arrest of the strike leaders that this action would make martyrs of them. Ironically enough, the man who most benefited from the martyrology of the government repression was J. S. Woodsworth, who had come late on the scene and whose seditious libel case had never actually come to trial. As Allan Mills has observed, 'in popular history Woodsworth has become the one figure identified with the Winnipeg General Strike. Such was his apparent importance, it might almost be believed that he instigated the strike, prolonged its life and, in the aftermath, was the primary victim of the judicial prosecution that took place.' The reason for this popular association, of course, was because Woodsworth was the only figure associated with the strikers who achieved a subsequent national reputation and whose name meant anything to the bulk of Canadians. Popular opinion was able to connect Woodsworth's participation in the strike with his later image of sanctity and reformist gradualism.

Although the odd scholarly study appeared in the generation after 1919 (Walter Ryder's unpublished M.A. thesis for the University of British Columbia in 1921, Wilfrid Crook's *The General Strike: A Study of Labour's Tragic Weapon in Theory and Practice in 1931*), it was through J. S. Woodsworth's career and reputation that the strike was kept alive at all throughout the 1930s and early 1940s. The establishment of the Winnipeg General Strike as a major event in Canadian history (and a major focus for Canadian scholarship, particularly in the field of labour studies) began in 1950 with the publication of Donald C. Masters' *The Winnipeg General Strike*. The Masters book was part of that influential series, funded ironically enough by the Rockefeller Foundation, of studies brought out in the late 1940s and early 1950s on the origins of the Social Credit movement in Alberta. The virtual absence in the book of any bibliography of secondary sources on the strike suggests just how open the topic was when Masters did his research and writing. Masters did his homework. His research in Winnipeg was substantial, and he read extensively in the local newspapers, including the detailed accounts of the trials. His conclusions were much like those of Judge Robson, whom he cited approvingly, in 1919. The strike was 'the result of a unanimous movement within the ranks of Winnipeg labour and was not instigated merely by a small radical group.' That radical group, many of whom had been arrested by the government, had 'obscure' motives but had not sought to overthrow the authorities. There was an atmosphere of governmental paranoia leading to repressive policies in 1919. 'It is therefore the opinion of the author that there was no seditious conspiracy and that the strike was what it purported to be, an effort to secure the principle of collective bargaining.'

Despite the seeming confidence of these conclusions, the Masters book left a lot of loose ends, some of which would continue to bedevil historians. Masters admitted that the strategy of the general strike meant that strikers took over authority from the government. He saw the One Big Union as almost totally outside his strike framework, although he devoted a number of pages to its post-strike organization. The returned soldiers were for Masters clearly a force of potential violence, but he never adequately explained their connection to the strike. Kenneth McNaught had a point when he commented in 1959 that Masters had vacillated between the interpretation of the strike put forward by the government and that presented by the strikers, concluding 'almost reluctantly, that the strike was not an abortive revolution.' There were, moreover, some serious omissions in the Masters analysis. For him, the 'aliens' were simply not important players. Neither for that matter were women, who appeared in the book only as the suffering wives of the arrested strike leaders. Nevertheless, Masters had identified most of the major issues and offered a series of conclusions with which later students of the strike for the most part agreed.

A detailed historiographic analysis of scholarship and writing on the strike since 1950 is well beyond the scope of this narrative. What is important is that although the strikers may have lost the battle in 1919, they won the verdict of subsequent historical study. Increasingly the prominent leaders of the strike became accepted as moderate gradualists, victimized by their opposition through the law and the courts. W. L. Morton set the tone by observing in his *Manitoba: A History*, 'the trials and the sentences were an abuse of the processes of justice by class fear and class rancour.' But in his next sentence, Morton had added, 'It is to be noted, however, that the strike had been a real challenge to public order; it had caused deep fears; the victors were comparatively lenient and the sentences in the circumstances relatively mild.' The perspective implicit in this comment was increasingly lost in the writing about the strike, however, and Morton never pursued it in detail. No one could be found after 1950 (indeed, except for Arthur Meighen nobody had appeared at any point after 1919) to defend seriously the role or policy of the federal government in the strike. The Citizens' Committee of One Thousand became little more than a caricature of unenlightened and conspiratorial plutocrats. The strike was seen not as an incipient revolution, but rather merely as a

modest attempt to win the right to collective bargaining. The number of scholars who suggested anything different could be counted on the fingers of one hand, and none of them took on directly the dominant interpretation. At the time the 50th anniversary of the strike was celebrated in 1969, among the large number of surviving opponents of the strike, only F. G. Thompson would come forward to defend his part, and he insisted vehemently that he had not been a member of the Citizens' Committee of One Thousand. The publication in 1973 of *Winnipeg 1919: The Strikers' Own History of the Winnipeg General Strike*, edited by Norman Penner, and in 1974 of David Jay Bercuson's *Confrontation at Winnipeg: Labor, Industrial Relations, and the General Strike* can be taken as the benchmarks of the growing acceptance of the strikers' 'own history.'

Since the early 1970s the number of studies that deal in whole or in part with the Winnipeg Strike has increased enormously, with perhaps the principal focus on the expansion of topics relatively neglected by previous work rather than upon any reconsideration of the general line of interpretation. Thus we now know far more than before about collateral matters such as: the role of the 'alien' and racism, the role of women, the repression of dissent during and after the Great War, the role of the police, the 1918 general strike, the legal aspects of the trials, Socialist ideology, and the subsequent history of Winnipeg municipal politics.

But as we approach the 75th anniversary of the Winnipeg General Strike, what remains the central feature of its historiography is the extent to which the strikers' own interpretation has come to be the accepted one. In the verdict of history, at least, it is not always the case that to the victor belong the spoils.

A

ADAMS, F. W.: Manager, Adams Brothers Harness Mfg., 154 Market St. Prominent member of Committee of 1000. Residence in 1919: Fort Garry Hotel.

AGENT No. 10: Royal North-West Mounted Police undercover agent who infiltrated Western Labour Conference at Calgary from 13 to 15 March 1919. He reported that the radical Socialists who had taken over the conference sought the overthrow of the existing order. They planned to use the One Big Union and a general strike to achieve their ends. These leaders — identified as Joseph Knight, J. Kavanagh, Victor Midgely, William Pritchard, Joseph Naylor, and R. J. Johns — made public declarations of non-revolutionary intentions, but privately they hoped to precipitate a breakdown of civil order which they could exploit. His superior officer argued that this assessment was 'over drawn,' and plans of revolution merely 'far fetched dreams', and No. 10's report was never forwarded to Ottawa.

AGENT No. 32: anonymous police spy reporting to Regina.

ALCIN, ROSE (MRS): Ran successfully for Winnipeg School Board in 1919 municipal election. Jewish, candidate from the North End. Her father worked for the Talmud Torah. Her opponent, Max Steinkopf, was president of the Torah and known to be a member of the Citizens' Committee of 1000. Criticized by the opposition for her limited educational attainments, she answered 'the existing educational system merely taught children to become "obedient" slaves to the existing capitalistic order and future good members of the committee of 1,000.'

ALIEN INVESTIGATION BOARD: Announced by provincial government in early 1919 to placate fears of returned soldiers in Winnipeg that aliens were taking their jobs. The Board was instructed to issue registration cards only to those enemy aliens who were 'loyal' Canadians, based on testimony of two reliable persons stating that during the past four years, the person in question had been a loyal citizen. Hearings of Board were alleged by critics to be 'kangaroo' courts at the Registration Hall. Many aliens termed disloyal were subsequently scheduled for deportation. Three thousand cases were processed by the Board by early May 1919. Phased out in summer of 1919, partially in response to pressure from the Ukrainian community.

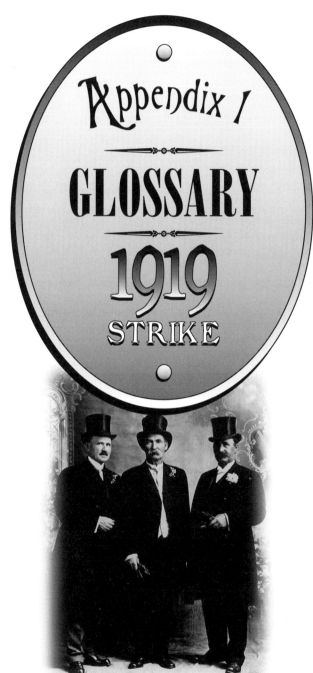

Appendix I
GLOSSARY
1919
STRIKE

GROUP IN FORMAL ATTIRE, 1914

ALIENS: A term usually reserved either for new immigrants from eastern Europe or for 'enemy aliens', those among the immigrants whose origins were in Germany or the Austro-Hungarian Empire. The term often was employed to refer to those 'who had not supported wholeheartedly Canadian participation in the war.' It was not clear who was referred to by the Citizens' Committee when it advertised in the *Manitoba Free Press* on 5 June: 'Choose between the Soldiers who protected you and the Aliens who threaten you!' The *Telegram* (Winnipeg) on 9 January 1919 editorialized: 'The deportation proceedings should not be confined to the enemy aliens that were interned. They should be extended to every alien enemy whose sympathy with the Allied cause has not been capable of the clearest proof from the beginning of the war.' On another occasion the Citizens' Committee defined the term 'undesirable alien' as one of foreign parentage, born in or outside Canada, who has (1) failed to observe the regulations for enemy aliens, (2) being a naturalized Canadian citizen, passed as an alien to evade the draft, (3) became a naturalized citizen by fraudulent means, (4) entered Canada against the immigration laws, and (5) been found disloyal by the Manitoba Alien Investigation Board or any official police record.

ALL PEOPLE'S MISSION: Established in 1898 by Methodists in Winnipeg's North End to serve traditional role of urban mission, including charitable work. J. S. Woodsworth served here 1907–1913, and developed many of his social principles in the process. Became a landmark of the social gospel in Canada.

ALLEN,_____: Member of central strike committee.

ALLISON, PROFESSOR WILLIAM TALBOT (1875–1941): Born in Unionville, Ontario. Worked as a journalist. Appointed professor at Wesley College in 1910, leaving there for position as head of the English Department of the University of Manitoba in 1920. In 1919 Treasurer of Christian Men's Federation of Canada. Regular contributor to local newspapers. Criticized government at Selkirk meeting in late May 1919. Recommended committee of 100 citizens to effect a settlement. Residence in 1920: 254 Furby.

ALMAZOFF, SOLOMON (SAMUEL) PEARL (MOSES) (1890–): Born in Rovne, Voliener Gubernie. Student at University of Manitoba, having come from Russia in 1913 age 23. Was from his arrival an organizer of the Social Democratic Party's Jewish branch. Studied economics and philosophy. Editor, *Die Volke Stimme*, member Social Democratic Party, a communist. An anti-zionist. Elected to Canadian Jewish Congress in 1919. Finished writing exams on 13 June, arrested 17 June. His application for bail pending a decision of the Board of Inquiry was dismissed by Mr Justice Mathers, who held that the court had no jurisdiction. Habeas corpus applied only to criminal proceedings, and these were not criminal. Freed after an impassioned speech before a special deportation commission, arguing he had no objection to deportation to Soviet Russia but not with undesirable tag, which would be an execution permit. His speech was fully reported in the Jewish Press, but has been forgotten. Allowed to leave for United States, where he subsequently resided.

ANDERSON, EDWARD, K.C. (1867–): Born in Dorchester, Quebec, and came to Winnipeg in 1879. Attended University of Manitoba, then practised law in Portage la Prairie before becoming a junior partner of 'Fighting' Joe Martin. Member of law firm of Moran, Anderson, and Guy. General Counsel, Winnipeg Electric Company. Objected on 24 June (and later) to appointment of provincial royal commission, insisting that only a dominion commission would do to 'investigate all matters connected with the plot to overthrow constituted authority in Canada.' Lived at 265 Wellington Crescent.

ANDERSON, G.: Member of central strike committee.

ANDERSON, HELEN: Appointed on 26 May to assist central strike committee with women's matters . Helped organized food kitchens.

ANDREWS, A. J., K.C. (1865–1950): Described by *Toronto Star* in late June 1919 as 'the principal human factor opposing the strike.' Born in Franklin, Quebec, son of a Methodist minister. Came with family to Winnipeg from Galt, Ontario in 1881. Articled with D. A. Walker, then Attorney General of Manitoba. Served in Saskatchewan during Riel Rebellion, admitted to Manitoba Bar in 1886. A Winnipeg alderman in 1893, mayor in 1898, re-elected in 1899. Founding member of Winnipeg Humane Society in 1894. Sought election to Manitoba legislature unsuccessfully on four occasions. Was Conservative candidate from Centre Winnipeg in 1914. Described by a contemporary as 'preeminently a trial lawyer, a strategist and tactician to be respected and

A. J. ANDREWS, 1909

feared but never hated by his opponents.' Obituary claimed he 'had a fund of common sense and a talent for practical affairs that also brought many of the city's leading businessmen to his door for advice.' Met at Thunder Bay with Meighen and Robertson in late May, convincing Robertson that the 'motive behind this strike undoubtedly was the overthrow of constitutional government.' Appointed representative of federal justice department on 26 May, charged with ascertaining 'whether or not the activities of these men [strike leaders] is of a seditious or treasonable character and to advise as to what should be done.' Became

special deputy minister of Justice and chief Crown counsel in trials. Pillar of Methodist church. Lived at 749 Wellington Crescent.

ANDREWS, G. W. (MAJOR) (1869–1943): Born in Oxfordshire, emigrated to Manitoba in 1890 and settled at Springfield to farm. In real estate business before the war. Elected to the Union Parliament for Winnipeg Centre as conscriptionist in 1917 with 21,000 vote majority. Supported strike in Commons debates on 2 June. Lived at 96 Academy Road.

APPEAL TO REASON, THE: Kansas-based radical journal circulating in Canada. Called facetiously by Canadian socialists 'The Appeal to Treason.'

ARBEITER RING (WORKMEN'S CIRCLE): Founded in 1900 by a group of radical East European Jews as the first Jewish labour and fraternal organization in the United States. Had 48,000 members in 1915 in 546 branches across North America, including Winnipeg. In Winnipeg, the Arbeiter Ring served as the umbrella organization for progressive and radical elements of Winnipeg's Jewish community. Operated at the social, cultural, and ideological level. It had three branches, each of which was permitted to practise its particular version of radicalism: (1) Branch 169, the revolutionary Marxists (Bundists); (2) Branch 506, the Nationists or Socialist Territorialists; and (3) Branch 564, the Anarchists. A co-ordinating committee within the city not only provided continuity for these disparate branches, but linked them to other cities.

ARCTIC ICE COMPANY: One of those firms allowed to operate by permission of the strike committee until 4 June. Address was 156 Bell Avenue.

ARMSTRONG'S POINT: Residential enclave in northern bend of Assiniboine River near Wolseley district. Developed as the 'Faubourg St. Germain of Winnipeg.' Home of many of Winnipeg's business and professional classes, contained large lots and limited access through its own gates. Some of its homes were of unusual (for Winnipeg) Arts and Crafts style. 'There were no houses...', recalled one Winnipegger, 'there were only castles, huge castles three full stories in height, some with leaded glass windows, and all, certainly, with dozens of rooms. They were built in an assortment of architectural styles and peopled by names from Winnipeg's commercial and industrial *Who's Who.*'

ARMSTRONG, A.: Arrested 21 June and charged with intimidation. Convicted December 1919 and given suspended sentence.

ARMSTRONG, GEORGE (1870–1956): Native of Scarborough, Ontario, descended from United Empire Loyalist stock. Came to Winnipeg in 1905. Member and one-time organizer of Carpenters' Union, founding member of the Socialist party in Winnipeg. Prominent Marxist exponent. Not to be confused with the George Armstrong working as motorman on streetcar. Regarded as a talented soap-box orator. After strike a member of the Manitoba legislature. His wife Helen was leader of Women's Labor League. Arrested on 17 June 1919. Found guilty on 28 March and sentenced to one year. Retired to Victoria in 1945 and died in Concord, California. Address in 1919 was on Edmonton St.

ARMSTRONG, HELEN (–1949): Leader of local chapter of Women's Labor League, referred to by *Toronto Star* as 'business manager for the Women's Unions' and later dubbed by eastern newspapers 'The Wild Woman of the West.' Organized several women's strikes during the War. In charge of arrangements for kitchen main-

tained by the Women's League, initially in Strathcona Hotel beginning 24 May, later in Oxford Hotel. According to Citizens' Committee spent much time in an asylum. Wife of George Armstrong. Described by contemporaries as 'feisty' and 'fiery.' Arrested several times during Winnipeg strike for urging shopgirls and female workers to join strike, including once on 30 May outside Canada Bread Company's plant. Her campaign begun on 26 May at 5:00 a.m. against smaller store employees was very successful. *Tribune* complained that 'employees going into the business places were accosted and efforts were made to persuade them to join the general strike.' Also arrested on 5 June on disorderly conduct charges while inciting strikers on Main Street near Market Square. Committed for trial later in June on charge of counselling to commit an indictable offense by inciting Ida Kraatz and Margaret Steinhauer to assault two *Tribune* employees selling newspapers on the street. She was held in jail until she obtained bail, which authorities refused to grant for some days. Told mass protest meeting on 7 September 1919 that 'Women's vote had given us the club. Now we wanted women to use it.' Visited Ontario frequently after her husband was arrested, to plead for assistance for arrested strike leaders.

Organized the children of Weston to sing 'Solidarity Forever' and old Scottish and English folk songs outside the walls of Stony Mountain Penitentiary. Resided in 1919 on Edmonton St.

ARMY AND NAVY VETERANS' ASSOCIATION: One of a number of veterans' organizations that sprang up at the end of the war. The Winnipeg branch refused to become involved with Central Strike Committee and remained officially neutral throughout the strike. Address was 312 Main St. Major officers were J. Hay, president, J. H. Holman, 1st vice-president, Captain E. Kay, 2nd vice-president, W. A. Shepherd, Business Manager.

J.H. ASHDOWN, 1909

ASHDOWN, J. H. (1844–1924): Pioneer Winnipeg hardware merchant. Opposed unsuccessfully the speaking tour of Emma Goldman in Winnipeg in 1907. Owned a huge mansion at 549 Wellington Crescent.

B

BAIRD, HUGH N. (1876–1963): Grain merchant in firm of Baird and Botterell. President of the Grain Exchange 1909–1910. Chairman, Finance committee of Citizens' Committee of 1000. Later (1924) was Chief Executive Officer of National Steel Car of Montreal. Resided in 1919 at 260 Wellington Crescent.

BAKERY AND CONFECTIONARY WORKERS: Struck in sympathy on 16 May 1919.

BARKER, H. E.: Chairman of Train Services Employees Committee and Chairman of Running Trades Mediation Committee, in which capacity at the end of May he approached Mayor Gray, the strikers, and the employers with an offer to mediate the dispute. Wrote on 7 June to the Metal Masters: 'If, as you state, our recommendation is virtually the proposition upon which you and your employees parted ways . . . we

are not surprised that a strike occurred. . . . it was our opinion that these principles of collective bargaining would be carried out by a proper recognition of the Union which would carry with it recognition of the Metal Trades Council.' Later signed statement released on 16 June that the offer of the Ironmasters to the Metal Trades Council constituted collective bargaining as practised on the railroads.

BARRETT, L. R.: Representative of Metal Trades Employers, vice-president of Vulcan Iron Works. A proponent of bonuses for excessive piecework production and a hard-core opponent of negotiating with unions under any circumstances. Refused in 1916 to meet a committee of his own employees, writing the chairman of the Munitions Board, 'This is a free country and . . . as far as we are concerned the day will never come when we will have to take orders from any union.' Resided in 1919 at 91 Edmonton.

BATHIE,_____: Sat as Great War Veterans' Association observer on strike committee.

BATSFORD,_____: Returned soldier got the floor at 31 May meeting with premier, asked for legislation on collective bargaining.

BERESLER, ELIZABETH: Mentioned by *Free Press* on 27 June as member of unlawful assembly of 10 June. Committed to trial.

BERROL, ADOLPH: Motorman on the Winnipeg Street Railway. Arrested on 21 June and charged with rioting. Sentenced on 11 November 1919 to 23 months.

BLAKE, DR M. R. (1876–1937): Born Ashfield Township, Ont. Studied medicine in London and Dublin. Medical officer and Captain, 106 Winnipeg Light Infantry. Elected to Union Parliament in 1917 as Conservative M.P. for Winnipeg North. Opposed strike in Commons on 2 June. Address in 1919 275 Burrows.

BLAND, SALEM (1859–1950): Born at Lachute, Canada, Bland taught at Wesley College from 1903 until his dismissal in 1917. Very influential in Winnipeg social gospel and labour reform circles before and during World War I. Served as columnist for *The Grain Growers' Guide* from 1917 until he moved to Toronto in 1919. An influential popularizer of the linkage between liberal theology and socialism. He urged a constant battle against slums, monopolies, and unearned profits. Exponent of Henry George's single tax ideology.

Influential teacher of Woodsworth, Ivens, and other social gospellers. Despite his radical enthusiasm, Bland was chary of general strikes and labour militancy. On 11 May 1919 he told a labour audience that he doubted labour could cause a revolution, though 'they could involve the country in great misery.' He told a Toronto audience on 25 May that he condemned syndicalism as an 'evil dream', which was 'not possible and not just.' Wrote *The New Christianity* in 1920.

BLASK, HARRY: See Zaneth, F. W.

BLUMENBERG, SAM: Popular Socialist in Winnipeg. During a meeting at the Columbia Theatre in Winnipeg in May 1918, he told his audience 'We are going to run this city and we will not consent to having any scab working beside us.' Blumenberg refused to explain away this remark, later saying 'I meant to go further than this. . . I was going to say, "We are going to run the Dominion of Canada. It is our aim to change the trades union into a Socialist industrial union. If the capitalistic class were not afraid that the strike in Winnipeg would spread throughout the country and grow into a social revolution they would not have settled the [1918 general] strike as easily as they did."' He told

the Majestic Theatre meeting in December 1918 that 'the map of Palestine was written on his face, and on his nose was the mount of Zion.' Delegate to Winnipeg Trades and Labor Council, formerly member of Socialist Party of Canada. Denounced Allied intervention in Russia at Walker Theatre meeting, where he wore a red tie. He insisted that 'Bolshevism is the only thing that will emancipate the working class. . . There are thousands of men coming back who went over to fight. They will say, "We have fought for this country and by the gods, we are going to own it." ' His business establishment (a cleaning shop, the Minneapolis Dye House) was wrecked by rampaging veterans in January 1919. Arrested 17 June 1919. Held for deportation. Left for the United States rather than be deported to Europe. Subsequently worked as labour organizer in Duluth and Minneapolis and ran for municipal office as a socialist. Resided in 1919 at 318 Good.

BOAL, K.: Arrested on 21 June and charged with rioting. Convicted in June and fined $10 and costs.

BOARD OF TRADE: See Winnipeg Board of Trade.

BOLSHEVISM: Term used to refer to the revolutionary actions in

Russia. On the one hand a term of opprobrium used to refer to all people and movements committed to revolution and the overthrow of established authority, on the other a term of praise employed to refer to genuine radicalism rather than gradualism. Term was derived from the Bolshevik section of the Russian Social Democratic Party, which was led by confirmed revolutionaries like Lenin and Trotsky who took the lead in the downfall of Russia's Kerensky government. Bolshevism was a programme around which some radicals in Canada hoped to unite their disparate factions in 1917. It became extended in Canada to all extreme industrial and political action, and even to anything radical. The strike leadership in Winnipeg attempted to argue that the term in Canadian radical usage did not refer to Russian Bolshevism, the *Strike Bulletin* insisting that 'all Labor men, and many others today are Bolsheviks meaning they are in revolt and using the word much as a policeman does when he says he is going after a man's scalp, meaning he intends to get his man.' It was, on the other hand, defined by Arthur Meighen in House of Commons on 2 June 1919 as 'a combination of all organizations of labour in the Dominion taking part in and determining the event of every dispute as to labour conditions and wages here, there, and at any other point, why then you have the perfection of Bolshevism', and popular jazz music was described by the *Tribune* as 'musical Bolshevism.' The Toronto *Globe* on 21 December 1918 called Bolshevism 'a label for any act or tendency which happens to offend our beliefs and prejudices.'

BONNER, R. A. (1860–1932): Born Ontario. Educated at Osgoode Hall, and came to Winnipeg in 1882. Called to the bar in 1889. Partner in Bonner, Trueman, Hollands, and Robinson. Counsel for the defence in trials of strike leaders. Resided in 1919 at 206 Langside.

BORDEN, ROBERT (1854–1937): Prime minister of Canada in 1919, by which time he was leading a Unionist government composed of members of the Conservative Party plus a number of pro-conscriptionist Liberals which had won the election of 1917 on a win-the-war pro-conscriptionist platform. Spent much of first half of 1919 as head of the Canadian delegation at the Peace Conference at Versailles. He basically left the administration of the country (and the handling of the Winnipeg Strike) to his ministers, although he shared their belief that the strike was a dangerous revolutionary situation. On 27 May announced in the Commons that his government would maintain law and order in Winnipeg, and would not permit the dislocation of 'the public service under the conditions that have arisen in the city of Winnipeg.' Wrote in his memoirs that the strike was based upon 'absurd conceptions of what had been accomplished in Russia.'

BOTTERELL, JOHN E. (1880–1924): Prominent grain broker, came to Winnipeg in 1913 and became partner of Baird and Botterell. President of the Grain Exchange in 1919. Member of St Luke's Anglican Church. Lived at 254 Wellington Crescent. Leading member of Citizens' Committee.

BRANDON TRADES AND LABOR COUNCIL: Protested arrests at mass meeting 17 June.

BRASTER, MRS PETE: Arrested on 5 June and charged with being a member of an unlawful assembly (at Main Street near Market Square).

BRAY, ROGER E.: Born in Sheffield, England, migrated to Winnipeg in 1903. Worked in butcher trade. A former Methodist lay preacher and socialist, who had discovered 'that Christianity was not the means of correcting social injustice.'

He had joined Canadian army in 1916 while unemployed, later explaining he had 'no job and a large family.' Returned to Winnipeg from England on 31 December 1918. Alleged by Citizens' Committee to be a Bolshevist seeking Soviet Government in Winnipeg. Along with A. E. Moore led veterans' meeting on 29 May to agree to demonstrations and parades in favour of strikers. Served as spokesman for returned soldiers meeting in Victoria Park, and as chairman of returned soldier strikers. On 4 June told the soldiers at the legislative building, 'Boys, you have signified confidence in your committee and its ability to handle the case. Please don't interrupt the speakers. If anyone tells lies there are enough of us here who know the facts to confound them without you butting in.' On 14 June a secret agent of Royal North-West Mounted Police informed Superintendent of Winnipeg District that Bray was 'at the present time the most dangerous person in the City.' He is alleged to have asserted that the strike would end with a fight, adding, 'Don't worry about guns, we'll have them.' Alleged to have 3,000–4,000 men ready to infiltrate Minto Barracks and get possession of rifles. Arrested on 17 June. Vice-president of Winnipeg Labor Council formed by One Big Union on 5 August 1919. Tried with 6 others for seditious conspiracy. Decision on 28 March 1920. Acquitted on first six counts and convicted only on seventh and less serious charge (conspiracy to commit a criminal nuisance); sentenced to 6 months. Subsequently became One Big Union organizer. Eventually moved to North Vancouver, where he raised gladioli. Resided in 1919 at 187 Eugenie.

BUILDERS' EXCHANGE:
Employers' organization in the Winnipeg Building Trades. In August 1916 worked out a progressive agreement with the Winnipeg District Council of Carpenters. Initially enthusiastic in 1919 about negotiations with Building Trades Council, which would mean one agreement would cover the entire industry. But claimed it could not afford demands of workers. Approached for funds by Citizens' Committee of 1000 in 1919. After strike, with construction in Winnipeg booming, settled with individual unions for wages retroactive to 1 July which were higher than before strike.

BUILDING TRADES COUNCIL:
Umbrella organization for unions in the building trades in Winnipeg. In January of 1914 forced to allow member unions to withhold payments because of their inability to collect dues from members. In spring of 1919 took on responsibility for negotiating working agreements with Builders' Exchange. Despite initial approval of employers to principle of industry-wide negotiation, the wage demands of the Building Trades Council for an across-the-board 20 cent per hour raise was rejected by the Builders' Exchange, which offered 10 cents. The Building Trades Council pulled its workers off their jobs on 1 May 1919.

C

CAHAN, C. H. (1861–1944):
Born Hebron, Nova Scotia. Educated at Dalhousie University. Active in Latin American tramway and electrical enterprises. Montreal lawyer. Appointed in September of 1918 by Prime Minister Borden to position as Director of Public Safety, charged with creating a centralized domestic security system. Resigned soon after because of frustrations with government, but succeeded in getting government to pass orders-in-council intended to suppress dissent and unrest, especially P.C. 2381. Cahan was convinced the Justice Department was 'soft on Bolshevism.' Regarded One Big Union and International Workers of the World as bedfellows. Later served as Conservative M.P. Described in 1929 by the British

high commissioner in Ottawa as the 'mouthpiece' of the Holt, Gundy and other big business interests of Montreal.

CALGARY CONVENTION OF MARCH 1919: Meeting of western delegates of labour locals affiliated to the Trades and Labor Council beginning 13 March 1919 at Labor Temple of Calgary. Convention endorsed reorganization of Canadian workers on basis of industrial organization rather than craft unionism. Also endorsed 30-hour week (six hour day, five day week) for all labour in dominion. It resolved for replacement of production for profit by production for use. It also resolved a recommendation to organized labour in Canada for the industrial organization of all workers, the name of the organization to be called 'The One Big Union', although it specified few details. The convention endorsed the Russian Bolshevik and Spartacan Revolutions, the principle of 'Proletariat Dictatorship.' A verbatim report of the Convention was published in the Winnipeg *Tribune* of 5 April 1919.

CALGARY RESOLUTION: Resolution passed in a Calgary theatre on 23 February 1919 by a meeting of returned soldiers, calling for 'full re-establishment' to civilian

conditions by the payment of a bonus of $2,000 for every soldier who had served overseas. The idea rejected by the Borden government because of its enormous cost.

CAMERON, MR JUSTICE JOHN DONALD (1858–1923): Born Woodstock, Ontario. Of Scottish ancestry. Came to Winnipeg in 1880. Active in the Liberal Party. Appointed judge of King's Bench in 1906 and judge of Court of Appeal in 1908. Denied first bail application of eight leaders charged with seditious conspiracy. Resided in 1919 at the Fort Garry Hotel.

CAMPBELL, _____: CONSTABLE: One of several police spies in Winnipeg reporting to Regina.

CANADIAN EXPEDITIONARY FORCE (C.E.F): The official umbrella title for the Canadian army in Europe in the Great War.

CANADIAN JEWISH CONGRESS: Met in Montreal in March 1919, composed of representatives (elected by secret ballot) of the various local Jewish communities. A Jewish parliament was regarded as necessary in the post-war world to preserve the Jewish existence which was threatened in so many places. Followed on the heels of the

birth of the American Jewish Congress on 15 December 1918. Delegates to the Canadian Jewish Conference represented 124 organizations. Twenty delegates were elected from Winnipeg at a meeting in the Talmud Torah Hall in December 1918 attended by 3,500 Jews. The Congress highlighted the extent to which the emergence of Zionism with the Balfour Declaration of 1917 tended at that time to isolate from their fellow Jews those Jewish radicals who did not accept the Zionist position.

CANADIAN LABOR CONGRESS (CLC): See Trades and Labor Congress of Canada.

CANADIAN LABOR PARTY (CLP): See also Labor Party of Canada. Attempts to form a Labor Party in Canada based upon the British Labour Party, independent of existing socialist and labour parties, were frequent in the early years of the twentieth century. The Winnipeg Labor Party was formed in 1903, *The Voice* reporting most attendance from 'old-countrymen who made evident their determination to support a movement similar to the one with which they had hitherto been associated.' The British Columbia section of the Canadian Labor Party was founded in 1906, the Ontario branch on Good Friday in 1907. In Ontario, the Canadian Labor Party first ran in a provincial general election in June of 1908 in four ridings in Toronto, contested by the socialists. It remained an organization on paper in Manitoba and Ontario until it disappeared in 1909. Attempts to rejuvenate a Labor Party in 1912 failed. The Trades and Labor Congress decided to encourage a National Labor Party in the 1917 election, but none was organized in time. A Labor Party contested a number of seats in that election in Ontario. In Manitoba, R. S. Ward and R. A. Rigg were nominated by the Manitoba section of the Canadian Labor Party at a convention of 600. Labor Party candidates did not win any seats and won no more than 20 per cent of the vote in any of the 27 constituencies they contested. A drive to organize a National Party in 1918 led to a convention in Toronto in March, which only organized an Ontario section of the Canadian Labor Party, with much debate between those who wanted a broad party and those who sought a workingman's party. Attempts to unite labour under the Canadian Labor Party banner failed on a number of occasions between 1919 and the 1920s. The difficulty of organizing a broad-based party in the face of much division and ideological squabbling symbolized much of the problems facing labour on the political front after the war.

CANADIAN PROBLEMS CLUB: Winnipeg organization composed of professional men which asked for information on strike and attempted to intervene with the city on behalf of strikers. Delegation of R. A. Rigg, F. M. Black, R. F. McWilliams, and Professor Chester Martin, asked City Council on 30 May to modify policy regarding the police, particularly the pledge the police were being asked to sign that they would never join any union.

CANADIAN RECONSTRUCTION ASSOCIATION: Post-war organization which attempted to bring harmony between labour and capital using plans of W. L. Mackenzie King acting as labour consultant to John D. Rockefeller.

CANADIAN SERVICE LEAGUE: Formed in 1916 at a conference of delegates from recruiting leagues meeting in Ottawa to press for registration and conscription. Its purpose was 'to promote any form of National Service which the need of the hour may demand.' Honorary president was Chief Justice T. G. Mathers of Manitoba.

CARRUTHERS, JAMES MALCOLM (1872–1947): Born Quebec, came to Winnipeg in 1900. An experienced and skilled cheese-

JAMES M. CARRUTHERS, 1909

maker. General Manager and Director of Crescent Creamery Company. Suggested use of controversial placards in which Strike Committee authorized milk deliveries. Resided in 1919 at 600 Macmillan.

CARTWRIGHT, S.: Head, Soldiers' and Sailors' Labor Party.

CASSIDY, ROBERT (1857–1947): Educated Queen's University, Belfast. Came to Canada 1875, called to Manitoba bar 1882. Practised in Victoria from 1892.

Defended Russell in R. v. Russell. Reputedly annoyed judge continually throughout the trial, particularly by raising the question of who was paying for the prosecution, which he insisted should be the business of the Province of Manitoba.

CENTRAL STRIKE COMMITTEE: The executive of the general strike committee nominated on 21 May 1919, included _____ Allen, George Anderson, Thomas Flye, W. A. Greer, W. D. Lovatt, W. Miller, J. L. McBride, R. M. Noble, Laurence Pickup, Ernest Robinson, R. B. Russell, _____ Shaw, _____ Smith, H.G. Veitch, James Winning.

CHAMBERS, COLONEL ERNEST JOHN (1862– 1925): Born in Penkridge, Staffordshire, England. Journalist, whose first important assignment for the *Montreal Star* was the reporting of the Riel trial. Between 1908 and 1921 he edited the *Canadian Parliamentary* Guide. Active in militia circles, he was appointed in 1915 as Dominion censor. According to radicals he allowed newspaper articles to be printed not on questions of accuracy but upon question of harmony with the policy of the government. Chambers believed that 'there is a limit' to the right to discuss political questions, adding, 'when people say that the war is none of our business,

they are unquestionably using treasonable expressions which should be stopped.' He closed in mid-July 1917 the offices of a radical (Social Democratic Party) anti-war newspaper published in Victoria, and recommended suppression of several other papers on the grounds that 'the developments along extreme Socialistic lines on the part of several newspapers in Canada is due to enemy support.' He firmly believed that collectivist ideology was duping the ignorant masses into revolution. Warned William Ivens in the autumn of 1918 that a failure to limit pacifist and radical articles in the *Western Labor News* would result in shutdown, but never acted. Prominent military historian of his day.

CHARITONOFF, M.: Former editor of *Robotchny Narod* (Working People), a weekly paper published in Russian and the organ of the Ukrainian Social Democratic Party. He was Jewish and had been tried in 1918 for possession of seditious literature but let off on a technicality thanks to defense of T. J. Murray. Suspected in 1919 of receiving funds from Bolshevist organizations in United States. Arrested 17 June 1919. Ordered deported but released after appeal to Ottawa.

CHOPPELREI, OSCAR: (see Schappellrei)

CITIZENS' COMMITTEE OF ONE HUNDRED: Composed of business and professional people, negotiated directly with workers in 1918 civic workers' strike in Winnipeg and helped settle all outstanding issues. The *Telegram* of 17 May listed the names of the members of this committee, to a total of exactly 100. The majority lived north of the Red River in Wolseley, the downtown area, St James, and the St John's district, and there was a large contingent in the less opulent sections of Crescentwood. Only a handful lived on Wellington Crescent and Armstrong's Point.

CITIZENS' COMMITTEE OF ONE THOUSAND: Composed chiefly of members from the Winnipeg Board of Trade, the Winnipeg Branch of the Canadian Manufacturers' Association, and the Manitoba Bar Association, although a number of office workers preferred to identify themselves with business rather than labour. Never did publicize its membership as had the Committee of One Hundred. Had headquarters in the Industrial Bureau at the Board of Trade building on Main Street. One lawyer, J. W. Wilton, who dealt with the executive of the Committee, subsequently reported, 'I sized up the personnel. There was not a returned soldier there. Newspaper editors, bankers, manufacturers and capitalists abounded.' Did not appear before Robson Commission. Never publicized its membership and the names of only a few members (mainly lawyers) are known. Membership was not included in any of the obituaries of its members. Characterized by R. E. Bray as representing 'the same bunch of boodlers who plundered this Province to the verge of bankruptcy.' Its intended aims were expressed in the following resolutions: (1) 'Resolved, that this Committee is opposed to the principle of sympathetic strikes by employees in Public Utilities, Departments of Public Service, and those which affect the distribution of milk and food.' (2) 'That no employees who are members of unions having affiliation with any outside organization, which purport to exercise authority over the employees in relation to their actions towards their employers, should be employed or retained in the City Police Department, Fire Department, Water Works Department, City Light and Power Department, Government Telephones or Postal Service.' (3) 'That this Committee, however, recognizes the right of any such employees as so desire to form unions or associations among themselves, and to bargain with their employers as to wages and working conditions

through their committee, without any interference whatever by any outside body, which may affect their allegiance to their employers, and the position of trust which they occupy toward the Public, and also the right in the case of disagreement to appeal to a duly constituted Board of Authority.' Its leaders subsequently insisted that its major function was to support constituted authority and to maintain public utilities through the use of volunteer labour. A totally ad hoc enterprise, the Citizens' Committee's table of organization was much like that of other Winnipeg volunteer operations, and indeed, it harnessed middle-class Winnipeg's celebrated 'volunteer spirit' for a purpose more overtly political than usual. Not surprisingly, Winnipeg's ethnic and labour communities have always been suspicious of volunteerism. At its height the Committee probably contained more than 1,000 'members.' Succeeded by the Citizens' League, which formed a 'non-partisan' political party contesting Winnipeg municipal elections for a quarter of a century in opposition to Labour candidates.

CITIZENS' COMMITTEE OF TWO HUNDRED: Formed on 16 May at meeting at Winnipeg Industrial Bureau. Succeeded by Citizens' Committee of One Thousand.

CITIZENS' LEAGUE: Successor to the Citizens' Committee of 1000, a purportedly 'non-partisan' political organization created in September 1919 'to permanently [sic] carry on the work of the Citizens' Committee of One Thousand.' Its constitution emphasized that it stood for 'the inculcation of the best Canadian ideals; the cultivation of respect for Canadian law; the proper maintenance of constitutional government and the combating of all forms of propaganda tending to subvert our established Canadian institutions.' Organized to prevent 'the Bolsheviks and red revolutionaries' from taking over city hall.

COLLECTIVE BARGAINING: The proper meaning of collective bargaining was one of the major issues of the strike, both at the beginning and at the end. The breakdown of negotiations between the metal industry employers (the 'ironmasters') and the Metal Trades Council in 1919 came partly over the refusal of the employers to agree to bargain with the Metal Trades Council instead of individual unions. The employers always insisted that they had not rejected collective bargaining, but merely the Metal Trades Council's definition of it. The Great War Veterans' Association on 23 May declared 'ignorance of what collective bargaining means is displayed by the labour people, citizens' committee and anyone else who draws the conclusion that the [association] backed the strike.' The Hamilton *Herald* in an editorial on 27 May had made the distinction: 'Collective bargaining, according to the common acceptation of the term, is negotiation between the employers in a particular industry and chosen workers representing the crafts engaged in that industry, with a view of agreeing upon wage scales and working conditions. That is the sort of collective bargaining that the Winnipeg employers will agree to. The strike committee's interpretation is that any agreement arranged by employers and the representatives of workers engaged in any craft must first be submitted to and endorsed by the central labour body before it becomes effective — the central labour body having the right either to accept or reject the agreement. Such an arrangement would, of course, deprive any union of craft workers of the power to make final agreements with employers.' The Citizens' Committee of 1000 passed a resolution recognizing 'the right of any of such employees as so desire to form Unions or Associations among themselves, and to bargain with their employers as to wages and working conditions through their

Committees,' adding 'without any interference whatever by any outside body which may affect their allegiance to their employers and the position of trust which they occupy towards the public.' The strikers always maintained that this interpretation of collective bargaining amounted to a principle of divide and conquer, forcing negotiating unions into weak positions. They preferred a system in which employers bargained industry-wide with a strong union bargaining agent. The employers and the Citizens' Committee of 1000 saw their version of collective bargaining vindicated in the agreement worked out between Secretary of Labour Robertson, the Ironmasters, and the running trades unions of the railroads, and released publicly on 16 June 1919. Employer policy on collective bargaining (which allowed for membership in unions but did not insist upon it; allowed the right of trade organizations to negotiate with the employers; allowed for settlement of disagreements by negotiation between employers and 'the committee representing all the trade unions employed by the firm or firms concerned'; and called in international officers of the unions involved when all else failed) was approved by Robertson as 'a full and complete recognition of collective bargaining,

as generally interpreted and applied, and is entirely in accord with the established practice on our Canadian railways.' The railway union heads concurred with Robertson that the Ironmasters' version of collective bargaining was the same as that of the railways.

CONFEDERATE, THE: Journal of Dominion Labor Party in Brandon, edited by A. E. Smith.

CONSPIRACY: According to T. L. Metcalfe, judge in the trials of the arrested strike leaders, conspiracy 'consists in the agreement of two or more persons to do an unlawful act or to do a lawful act by unlawful means.' More controversially, Metcalfe — who told the jury that it ought to follow his directions in matters of law — insisted that while in conspiracy cases the parties must be shown to be pursuing one common intention, it was not necessary that evidence be presented that the individuals accused had actually joined in concert or had met the others charged. Agreement, in short, could be implicit as well as explicit.

CONSUMERS ARTIFICIAL ICE COMPANY: W. S. Thomson was president and general manager, and the address was 504 Main Street. This was one of the firms delivering essential services allowed to operate by strike committee until 4 June.

COOPER, WILLIAM (1858–1935): Winnipeg resident who wrote often in the *OBU Bulletin* in 1919 and 1920, producing much of its distinctive ideology. Cooper was an Aberdonian cabinetmaker who had helped form the Aberdeen branch of the Social Democratic Foundation, served 11 years as a member of the Aberdeen City Council, and was active in much municipal reform. He came to Winnipeg in 1907. Besides extensive writing, he conducted classes at a Workers' University on Monday afternoons, influencing many including Woodsworth and Ivens. He helped bring the philosophy of British industrial unionism to Canada and adapted it to Canadian conditions. Resided in 1919 at 666 Jessie.

COPPINS, SERGEANT FREDERICK GEORGE: Former sergeant-major in Canadian Expeditionary Force. One of few casualties of 10 June melee. Injured by somebody and two ribs broken. Daily newspapers claimed beaten by foreigners; *The Tribune* said 'enemy ruffians', while *The Winnipeg Citizen* blamed 'three Austrians', men 'whose blood relations he and every other returned fighter fought in France' —

but others claimed Coppins swore his minor injuries were inflicted by returned soldiers. A returned soldier himself, he had won the Victoria Cross in 1918 as the surviving member of a group of five who had volunteered to destroy 24 enemy machine gun nests; he not only succeeded but marched back with prisoners. He had enlisted a few days earlier as a special constable.

COX, W. T.: A car inspector for the Canadian Pacific Railway, he was a self-confessed member of the middle class who told City Council he was learning to drill and shoot at Minto Barracks and wanted to tell Robertson and Meighen to go back to Ottawa. Resided in 1919 at 510 Riverton.

COYNE, JAMES BOWES (1879–1965): Winnipeg lawyer and prominent member of Citizens' Committee of 1000. Wrote in October of 1918 that the Winnipeg Trades and Labor Council was 'now largely dominated by labour leaders who are acknowledged Bolsheviki and whose desire I believe is to substitute a workmen's council with the Russian motto as the governing force in the municipality instead of the representative bodies now constituted by law.' Member of law firm of Coyne, McVicar and Martin. Resided in 1919 at 230 Yale.

CRESCENT CREAMERY COMPANY: Required permission card used on milk wagons to indicate sanction of strike committee for delivery. Its manager had first suggested the use of placards. Located on Sherburn St., in Killarney district of city.

CRESCENTWOOD: Residential district in south Winnipeg developed just before the Great War. Winnipeg developer Charles Henry Enderton began marketing his new subdivision in 1902. Adjacent to Wellington Crescent, the cachet of which the name 'Crescentwood' (chosen in a public contest) tried to capture. Enderton required dwellings to have a value of at least $3,500 and be set at least sixty feet back from the front street. Home of many of Winnipeg's professionals.

CROSSIN, A. L (1868–1956): Born in Waterloo, Ontario. Moved from Toronto to open branch for Toronto General Trust Corporation. Member of the Institute of Chartered Accountants. In 1919 was investment manager of Oldfield, Kirby & Gardner. Member of Citizens' Committee of 100 that in 1918 negotiated directly with civic workers on strike. He reported to Council that strikers and committee agreed on every point except whether members of the fire

A. L. CROSSIN, C. 1912.

brigade should be unionized, and this problem was soon overcome. Leader (chairman) of Citizens' Committee in 1919. Address: 240 Harvard.

D

DAFOE, JOHN (1866–1944): Born Combermere, Ontario. A great liberal and usually supporter of Liberal Party, he was a moderate who opposed extremes of all kinds. He had been an ardent supporter of the Great War as Editor of *Manitoba Free Press*, a position he held from 1901 to his death. Opposed strike but warned government against a 'Strong Arm policy of breaking the strike.' According to a colleague, Dafoe was singularly unhappy at news of the arrests of the strike leaders; 'the air was blue around the *Free Press* building.' In an editorial on 18 June, Dafoe argued that the arrests of strike leaders 'may do the extremists an actual service. They were in the position of leaders of a senseless criminal strike which was nearing the point of collapse. . . Their arrest will enable them to pose as martyrs in the cause of the workingman and will also supply them with a plausible excuse for failure.' Resided in 1919 at 509 Spence St.

DAILY STRIKE BULLETIN: Published by strike committee. Edited by William Ivens until his arrest, then by Dixon and Woodsworth until they were arrested.

DAVIEATKIN (DEVYATKIN), B.: Away on farm and not arrested on 17 June. Instead, the mounted police arrested at Davieatkin's house one Mike Verenchuck (q.v.).

DEACON, T. R. (1865–1955): Head of Manitoba Bridge and Iron Works. Born 3 January 1865 in Perth, Ontario. Had elementary education, worked in country store, then in lumber camps of Northern Ontario. Returned to school in Pembroke, Ontario, aged 20, and after serving as assistant on a survey crew in Banff he enrolled at University of Toronto, graduating with degree in Civil Engineering in 1891. Moved in 1892 to Kenora as manager of the Ontario Gold Commission for the district of Rainy River, also serving as managing director and consulting engineer for Mikado Gold Mining Company. Tagged by local natives 'Chief no-Gold.' Moved to Winnipeg in 1902 and founded Manitoba Bridge and Iron Works with H. B. Lyall. Deacon was active in insurance, Winnipeg Builders' Exchange, the Manitoba Club, and the Winnipeg Motor Club. City councillor in 1906 when Shoal Lake water supply discussed. Promoted Shoal Lake for years thereafter. Elected mayor in 1913 on Shoal Lake platform and implemented project. Always hostile to trade unions. At one point advised city's unemployed to 'hit the trail.' Was accused by *The Voice* in early 1914 of having a 'contemptible dog-in-the manger spirit'. Opposed any limitations on immigration in spring of 1914 on the grounds that there were millions of acres of land still available for settlement. In 1917 employed private detective agency to supply strikebreakers from Montreal, and when this failed obtained an antipicketing injunction, combining it with a suit for damages against one of the striking unions. Told Mathers' Commission in May 1919 that his firm, despite a programme of plant expansion, was not making money and could not afford to pay its workers any more money. Nevertheless he planned introduction of an expensive new metallurgical process that would obviate need for imported American coal, at a cost of several hundred thousand dollars. Reputed a leading member of Committee of 1000. In November 1919 introduced a 'Work's Council' system of employees' advisory boards into his shop. Died 29 May 1955. Often employed as the classic symbol of the anti-union strike-breaking Winnipeg employer. Resided in 1919 at 194 Yale.

DILUTION OF LABOUR: The introduction of female workers or semi-skilled workers (from rural districts or the immigrant community) at lower wages before steps had been taken to employ available skilled workers. Organized labour opposed this policy during the war, on the grounds that 'after the war the wages of the men will be brought to the women's wages and not the women's wages to that of the men.' The concern of labour that immigrant workers would be used by employers to undercut the union movement was a constant in this period.

DIRECT LEGISLATION: Political reform originally advocated by American populists, calling for law-making by the direct vote of the people, including voter initiative of legislation, use of referendums on important issues, and recall of elected officials. Supported in western Canada by a broad spectrum of reformers, ranging from J. H. Ashdown to William Hoop. It was intended to short-circuit legislative corruption. Direct legislation challenged the parliamentary system and the concept that the legislature was supreme, however. An Initiative and Referendum Act was passed by the Manitoba legislature in 1916, allowing any petition composed by eight per cent of the electors at the last election could put forward legislation for the Assembly to consider, and ordering all legislation passed by the Assembly to be held in abeyance for three months to see if the electorate wanted to ask for a referendum. The Manitoba Court of Appeal unanimously declared it *ultra vires*, because 'the king and the ballot box cannot make laws.'

DIRECT LEGISLATION LEAGUE: Founded in 1908, merged with Single Tax League in 1910, and revived in November of 1910 with broad support. The new League was supported by the Grain Growers' Association of Manitoba, the Royal Templars of Temperance, the Winnipeg Trades and Labor Council, and the Single Tax League. It included as members a varied cast, ranging from J. H. Ashdown to Arthur Puttee, J. L. Richardson, R. Rigg, and Fred Dixon. Provides some evidence that Manitoba was not totally divided along class lines.

DIXON, F. J. (1881–1931): Born in Englefield, England, apprenticed as a gardener. Came to Winnipeg in 1903, trained as draftsman, and worked for the Bemis Bag Company as an engraver. Although a social reformer, highly critical of socialism because collective ownership of means of production would lead to tyranny over the individual, whose rights he always held to be critical. Active in the direct legislation movement, and ran for office on several occasions. Active in Political Equality League, Direct Legislation League, League for the Taxation of Land Values. Elected to Manitoba legislature in 1915 as labour member for Centre Winnipeg. His platform in 1915 included direct legislation (initiative, referendum, recall), home rule for Winnipeg, referendum on temperance, women's suffrage, public ownership of public utilities, opposition to subsidies for private enterprise. In the legislature, Dixon forced an investigation into the corrupt relationship between the construction firm building the Manitoba legislative building and the government of Sir Rodmond Roblin which led to Roblin's resignation. First president of the Dominion Labor Party, re-elected to legislature in 1920. Insurance salesman. Contributed column to *The Voice*. In 1917 addressed meeting in Market Square urging listeners to burn their registration cards and resist conscription. Most popular strike leader. Published *Western Star* and *Enlightener* after *Strike Bulletin* suppressed and arrested 17 June. Tried for seditious libel, defended himself and was found innocent on all charges. A great orator. Retired because of ill health and died of cancer in 1931. His papers lost in 1950 Manitoba Flood. Resided in 1919 at 60 Lipton.

DOHERTY, CHARLES (1855–1931): Born Montreal. Educated at McGill University, called to bar in 1877. First elected to Commons in 1911. Dominion minister of justice at time of trials of strike leaders, but also Canadian delegate to peace conference in Versailles, so left most business to acting minister Meighen until after arrest of strike leaders, when he took the lead in insisting on showpiece court trials.

DOMINION BRIDGE COMPANY: One of eight Winnipeg firms granted shell production contracts by Canadian government in 1915. Located at corner of Notre Dame and Dublin. In 1919 one of the three metal shops that refused to negotiate with the Metal Trades Council, leading to the strike.

DOMINION LABOR PARTY (DLP): One of several labour parties in Manitoba during and after the war. Formed after the passage of a resolution of the Trades and Labor Congress of Canada in 1917 calling for a national labour party. Organizational meetings were held in Winnipeg in October 1917 and January 1918, and the Dominion Labor Party was created as the Manitoba section of the national labour party. Its organization was violently opposed by leaders of the Socialist Party of Canada, headed by Russell and Armstrong. Dixon was elected chairman of the Winnipeg branch of the party on 15 July 1920. During the war, the party espoused the single tax and sought reconstruction of capitalist system rather than revolution. Nominated F. J. Dixon, William Ivens, W. A. James, and F. G. Tipping in 1920 provincial elections. See also Canadian Labor Party, Labor Party of Canada.

DOMINION POLICE FORCE: During Great War had national responsibility for enforcing federal laws and security parts of the War Measures Act. After 12 December 1918 became the federal police agency east of the Lakehead charged with intelligence work and suppression of agitators, while Royal North-West Mounted Police became responsible for western security. Reported to the dominion minister of justice. Consisted in 1919 of 146 men. Amalgamated with Royal North-West Mounted Police into Royal Canadian Mounted Police on 1 February 1920.

DONALDSON, F.: Post office carrier, arrested on 21 June for rioting and convicted in June, fined $5 and costs. Resided in 1919 at 647 Beverley.

DUNCAN, JAMES (1879-   ): Born in Fife, moved to Seattle in 1904. The only American labour leader actively involved in the Winnipeg strike, Duncan addressed a mass meeting at Victoria Park on 4 June. He was on his way east to the 1919 American Federation of Labor convention – where he would cast the sole vote against the re-election of Samuel Gompers as President – and was persuaded to stop off in Winnipeg to investigate the local situation there. Duncan was secretary of the Seattle Central Labor Council and president of the Machinists' District Council at the time of the Seattle General Strike of February 1919. He was responsible for a conservative philosophy in Seattle known as 'Duncanism', which substituted for industrial unionism a policy of central control by labour councils in a particular industry and the effort to get agreements within a single industry coordinated to expire simultaneously so that labour could bargain as a single unit. Whether or not the Winnipeg Metal Trades Council and Building Trades Council had modelled their industrial strategy on Duncan's views is not known, but there were obvious similarities.

DUNN, F. H.: Spokesman for returned soldiers meeting in Victoria Park. Met with Gideon Robertson and Mayor Gray on morning of 21 June and refused to call off parade.

E

EASTEN,_____: Arrested on 21 June and charged with intimidation. Convicted December 1919 and fined $25 and costs.

EATON, T., COMPANY: Major Winnipeg department store, which refused to recognize strike, organizing 'scab' labour in the East and offering employees $4 wage increases to stay on. Allegedly supplied some of the horses used in the specials' charge of 10 June.

F

FAIR WAGE ACT OF 1916: Manitoba legislation of the Liberal government under T. C. Norris that provided a three-man government board to determine equitable wage standards. One member represented employers, one represented workers,

and the third the Department of Public Works. Board's decisions tended to influence all agreements and settlements in the province.

FARMER, SEYMOUR JAMES (1878–1951): Born in Cardiff, Wales, came to Canada in 1900. Employed at Winnipeg Grain Exchange 1913–1927, clerking at International Elevator Corporation in 1919. Supported direct legislation in 1915, and was a single taxer. A pacifist. Active in founding of Labour Church in 1918. Chairman of Dominion Labor Party in Manitoba in 1918. One of founders of Independent Labor Party in 1921. Later a Co-operative Commonwealth Federation MLA in Manitoba, Manitoba leader of the CCF, and served as provincial Minister of Labour in World War II. Resided in 1919 at 691 Alverstone.

FARNELL, J.: Returned soldier who assumed leadership of pro-strike veterans after the arrest of R. E. Bray, spoke to mass meeting at Market Square in front of City Hall on 20 June. He said that 'if the Government won't settle the strike, returned soldiers will.' He announced nightly meetings in the square until strike was settled. Subsequently met on morning of 21 June with Gideon Robertson at Royal Alexandra Hotel,

and along with other soldier-strikers (J. A. Martin, F. H. Dunn) refused to call off the demonstration. He was charged with 'seditious utterances.' Grand jury returned indictment.

FEDERENKO, SAVVA: Russian revolutionary of 1905, escaped to Winnipeg in mid-July 1910. Arrested on 14 August and charged with murder and arson under 1886 extradition treaty between Russia and Canada. Various labour and socialist leaders spoke out on his behalf, but he was convicted in a court presided over by Chief Justice Mathers in October 1910. *Manitoba Free Press* and Winnipeg *Tribune* both carried editorials on his behalf, and at a Walker Theatre rally on 20 November, a nonpartisan group which included the Reverend C. W. Gordon (Ralph Connor) resolved that extradition should be refused if there was a political motive behind Russia's request for it. On 23 November 1910, the court under Mr Justice Robson decided that Federenko's crime was political. He was eventually given his unconditional release.

FICHENSCHER,_____: Striking metal worker of German birth arrested on 6 May 1919 for visiting shops on behalf of his local to advise workers to withdraw their services. Released, he was to appear in court on 7 May.

FISH,_____ CORPORAL: One of police spies reporting to Regina.

FLETT, J. G.: Arrested on 21 June and charged with intimidation. Convicted December 1919 and given suspended sentence.

FLYE, THOMAS (TOMMY) (1874–1943): Born in Dowlais, Wales. Blacksmith and steeplejack, came to Canada in 1910. Foreman at Dominion Bridge during the war, then blacksmith at Canadian Pacific Railway. Originally a member of the Labour Party, carrying over his British affiliation to Canada, later broke with the Independent Labor Party and ran as an independent. Member of Central Strike Committee. Member of Winnipeg City Council from 1921. Resided in 1919 at 1554 Ross.

FORT OSBORNE BARRACKS: Built in 1871–1872 at Broadway and Osborne. The site was donated by the Hudson's Bay Company for military purposes. Named after Colonel Osborne Smith, C.M.G., first commanding officer of Military District 10. Used in 1919 to house reserves called up in anticipation of violence in the strike.

FORT ROUGE: The one working-class residential area of south Winnipeg, surrounding Fort Rouge Canadian National Railway shops and yards off Pembina Highway.

FOWLER, FRANK OLIVER (1861–1945): Born in Ontario, came to Manitoba in 1881. Winnipeg grain dealer, became secretary of North West Grain Dealers' Association. In 1919 manager Winnipeg Grain and Product Exchange Clearing Association. City councillor from 1908. Alderman who introduced in 1918 a motion denying to all civic employees the right to strike, which narrowly passed Council by 9 to 8 vote. This position made settlement of the 1918 civic employees' strike virtually impossible, and was opposed by labour representatives on the council, supported by the federal minister of labour, Gideon Robertson. On 26 May 1919 cointroduced in City Council motion prohibiting firemen from belonging to any union affiliated with an organization which could give it commands contradictory to Council's orders. It passed by a vote of 9 to 5. Later mayor of Winnipeg. Resided in 1919 at 422 Assiniboine.

G

GALT, MR JUSTICE A. C. (1853–1936): Born in Ontario. Judge in trial of Fred Dixon. Lived at 86 Donald St.

GENERAL STRIKE: Usually seen as the ultimate weapon in the arsenal of labour engaged in the class struggle. Involved a sufficiently total withdrawal of services to topple the capitalistic state. Some theorists insisted that without a revolutionary intent there was not a genuine general strike. Because of the confusion over terminology, as well as the extent to which a general strike inevitably had to challenge the existing authorities, its adoption as a labour strategy in 1919 was fraught with danger.

GEORGE, HENRY (1839–1897): American reformer responsible for single tax ideology. Author of one of the best selling books of the nineteenth century, *Progress and Poverty* (1879), which called for tax on the 'unearned increment' on land.

GODFREY, ALVIN K. (1871–1951): Born St Louis, Missouri. Educated at University of Minnesota. LL.B. Organized Canadian Electric Company and Monarch Lumber. Naturalized in 1913. Active in national lumber associations. Prominent member of Citizens' Committee. Resided in 1919 at 144 Kingsway.

GODSMARK, ARTHUR E. (1871–1951): Born in England. Arrived in Winnipeg in 1902. Architect and builder in private practice before becoming Secretary of the Building Trades Association. In 1919 manager Metal Shingle Siding Company. Resided in 1919 at 108 Eugenie.

GOULDIE, FRED: Testified at trial of women picketers from Weston that 'He would rather face the Huns than the women of Weston. He wanted to go to work at Eaton's, but they stopped him on the path and for nearly three weeks he did not try to pass their pickets. They were fierce — and then some. They didn't touch him but "they were determined I shouldn't go to work."'

GRAHAM, ROBERT B.: Born Brookfield, Nova Scotia. Educated at Dalhousie University. Settled in Killarney in 1897. Crown Prosecutor for the eastern judicial district. Lived at 80 Roslyn Road.

GRANT, JAMES: Returned soldier charged with seditious utterances. Grand jury found no bill.

GRANT, W.: Warden of Stony Mountain.

GRAY, CHARLES FREDERICK (1879–1954): Born London, England. Mayor of Winnipeg in 1919. A consulting electrical engineer, he had no apparent connections with the city's commercial elite before his election to the Board of Control in 1917. During the 1918 municipal workers' strike, he began by favouring a compromise with the unions and ended up supporting the Fowler Resolution. His change of vote at the last minute enabled the Fowler

CHARLES GRAY, UNDATED

Resolution to pass council 9 to 8. Soon after he ran for mayor on a platform of honest government. Described as a 'dapper' man who had never pronounced on the class issues of Winnipeg. He first confronted the strikers over the issue of the need for essential 'necessities of life', then over the placards being issued to make their delivery possible, on the grounds that they suggested to the outside world that the strike committee had usurped the authority of the city government. Eventually persuaded that the strike was Bolshevism run rampant, he gradually became an implacable supporter of the Citizens' Committee of 1000. He met daily in conferences with General H. D. B. Ketchen, Commissioner Perry of the Royal North-West Mounted Police, Premier Norris, and the attorney-general of Manitoba. Early in the strike he had been rebuffed by Norris over requests for provincial mediation, but he made several efforts at conciliation meetings. On 20 May he told a deputation of large property owners: 'Law and order have been maintained. Law and order will be maintained at all costs. If any radical element attempts to interfere with enforcement of law and order, we are prepared to smash it immediately. The mayor is directing affairs from his office in the City hall, and the British flag is flying over the building.' Gray told the press before the City council meeting of 26 May that he could no longer remain neutral and thereby disqualified himself as a mediator. He supported the efforts of council to force its employees back to work through 'yellow dog' tactics, and became increasingly concerned over the situation as the returned soldiers confronted him at City Hall in early

June. Gray welcomed the anti-strike veterans on 4 June, then on 6 June issued (on the advice of General Ketchen) a public proclamation forbidding further street demonstrations. On 5 June he ordered the use of special constables and a day later invited the anti-strike veterans meeting at the Auditorium Rink to join the police force as 'special' at $6 per day. He reissued his proclamation against parades on 20 June, and Gray met with pro-strike veterans on the morning of 21 June, but was unable to convince them to call off their demonstration in support of the arrested strike leaders. When informed that the specials could not manage the crowd gathering near city hall, he drove to Royal North-West Mounted Police headquarters to request personally the intervention of the Police. Resided in 1919 at 680 Jubilee Avenue. Later lived at Elm Park. Founder of the Cutty Sark Club.

GREAT WAR: The contemporary name for World War One, before people knew that there would be another World War to be numbered World War Two. Was an important influence on the Winnipeg General Strike in a number of ways. It created an inflationary economy which led labour to demand higher wages, often granted under wartime emergency conditions. It also led to government limitations on free speech and other rights, as well as to conscription, policies to which some elements of labour objected.

GREAT WAR VETERANS' ASSOCIATION (GWVA):
Organized in Winnipeg in 1917, originally as ladies' auxiliary. Claimed 10,400 Winnipeg members. Its secretary estimated that it was composed locally of 37 per cent employers and 57 per cent of employees and the other 15 per cent of different classes. Officially neutral in strike, although three delegates (F. W. Law, _____ Bathie, and A. E. Moore) sat on strike committee as observers, and many of its members supported the strike. An emergency committee denied vehemently on 23 May that the Association had endorsed the strike, insisting that it had only endorsed the principle of collective bargaining. It added, ignorance of what collective bargaining means is displayed by the labour people, Citizens' committee, and anyone else who draws the conclusion that the meeting backed the strike. Later the national association helped persuade Parliament to provide benefits for disabled veterans, but never was able to come to terms with the demands of the able-bodied ones, including the $2,000 bonus for all overseas soldiers called for by a February 1919 Calgary meeting. The bonus campaign raised national membership to 200,000, but in 1925 the GWVA faded into the Canadian Legion.

GREER, W. A.: Member of central strike committee. Resided in 1919 at 324 Lipton.

H

HAMILTON, CHARLES FREDERICK (1869–1933):
Journalist and historian. Assistant comptroller of Royal North-West Mounted Police in 1919, recently returned from post of deputy chief censor for Canada. Author of an April 1919 Memorandum on Revolutionary Tendencies in Western Canada which saw a sinister conspiracy to subvert the existing order and replace it with a Soviet Government based upon the dictatorship of the proletariat.

HANCOX, E. (MRS.): Ran unsuccessfully for Winnipeg School Board in 1919 municipal elections.

HAZLETON, HERBERT. T.: President of Winnipeg Builders' Exchange and probably member of the Citizens' Committee of 1000. Secretary-treasurer of Hazleton & Walin Ltd. Resided in 1919 at 342 Wellington Crescent.

HEAPS. A. A. (1885–1954): Member of Winnipeg City Council from Ward 5, member of Upholsterers' Union and a furrier by trade, foreman of a city concern, Robinson and Company. Arrested and acquitted as strike leader. Born in Leeds, Jewish, of Polish descent. Came to Canada in 1910 and Winnipeg in 1911. Member of Social Democratic Party. Pacifist, opposed conscription in 1917 with F. J. Dixon and John Queen. Supervised commissariat for strike committee. In council advocated banning of all parades. Suspected of leaking 'telegraphic news' to strike committee. Elected to House of Commons from Winnipeg North in 1925. Served to 1940. Arrested on 17 June. Conducted his own defence. Verdict on 28 March 1920. Found innocent on all counts, after a masterful address to the jury. In the House of Commons, he confronted Arthur Meighen over 'Heenan' disclosures of 1926. Resided in 1919 at 562 Burrows.

HEENAN, PETER (1875–1948): Born in Ireland. Former Labour member of Ontario legislature and Liberal Member of Parliament for Kenora/Rainy River in 1926. Raised question about government use of troops in strike areas, instancing Winnipeg Strike and quoting files. Heenan, probably acting with government approval, charged that the government policy of 1919, especially the action of then minister of Labour Gideon Robertson, had prolonged the strike and provoked bloodshed. Robertson denied these charges in the Senate and Heenan subsequently asked for unanimous permission to present the relevant documents, which was denied him. In debate, Arthur Meighen denied that troops had been 'ordered' from outside, but otherwise merely defended the necessity of government action.

HEIR, IRENE: Arrested in connection with 21 June riot, arraigned 23 June and remanded.

'HELLO GIRLS': Telephone operators, ninety per cent females, who were first strikers when they punched off duty at 7:00 a.m. on 15 May 1919. First unionized in February 1917, staged first strike on 1 May 1917, joined sympathetic strike in May 1918. By 26 May, telephone lines were closed across the province.

HOLLANDS, WARD (1883–1953): Born in Chisholm, North Dakota. Came to Beaudry, Manitoba in 1900, later articled as law student. Lawyer, member of firm of Bonner, Trueman, Hollands, and Robinson, counsel for defence in trials of strike leaders. Resided at 400 St John's.

HOOP, W. H. (1876–   ): Born in Durham County, an ex-steelworker in London, then postman in Winnipeg. Came to Winnipeg in 1893. Began as impossibilist member of Socialist Party. Helped organize party in Winnipeg in 1906. Supporter of the revised Direct Legislation League. In 1912 municipal election ran for alderman in ward four, declaring 'Race-protection, race-progression, and race-perfection are the ideals of my religion, and if elected I will put them into practice.' An ardent conscriptionist during the Great War. Listed as organizer of Retail Clerks in 1919 in Henderson Directory. Moderate member of Trades and Labor Council. Alleged in 1920 to have described the strike as an attempt to set up a Russian soviet government, which he denied. Residence at Amulet Apartments (640 Westminster St).

HUGG, J. B., K. C.: Counsel for Prairie Provinces Branch of Canadian Manufacturers' Association. Wrote in April 1919 issue of *Industrial Canada* (the journal of the Canadian Manufacturers' Association) that manufacturers were tired of shilly-shallying by the state. He called upon the government to 'assert the authority of the state and . . . repress all lawfulness no matter by whom committed.' Member Canadian Manufacturers'

Association (Prairie Branch) committee to investigate industrial relations, formed in 1919. Testified at Mathers Commission, where he opposed strike action imposed by majority rule. Member of law firm of Hugg and Johnston. Address in 1919: 397 River.

HYMAN, MARCUS (1883–1938): Born near Vilna, Poland, emigrated to London in 1885, came to Winnipeg in 1913. Lawyer appointed by Winnipeg Trades and Labor Council to defend radical aliens before Board of Inquiry in 1919. Had deportation orders of five strike leaders reversed. Later taught law at Manitoba Law School. Lived at 213 College in 1919.

I

IMMIGRATION ACT AMENDMENT OF 1919: Allowed for the deportation of British subjects under certain conditions, especially 'undesirability' or subversive activities. Applied to virtually all persons of British birth since, as *Free Press* noted, few troubled to be naturalized in Canada. Government was rejecting the traditional definition that a Canadian was a British subject resident in Canada. This amendment met with little discussion or opposition, wrote Robert Borden in his memoirs. It was 'read first, second and third times and adopted with unanimity in about twenty minutes.' It passed the Senate and received royal assent the same day.

IMMIGRATION HALL: Building of provincial immigration department at 83 Maple Street. Demolished in 1947.

IMPERIAL VETERANS OF CANADA: Delegation of strike committee urged on 16 May that the association should support the strike. A meeting was called, and according to the organization's secretary-treasurer, H. B. Willing, 'unanimously turned down and refused to have anything to do with the labour side or the citizens' committee.'

IMPOSSIBLISM: The theory that capitalism was not reformable and that attempting to achieve reform would divert the worker from the class struggle. Came partly from Marx, partly from the British Socialist Democratic Federation, and partly from frontier working conditions in British North America.

INDEPENDENT LABOR PARTY (I.L.P.): Organized in Winnipeg in 1895, its platform calling for eight-hour working day, the nationalization of public utilities, and the municipal ownership of all franchises. Elected Canada's first M.P. in 1900, A. W. Puttee. Reorganized in 1905, and according to *The Voice* became 'the British expression of the socialist aim of other countries.' Strongly influenced by British non-conformity. Name was resurrected in 1920 when Independent Labor Party was formed as a Social Democratic Party, the leaders of which were F. J. Dixon, J. S. Woodsworth, and S. J. Farmer. The new Party was provincial in nature, with branches in Winnipeg, Brandon, The Pas, Souris, and Dauphin. Its support came from socialists, trade unionists, and politicized Methodists, and it became heir in Manitoba to the Socialist Party of Canada, the Social Democratic Party, and the Dominion Labor Party, none of which survived after 1920. The Independent Labor Party, which elected Woodsworth to the Commons in 1921, pressed for social reform. Manitoba Labor Party merged with the Independent Labor Party in the provincial election of 1920. The Independent Labor Party also operated in Winnipeg in municipal politics.

INDUSTRIAL BUREAU: Headquarters of Committee of 1000. In Board of Trade Building on Main Street.

INDUSTRIAL DISPUTES INVESTIGATION ACT OF 1907: Called for compulsory conciliation and a cooling-off period in utilities, railroads, and coal mines. Established boards of arbitration. Served as model for industrial relations in Canada in the early twentieth century, but was increasingly opposed by organized labour because of its lack of protection for unions and workers.

INDUSTRIAL UNIONISM: Originated in Britain in the nineteenth and early twentieth centuries. Defined by Irish labour leader James Connolly as the creation of 'an industrial republic inside the shell of the political State, in order that when that industrial republic is fully organized it may crack the shell of the political State and step into its place in the scheme of the universe.' According to another exponent, when workers controlled the tools of production, 'by the power of the internationally organized Proletariat, capitalist production shall entirely cease, and the industrial socialist republic will be ushered in, and thus the Socialist Revolution realised.' Basic to this philosophy was the division of society into only two classes, the capitalists and the workers. Although industrial unionists could talk in a Marxist vocabulary, they were not necessarily revolutionaries in a Russian sense. Industrial unionism's institutional expression in Canada was the One Big Union, its tactic the general strike (which Labour tried in Britain in 1926). The principal Canadian opponent of industrial unionism within the ranks of organized labour was the Trades and Labor Congress.

INGRAM, W. M.: On Winnipeg Board of Control in 1914. Member of Citizens' Committee. Assistant manager of Swift Canadian. Address in 1919: Suite 6, Panama Apartments, 229 Mackay.

ISRAELITE PRESS, THE: Yiddish newspaper published in Winnipeg 1914–1920. Founded by Faivel Simkin, a leading Jewish anarchist in the city.

IVENS, REV. W., (BILL) B.D. (1878–   ): Born at Batford in Warwickshire, had come to Canada in 1896. Early worked as market gardener, but had attended University of Manitoba as a Methodist ministerial candidate. Methodist minister at McDougal Church, broke with church over his pacifism and was expelled from the ministry for his refusal to accept church authority. An active social gospeller. Member of Central Strike Committee. Founded Labour Church. Had become editor of *Western Labor News* in 1918 and edited daily strike bulletin. Member of Manitoba legislature from 1920.

Arrested on 17 June as editor of *Western Labor News*. Found guilty by jury of seditious conspiracy on 28 March 1920 and sentenced to one year. Before his trial, he was charged with contempt for statements he had made regarding the trial of R. B. Russell. He was found guilty. His address to the jury in his trial lasted for fourteen hours. Address in 1919 was 309 Inkster.

J

JACQUES, WILLIAM H: Returned soldier gassed and consumptive, thrown into jail without a charge. Address in 1919: 189 Jarvis.

JELLEY, THOMAS: Mentioned as member (eligible) of special immigration board held June 1919.

JENNINGS, MAJOR: Commander of a squadron of mounted police, recently returned from Russia and demobilized in Winnipeg, adding 172 men to Royal North-West Mounted Police.

JOHNS, RICHARD J.(DICK) (1889-   ): English (Cornwall) machinist (toolmaker) for the Canadian Pacific Railway in 1919, member of Social Democratic Party and leader of One Big Union. Came to Canada in 1912. Spoke to Majestic

Theatre meeting. Later helped organize Toronto general strike. In 1917 had urged a general strike against conscription and national registration. In 1918 told a strike meeting in Winnipeg, 'I am a Socialist and proud of it. You can call me a Bolsheviki if you want to. You must have nothing that flavours of compromise in this proposition. I say strike today, this has resolved itself into a question of right. You have the right to demand anything you have the power to enforce.' Delegate to Calgary Convention of 1919, elected to committee to 'carry on the propaganda' to establish the One Big Union. In Montreal at sittings of National Railway Board as elected representative of machinists when warrant issued for his arrest on 17 June. Found guilty by jury on 28 March 1920 of seditious conspiracy and sentenced to one year. Subsequently became an industrial arts teacher and eventually was appointed Director of Technical Education for the Province of Manitoba.

JONES, GEORGE E.: Arrested on 21 June for rioting. Convicted in July 1919 and fined $300 or thirty days in jail.

K

KAISERISM: Charges that Canadian government was behaving with the same sort of heavy hand as the German government under the Kaiser, an obvious attempt to connect the Great War with the strike.

KELLY, T. & SONS: Construction firm that was awarded contract for Manitoba legislative building. Trades Council was able to demonstrate in January of 1915 that lower wage schedules for workers on the project were the result of direct government intervention, and Fred Dixon in the legislature forced an investigation into the financial arrangement between T. Kelly & Sons and the government of Sir Rodmond Roblin which revealed much graft and corruption. Roblin was forced to resign over the revelations and retire to Florida.

KERR, CHARLES M. PUBLISHING COMPANY OF CHICAGO: 'Our main source of the classics of working class philosophy', according to one Canadian socialist, its books were banned by the dominion government from entry in Canada in 1919.

KETCHEN, BRIG.-GEN H.D.B., O.C., M.D.(1872–1959): Born India, educated at Sandhurst. Came to Winnipeg in 1894. Lieutenant in Boer War, Brigadier-General of 6th Canadian Infantry 1915–1917.

Relieved from active command after a military fiasco at St Eloi (Flanders) in 1915. Commanding officer of military district in which Winnipeg was located, 1919–1929, when he retired. Spoke at Citizens' Committee of 1000 meeting on 6 June 1919 at Auditorium Rink. Told audience that all undesirables, veteran and otherwise, would be dealt with. About the same time he wired Ottawa that federal government should use War Measures Act to deal with cost of living problems, by appointing a prices board to investigate complaints and with power to prosecute. Such action 'would allay universal indignation and unrest and go far to save the situation.' Met daily with mayor and other officials over strike conditions and response. Opposed bail for arrested strike leaders on the grounds that the militia would be unhappy. Address in 1919: 111 Nassau.

KIRK, JESSIE (MRS): Ran as labour candidate for Winnipeg School Board in 1919 municipal election. Had lost her job as schoolteacher for her labour activities. Lost in 1919, but was elected to municipal council in 1920. Withdrew from 1920 provincial election in favour of male strike leaders. Elected to executive committee of Dominion Labor Party in March 1920 as one of two woman representatives.

KRAATZ, IDA: Arrested on 5 June for inciting strikers on Main Street near Market Square. Entered no plea and remanded. Late in June Helen Armstrong was arrested for inciting Kraatz to assault a *Tribune* employee selling newspapers on the street. Kraatz fined $5 plus costs.

KRAEL, MICHAEL: Arrested and charged with rioting and unlawful assembly. Convicted on 27 November and sentenced to two years in prison.

L

LABOUR CHURCH OF WINNIPEG: Organized by W. Ivens in late June 1918 as church for workers meeting in the Labour Temple. At first meeting on 30 June in Labour Temple, 200 of those present signed cards declaring: 'I am willing to support an independent and creedless Church based on the Fatherhood of God and the Brotherhood of Man. Its aim shall be the establishment of justice and righteousness among men of all nations.' Platform was open and subjects pertaining to fundamental problems of the day were discussed. Moved to Dominion Theatre in October 1918. Large proportion of collections donated to labour causes. Church in April 1919 planned a building fund for a new building, a people's university, and a conven-

tion in Winnipeg. Government was suspicious. Popular with workers, 10 branches in Winnipeg by 1919. Labour Church organized later in other cities. In the short run its involvement in the strike contributed to its upward growth in Winnipeg.

LABOR PARTY OF CANADA: See Canadian Labor Party, Dominion Labor Party.

LABOUR TEMPLE: On James Avenue. Searched on 17 June for seditious literature; half a truckload found. Searchers allegedly looted cigar stand on premises.

LANGDALE, FRANCIS E.: Military intelligence representative who took notes at Walker Theatre meeting of 22 December 1918 and was a key government witness in hearings for seditious conspiracy. Address in 1919: 156 Donald.

LAW, F. W.: Born Rushton, England. Came to Winnipeg in 1907, secretary of Great War Veterans' Association. Told preliminary hearing for William Ivens, 'When you have an association composed of possibly 37 per cent employers and 57 per cent of employees and the other 15 per cent of different classes, if you take any stand other than neutrality you are going to make enemies

in the association.' Sat as observer on Strike Committee, but he clearly privately supported the Citizens' Committee. He also testified that 'We are opposed to the alien and will be opposed to him until he gets out of the country', because 'these men have been holding down good jobs while our men have been overseas.' Argued on 26 July 1919 in *Tribune* that most of those who had followed the leadership of 'pro-Germans' like F. J. Dixon and John Queen were 'conscripts' rather than volunteers. Address in 1919: 163 Cathedral.

LEGISLATIVE BUILDING: Site of a number of confrontations between returned veterans and the provincial government during the strike. In 1919 the government was still using the old legislative building on Kennedy Street, since the new building remained under construction, having been delayed by corruption and embezzlement. The new building had been agreed upon by the legislature in 1911, and the design of a Liverpool, England, architect (F. W. Simon) was chosen from a competition of 65. The building was part of the 'City Beautiful' movement, intended to reflect the prosperity of the era. First estimates for its construction were voted in 1912. Work was begun in 1913 by the firm of

Thomas Kelly and Sons, and the original estimates were soon substantially overrun. In 1915 a Royal Commission under Chief Justice T. A. Mathers held an enquiry into the construction operations which found sufficient evidence of fraud and political corruption to force the resignation of Premier Rodmond Roblin, and later his trial on criminal charges. The new legislative building served as a symbol for many returning veterans of the profiteering made by the business elite while ordinary soldiers were dying in the trenches.

LENIN, NICHOLAI: His pamphlet *Lessons of the Russian Revolution* sold for 10 cents at Victoria Park during soldiers' meetings.

LIBERTY TEMPLE: Sometimes called 'Liberty Hall.' Social and cultural centre of the 'Arbeiter Ring' membership at Pritchard and Salter, the home of Winnipeg's progressive Jewry. Opened on 19 September 1917. L. Orlikow was president of the temple's first executive. Permanent headquarters after 1917 of the Jewish branch of the Social Democratic Party. Searched on 17 June 1919 for seditious literature.

LIEBKNECHT, KARL: Radical German socialist killed in political violence of post-war Germany. He was cheered by audience at Walker Theatre meeting. A memorial service announced for him and Rosa Luxemburg on 26 January 1919 at Market Square never took place because the Square was invaded by 200 returned soldiers looking for speakers.

LOCKE, CORBET H. (1854–1932): Born Barrie, Ontario. Irish. Called to Ontario bar in 1877 and Manitoba bar in 1881. Appointed a judge of the southern district in 1894. Assisted H. A. Robson on Royal Commission to investigate strike. Resided in Morden.

LOGAN, W. H. C.: Chairman of general strike committee. Machinist for Canadian Pacific Railway. President of the Winnipeg Labor Council formed by the One Big Union on 5 August 1919. Resided in 1919 at 137 Glenwood.

LOVATT, W.D.: Officer of the Building Trades Council. Chosen at Calgary convention as one of five Manitoba representatives 'to carry out the propaganda' for the One Big Union. Secretary of General Strike committee and member of its executive, the central strike committee.

LOYALIST VETERANS ASSOCIATION: (also known as Loyalist Returned Soldier Association). Organized by Citizens' Committee of 1000. Used to recruit special constables at $6 per day. Begun by lawyer F. G. Thompson.

LUXEMBURG, ROSA: German radical socialist killed in post-war violence in Germany. A memorial service announced for her and Karl Liebknecht on 26 January 1919 at Market Square never occurred because the Square was invaded by 200 returned soldiers looking for speakers.

LYALL, HUGH BURTON (D. 1948): Born Sutton West, Ontario. Assistant manager and secretary-treasurer of Manitoba Bridge and Iron in 1919, representative of Metal Trades Employers. Resided at Lockport in 1919.

LYLE, MAJOR HILLYARD: Appointed by Winnipeg mayor Gray to recruit and command special police 5 June 1919. Allegedly met with strikers on 9 June after 6 June scuffle and admitted 'I know there are a number of thugs amongst them.' Did attempt to reduce the size of the clubs carried by the 'specials.' According to both Bob Russell and Andrew Scoble, Lyle sought to avoid bloodshed and warned the strikers that the military would intervene and shoot if necessary. On 10 June ordered the Mounted Police and the Specials withdrawn from the streets after rioting began. Replaced on 11 June at insistence of the Citizens' Committee, which agreed with General Ketchen that the situation had been 'badly handled' by Major Lyle. According to later records, Lyle was sent out of the city to Minneapolis on 17 June. He could not be located at the time of the trials of the arrested strike leaders.

Mc

MCBRIDE, J. L.: Secretary, International Brotherhood of Electrical Workers. Appointed member of interim central strike committee by Trades and Labor Council. An opponent of industrial unionism and radicalism. On 21 May nominated to the central strike committee. Resided in 1919 at 160 Golf Boulevard.

MCCROM, MRS J.: *Toronto Star* reported on 13 June that she had been fined $20 plus court costs for assault on a delivery driver.

MACDONALD, SIR HUGH JOHN (1850-1929): Partner in firm Macdonald, Cray, Tarr and Ross. Judge who sentenced Matthew Charitinoff to three years imprisonment and fine of $1000 in 1918. Son of Sir John A. Macdonald. Presided at the preliminary trials of the eight strike leaders in July 1919. His stately home (Dalnavert at 61 Carlton) in downtown Winnipeg is now a museum.

MCINTYRE, PETER CAMPBELL (1854–1920): Represented North Winnipeg in Manitoba Legislature 1892–1900. Chairman Winnipeg School Board. Winnipeg postmaster. Address in 1919: 21, 105 Roslyn Rd.

MCKENZIE, H.: Arrested on 21 June and charged with rioting. Convicted in June and fined $20 and costs.

MCLAUGHLIN, W. H. CONSTABLE: One of police spies reporting to Regina. Called R. E. Bray most dangerous man in Winnipeg and alleged that he was planning takeover of militia.

MACLEAN, A. A.: Comptroller (administrative head) of Royal North-West Mounted Police in Ottawa.

MACLEAN, JOHN, REV. DR (1851–1928): Methodist minister in charge of MacLean Mission, 719 Pacific. Kept diary during strike (now in Victoria University Archives, Toronto). Critical of Woodsworth and Methodists

supporting 'Bolsheviks.' Believed that the strike was the beginning of a revolution 'contemplated for the whole Dominion' to begin at Winnipeg.

MCMURRAY, EDWARD JAMES (1876–1954): Born Oxford County, Ontario. One of Winnipeg's leading criminal lawyers, defended many accused of capital crimes. Partner in McMurray, Davidson, Wheldon and McMurray. Lawyer appointed by Winnipeg Trades and Labor Council to defend radical aliens before Boards of Inquiry in 1919. Elected to Parliament in 1921. Resided in 1919 at 167 Polson.

MCNAUGHTON, CHARLES H.: managing director of Arctic Ice Company. Resided at 136 Clarke.

MCPHERSON, DONALD (1876–1954): Chief Constable of Winnipeg Police Force. Replaced on 5 June by former Deputy Chief C. H. Newton at the time that the special police were being organized. Address in 1919: 320 Aberdeen.

MCWILLIAMS, W. H.: Chairman of Compensation Fund of Citizens' Committee of 1000. General manager, Canadian Elevator Co. Ltd. Lived in 1919 at 65 Kennedy.

M

MAJESTIC THEATRE: At 363 Portage.

MAJESTIC THEATRE MEETING: of 10 January 1919, called by Socialist party of Canada after Trades and Labor Council withdrew joint sponsorship. Attended by Messrs Russell, Johns, and Armstrong, who attacked capitalism and defended the Soviet government of Russia 'against the attacks of the press and pulpit and organized propaganda throughout the world against it.' The chairman announced a memorial service in Market Square on 26 January for Karl Liebknecht and Rosa Luxemburg, who had died in post-war German political turmoil.

MANITOBA BRIDGE AND IRON WORKS CORPORATION: One of three major metal shops in Winnipeg doing contract work at 875 Logan Avenue West. Struck by ironworkers in 1906 but quickly settled with workers. Received contract from federal government for shells in 1915, and had much continued labour unrest until struck along with Vulcan Iron Works and Dominion Bridge Company by Metal Trades Council in 1919. Only business corporation represented at Robson Commission hearings.

MANITOBA FREE PRESS: Influential Winnipeg newspaper owned by Clifford Sifton and edited by John Dafoe. Not very sympathetic to labour or enemy aliens. A great supporter of Canada's participation in World War One.

MANITOBA LABOR PARTY: Organized in 1910 as reform party of moderate constitutional reform. Merged with the Independent Labor Party in the provincial election of 1920, and elected eleven of the seventeen candidates it ran, including William Ivens, John Queen, and George Armstrong. Dixon was re-elected. 'You will have noted the results of the Manitoba Election', wrote Dixon in a private letter. 'The outstanding feature, of course, was the strength displayed by labour. They will have nearly 25% of the membership of the next legislature and, with perhaps one exception, all the labour members elected are reds.'

MANITOBA LEAGUE FOR THE TAXATION OF LAND VALUES: Organization based on Henry George's single tax ideology, which appealed to reformers in the early 20th century. Formed from the Manitoba Single Tax Association and the Manitoba Direct Legislation League, both organizations having Fred Dixon as principal leader.

MANITOBA VETERAN: Official organ of Great War Veterans' Association, issue published on 6 June.

MARKET SQUARE: Area of downtown Winnipeg next to City Hall, contained the market building, hotels, stores, and livery stables. It was a popular location for outdoor meetings and demonstrations.

MARTIN, CHESTER, PROFESSOR (1882–1958): Born in Nova Scotia. Leading Canadian historian, member of faculty of University of Manitoba (1909–1929) and later of the University of Toronto. Member of Canadian Problems Club that at the end of May 1919 unsuccessfully requested City Council to modify its policy on signed pledges of policemen. Resided in 1919 at 53–106 Roslyn Rd.

MARTIN, J. A.: Returned soldier charged with seditious utterances. At Victoria Park on 12 June he warned strikers to 'beware of camouflage and buncombe.' Rental agents were threatening to eject workers behind in their rent. 'Well, they can't throw us all out', declared Martin, amid laughter and cheers. At rally on 20 June, he referred to Saturday's proposed parade as 'the only weapon we have left.' Part of soldier-striker delegation which met with Gideon Robertson and Mayor Gray on morning of 21 June and refused to call off the parade. Grand Jury found no bill.

MATHERS' COMMISSION (ROYAL COMMISSION ON INDUSTRIAL RELATIONS): Industrial Commission of 1919 chaired by Judge T. G. Mathers. Appointed by Order-in-council PC 670 on 22 March 1919. Opened hearings in Victoria, B. C., on 16 April and completed them in Ottawa on 13 June. It was in Winnipeg June 10–13, but was boycotted by the Winnipeg Trades and Labor Council on the grounds that as a federal committee appointed by the federal government, it was part of the problem it was trying to investigate and rectify. At the same time, it was regarded by business as too sympathetic to labour, a built-in recipe for being ignored, particularly when it concluded that economic conditions rather than foreign aliens were responsible for the civil unrest and recommended a package of reform measures (minimum wage, 8-hour day, unemployment and health insurance, free collective bargaining) as the way to a better future.

MATHERS, JUDGE T. G. (1859-1927): Born Lucknow, Ontario, Solicitor for Manitoba

JUDGE T. G. MATHERS, C. 1915

Government Railroad, 1880–1890. Manitoba Supreme Court chief justice from 1910. Chairman of Krafchenko Commission in 1914. An ardent conscriptionist in the early days of the war. Made honorary president of Canadian Service League in 1916. Chairman of Industrial Commission of 1919. As judge granted bail application to eight leaders charged with seditious conspiracy. Defence argued that only question was likelihood of men to appear at trial. Mathers insisted that bail could be refused if public safety was at stake, but he did not think public safety endangered. Resided in 1919 at 16 Edmonton.

MEADE, INSPECTOR: Sent by Royal North-West Mounted Police from Regina with twenty men to Winnipeg.

MEAKIN(G), DORIS: Worked from 26 May with women in Winnipeg. Representative of IBEW (International Brotherhood of Electrical Workers), complained at the end of June that only half of the telephone operators had returned to work without seniority. They had to work overtime to maintain service. Demands for a protest strike had been ignored by their union.

MEIGHEN, ARTHUR (1874–1960): Born in Anderson, Ontario, Meighen migrated to Manitoba and established a law practice at Portage la Prairie before entering the House of Commons in 1908. A dominant figure in the 1917 Union government, he was associated with conscription and the wartime elections act, which disenfranchised many. He was in 1919 Minister of the Interior and Acting Minister of Justice. Met with A. J. Andrews at Thunder Bay in late May. Told Andrews on 26 May that the goals of strike leadership were 'of a most sinister character and far different from those that the ordinary sympathetic striker has in view.' Meighen told House of Commons on 2 June, 'a general strike to succeed or, indeed, to continue, must result in the usurpation of governmental authority on the part of those controlling the strike. It did so result in Winnipeg; it must ever so result.' Were the Winnipeg strike to succeed, it would produce 'a combination of all organizations of labour in the Dominion taking part in and determining the event of every dispute as to labour conditions and wages here, there, and at any other point, why then you have the perfection of Bolshevism.' Summarized his position on strike in House of Commons debate of 1926: 'Winnipeg was in charge of a strike committee; not a child could have milk to drink except by permission of that strike committee. The regularly constituted authorities were no longer in control in connection with the distribution of necessities. If that is a state of affairs to be sneered at and considered quite the incident of a day, well and good; but I would never care to be a member which so regarded anything of that importance.'

METAL TRADES COUNCIL: Central body in Winnipeg in which all nineteen craft unions of the metal trades, mostly in the railway shops, were represented. Council also represented the contract shops, independents that filled railway orders on a contract basis. The major contract shops in Winnipeg were Vulcan Iron Works, the Dominion Bridge Company, and the Manitoba Bridge and Iron Works, which refused in 1918 to agree to negotiate with a body composed partly of railway employees, leading to a strike, a subsequent injunction in restraint of picketing, and a vote of the Council for a general strike.

METCALFE, J. T., MR JUSTICE (1870–1922): Articled in Manitoba. Called to Manitoba bar in 1894. Leading figure in Liberal Party. Appointed to Manitoba Court of King's Bench in 1909. Named by federal government in May 1919 to be chairman of the Winnipeg Electric Railway Board of Arbitration. Judge in trial of Robert Russell and in trial of remaining 7 strike leaders. His charge to the jury in the Russell case was probably responsible for the subsequent convictions. Metcalfe began by emphasizing that it was his duty to instruct the jury in matters of law, 'and in such matters you ought to follow my directions', adding, 'In all matters of fact you are the sole judge.' He went on to insist that if jury believed the parties accused did 'not intend any real mischief, and did not desire to bring about the things that were brought about', he advised a verdict of not guilty. Although Metcalfe several times emphasized the need for intent, his characterization above, combined with his citation of an unnamed 'eminent authority' — that 'something must be allowed for feeling in men's minds and for some warmth of expression, but an intention to incite the people to take the power into their own hands and to provoke them to tumult and disorder is a seditious intention. The character of the words or acts may form an irresistible evidence of the nature of the intention…' — was doubtless influential with the jury, composed entirely of males from rural Manitoba. Metcalfe also commented in trials of those arrested on Bloody Saturday on the use of force against women, 'In these days when women are taking up special obligations and assuming equal privileges with men, it may be well for me to state now that women are just as liable to ill-treatment in a riot as men and can claim no special protection and are entitled to no sympathy; and if they stand and resist officers of the law they are liable to be cut down.' Resided in 1919 at Cornwall Apartments, 263 River.

METHODIST CHURCH OF CANADA: The Methodist Church had been active in the settlement of the Canadian West, promoting a Protestant Canadian culture which was both pervasive and reformist. It was extremely supportive of

Canadian participation in the Great War, which it saw as a moral crusade. It also had a radical wing associated with the social gospel movement, and was virtually the only prominent religious denomination which had some ministers (mostly ex-ministers) involved in the labour movement.

J. S. Woodsworth, William Ivens, A. E. Smith, and R. A. Rigg had all been Methodist clergymen. A more conservative Methodist, the Reverend John MacLean, observed in his diary on 9 June, 'it is a sad thing that the Bolsheviks are supported by three Methodist ministers.' MacLean was probably referring to Woodsworth, Ivens, and Smith.

MILLER, W.: Member of central strike committee.

MINIMUM WAGE ACT: Manitoba legislation of 1918 that provided for a government board of five (the Minimum Wage Board) to fix minimum wages for female workers in the province. A piece of milestone labour legislation by the Norris Liberal government, although the Board's rulings on salaries and hours had not been complied with by all employers at the time of the Winnipeg strike, thus helping explain the participation of women workers in it.

MONCREIFF, JOHN JOSEPH (1865–1939): Born Scallaway, Shetland Islands. Came to Manitoba with father, a Hudson's Bay Company employee, in 1875. Grew up in St Andrew's. Cofounder *Winnipeg Daily News* and *Tribune* in 1890. Served as managing editor of *Tribune* 1903–1920. Noted musician, a singer and producer of oratorios.

MOORE, ARTHUR ERNEST (JACK) (1882– 1950): Born Lewisham, Kent. Royal Navy. Came to Winnipeg in 1910. Ex-sergeant of Canadian Expeditionary Force, employee of government of Manitoba as member of Alien Investigation Board and president of provincial command of Great War Veterans' Association. With Roger Bray, led discussion at meeting of 29 May of veterans which led to decision to undertake soldier demonstrations and parades in support of the strikers. Later dominion head, Canadian Legion, from its founding in 1925. Lived in 1919 at 671 Rathgar.

MOORE, TOM: President, Dominion Trades and Labor Congress. His offer to address union workers in early May before strike rejected by Winnipeg Trades and Labor Council. Refused to interfere in arrests of 17 June by calling a one-day strike across Canada, on the grounds that a general strike was contrary to the policy of the Trades and Labor Council. He insisted strikers must have fair hearing, however, and warned the government that organized labour would not 'stand for strong arm methods for the suppression of legitimate labour demonstrations, and if the proof is not sufficient to show the Winnipeg labour leaders were plotting danger to the state, the government will be held strictly accountable.' At the same time, Moore told the 1919 convention of the Trades and Labor Council that 'Winnipeg was determined upon its own line of action, which harmonised strongly with the policies laid down in the propaganda of the One Big Union, and by the usurpation of the power of the international union executives by the Winnipeg Trades Council in the calling of the strike made it very plain that Winnipeg was determined to demonstrate the efficiency of the principle of massed action, sympathetic strikes and economic dictatorship as superior in achieving results to the policies of the international trade unions, the Trades and Labor Congress of Canada and the American Federation of Labor which are, and have been, a policy of negotiation and the using of the strike weapon as a last resort only.'

MORAN, W. J.: Partner of Moran, Anderson, and Gray. Appeared before

Robson commission on behalf of Manitoba Bridge and Iron Works.

MURRAY, THOMAS JOSEPH (1875–1954): Solicitor for the Trades and Labor Council. Counsel for accused strike leaders in June 1919. Also defended radical aliens before Board of Inquiry and individuals arrested on 21 June and prosecuted. Member of law firm of Murray & Noble. Appeared before Robson Commission on behalf of certain labour interests. Address in 1919 at 148 Harrow.

MYERS, R. E., JUDGE: County court judge appointed to Alien Inquiry Board in spring of 1919.

N

NANTON, SIR AUGUSTUS (1860–1925): Senior partner, Osler, Hammond and Nanton. President, Dominion Bank of Canada. Winnipeg investment dealer, influential member of business elite and Citizens' Committee of 1000. His wife, Lady Nanton, was auxiliary president of army battalion. Lived in 1919 at 229 Roslyn Rd.

NEWTON, CHRIS H. (1871–1953): Born Sleaford, England. Deputy Chief of Police in Winnipeg to 5 June, when replaced Chief of Police Donald Macpherson.

Was assigned the job of reorganizing the force. Resided in 1919 at 878 Bannatyne.

NEWTON, JOHN O.: President of Winnipeg chapter of Great War Veterans' Association. Managing director of Inter-provincial Coal Co. Ltd.

NOBLE, R. M.: Part of law firm of Murray & Noble. Police Magistrate (appointed in 1916) before whom the preliminary hearing of the strike leaders occurred in July and August 1919. Allowed evidence relating to the parade of 21 June against objections of defence, arguing, 'It having been shown that the accused were ringleaders during the strike which began on the fifteenth of May, having taken an active part throughout the strike, evidence of what others did, sympathizers or cooperators in that strike, what they said and did is admissible. It is true they are not charged as conspirators here, but for the purpose of the admissibility of the evidence, I think their words and acts in connection with the strike are perfectly admissible.' The question revolved around whether or not a conspiracy had already been proved, but Noble's interpretation was upheld by higher courts at the time and has often been criticized since. Address in 1919 at 200 Montrose.

NORRIS, T. C (1861–1936): Born in Brampton, Ontario, Norris was Premier of Manitoba from 1915–1922. His wartime government was a reformist one, responsible for temperance legislation, female suffrage, compulsory education, workmen's compensation, minimum wage legislation, as well as the establishment of a public-nursing system, rural farm credit, regulation of industrial conditions, and a mother's allowance for widowed dependent mothers. In 1919, the Norris govern-

T. C. NORRIS, UNDATED

ment depended heavily on rural support in the legislature, and Norris found himself caught between his own progressive instincts and more conservative forces. As a result, he ended up doing virtually nothing. The Manitoba provincial government retained a very low profile during the Winnipeg strike. Virtually its only concrete action was to keep the telephone system – which it owned and operated – going, even if that involved using volunteers from the Committee of 1000 and subsequently 'scab labour.' Norris met publicly with several large groups of returned veterans, but refused to commit himself to anything. He angered the veterans by mouthing platitudes but offering no concrete proposals. When urged to announce legislation to enforce collective bargaining, he replied, 'No, I can't see my way clear to do that. I think we'd better keep out of the fight.' Resided in 1919 at Royal Alexandra Hotel.

NORTH END: The residential area of the new immigrant in Winnipeg. Usually defined in the early 20th century as the area north of the Canadian Pacific Railway tracks to Burrows Avenue and west of the Red River to McPhillips Street. Also known as the 'Foreign Quarter', 'New Jerusalem', and 'CPR Town'. One Winnipegger characterized it as 'one gigantic melting pot north of the Canadian Pacific Railway tracks.' It was before the Great War virtually isolated from the remainder of the city by a level crossing of the main line of the Canadian Pacific Railway which intersected Main Street, the major access to the district from the south. Traffic on Main street was often blocked for hours and street cars did not cross the Canadian Pacific Railway tracks; instead, passengers had to transfer at level crossings like the Main Street one, often being forced to wait in inclement weather. The North End contained few large houses and large numbers of ethnics: Jews, Slavs, Scandinavians, and Germans. While some of the British working class lived in the North End, they tended to have their own neighbourhoods, particularly around St John's College and Cathedral and in the Weston area. The North End had its own business, culture, and social life. James Gray, who grew up in working class neighbourhoods to the south and west, recalled somewhat wistfully in his autobiographical account of his childhood that every block in the North End had a music teacher.

O

ONE BIG UNION (O.B.U.): Institutional expression of labour's demand for industrial unionism. Was based on the geographic (i.e. provincial) organization of all workers regardless of skills into one working class organization, which in turn was rooted in the assumption that there were only two classes in society, 'those who possess and do not produce, and those who produce and do not possess.' The long run objective of the One Big Union, according to one writer in the *O.B.U. Bulletin*, was 'to use our organization to secure the conquest of political power in order that the control of industry shall be brought into our own hands.' The One Big Union was consciously imitative of recent Russian examples. 'The Soviets are Trade Councils in reality, a new form of political machinery', declared the *Bulletin*. Ballots issued simultaneously with the vote on the General Strike about the One Big Union. The ballot, to be returned by 20 May , asked 'Are you In Favour of a General Strike to Establish a Six-Hour Working Day?' 'Are you in Favour of Severing your Affiliation with Your Present International Craft Union and Becoming Part of One Big Industrial Organization of All Workers?' The One Big Union was not actually established until after the Winnipeg General Strike had run its course, but the threat of its coming helps account for the hostile attitude toward the strike of the business classes of Winnipeg and of the Dominion government. The One Big Union grew rapidly in 1919 across the Canadian West. In Winnipeg, the Trades and Labor Council voted in early July 1919 in favour of the One

Big Union constitution by a vote of 8,841 to 705. The One Big Union formed the Winnipeg Labor Council on 5 August 1919, and began publishing the *O.B.U. Bulletin* after the former officers of the Trades and Labor Council refused to surrender the *Western Labor News*. Headquarters of the One Big Union were moved to Winnipeg in September 1920, and the city remained the centre of the movement for some years. During the 1920s it survived chiefly on the sale of its newspaper, which carried the results of the British football pools.

OXFORD HOTEL: Later home of food kitchen for women sponsored by Women's Labor League.

P

P.C. 2381: Was a postwar modification of wartime censorship, creating a ban on all 'enemy language' publication, including for first time Russian, Ukrainian, and Finnish.

P.C. 2384: Was another postwar regulation, defining unlawful associations, mentioning fourteen (mostly labour and left-wing groups in Russian or Ukrainian community) by name.

PARNELL, EDWARD (1859–1922): Born Dover, England. Came to Winnipeg in 1910.

Manager Parnell Bread Company. Prominent member of the Citizens' Committee of 1000. Elected Mayor of Winnipeg in 1920. Resided in 1919 at 826 Wolseley.

PENNER, JACOB (c.1880–1965): Prominent Winnipeg Marxist. Drafted Social Democratic Party Platform.

PEOPLE'S VOICE, THE: Predecessor of *The Voice* began publication in 1894.

PERRY, A.B. (1859–): Commissioner of Royal North-West Mounted Police in Regina. One of first graduates of Royal Military College, Kingston, Ontario, had served in North-West Rebellion. Early in 1919 had drafted operational directives for his divisions, emphasizing need to concentrate on those who espoused Bolshevism, chiefly in Winnipeg, Edmonton, and Vancouver. He was always clear that 'reds' were socialist 'agitators'. Having talked with radical leaders, he believed that they were 'Revolutionary Socialists' who were 'opposed to force or violence.' He added, 'I am not prepared to say that they are aiming at a revolution, but they were unchanging forces which, even if they so desire, some day they would be unable to control.' A breakdown

of civil order could be exploited by extremists into a revolution, he thought. Mentioned as eligible member of special immigration board of June 1919. After strike recommended to Borden that Royal North-West Mounted Police be given security jurisdiction over all of Canada. Was appointed first head of Royal Canadian Mounted Police in 1919.

PICKUP, LAURENCE: Member of central strike committee, representing the postal workers. Addressed Victoria Park meeting of Labour Church on Sunday 25 May. Address in 1919: 675 Home St.

PITBLADO, ISAAC (1867–1964): Of Scottish origin born in Glenelg, Nova Scotia. Family came to Winnipeg in 1881. Called to

L-R: ISAAC PITBLADO WITH J. A. M. AIKINS AND E. K. WILLIAMS, 1926

bar in 1890 and formed partnership with A. J. Andrews. Leader of Citizens' Committee of 1000. Declared that 'they are not going to have a Soviet Government here in Winnipeg.' Address in 1919: 523 Wellington Crescent.

PLEWMAN, W. R.: Reporter for the *Toronto Star* who wrote on the strike.

POPOVICH, MATTHEW: Editor of *Robochny Narod* in 1917, having been appointed in 1916 as part of a shift of control from an older to younger generation of Ukrainian Socialists. Highly critical of Socialist Party of Canada as 'an organization of academic philosophic debating clubs, incapable of guiding the political and economic struggle of the working class.' Before his appointment had been active in New York socialist circles, and was personally acquainted with Bolsheviks like Bukharin and Trotsky who were in New York at the same time. Later active in Winnipeg municipal politics. Remained aloof from general strike, reportedly spending the period of the strike in Gimli. Address in 1919: 246 Salter.

PORTAGE AND MAIN: Winnipeg's most famous intersection, the site of the 'riot' of 10 June. On three of its corners were the Bank of Montreal, the Canadian Pacific Railway ticket office, and the offices of Osler, Hammond, and Nanton. On the fourth corner (northeast) stood a rank of small buildings housing the Bank of Ottawa, the Central Shop, and the C.V. Cafe, which had above it the celebrated lighted billiard player who drove balls into pockets every evening.

PRITCHARD, WILLIAM A. (1889–): Head of Vancouver Longshoremen's Union, executive member of Vancouver Trades and Labor Council, member of Socialist Party of Canada, organizer of One Big Union. Born in England of Welsh descent. Athletic and musical, he was extremely well-read and a brilliant orator. Apprenticed to a building contractor in England, he had come to Vancouver in 1911. Responded to police actions against a draft evader in British Columbia in 1918 by querying, 'if the military authorities, in the round-up of evaders, will shoot a man on sight for his labour activities.' First spoke in Winnipeg on 12 June 1919. On Victoria Park platform with several clergymen, warned crowd to much laughter, 'beware of lawyers without briefs and parsons without pulpits.' On way home to British Columbia when warrant issued for his arrest on 17 June.

Arrested on train at Calgary. Took over chair of Winnipeg Trades and Labor Council from James Winning on 15 July 1919 as a member of the central executive of the One Big Union, when that council voted to affiliate with the One Big Union. Found guilty of seditious conspiracy on 28 March 1920 and sentenced to one year. His speech to the jury was a famous illustration of working-class oratory. Subsequently had lengthy career in provincial politics in British Columbia, serving as Reeve of Burnaby, chairman of Union of British Columbia Municipalities and Unemployment Committee of the Union of Canadian Municipalities.

PREUDHOMME, JULES (1877–): Winnipeg lawyer. Born in England, emigrated to Brandon and then became Assistant City Solicitor in 1912. Hostile to the strike. Represented city of Winnipeg at Robson hearings.

PRODUCERISM: Ideology demanding producers' 'natural rights to the fruits of labour', a strong ideological force in Western Canada.

PUTTEE [PRONOUNCED 'PETIT'], A. W. (1868–1957): Born in Folkstone, Kent, 25 August 1868. Apprenticed as printer. Immigrated to Brandon in 1888 but worked for some years in the United States in Seattle and St Paul. Settled in Winnipeg in 1891 and active in International Typographical Union.

A. W. PUTTEE, C. 1900

Elected Canada's first labour M.P. (Independent Labor) by ten votes in hotly-contested by-election in January 1900 against Edward Martin. One campaign jingle went, 'The Martin is a summer bird/Uncertain of his flight,/But year round Puttee sticks and hears/The stalwart's "Voice for Right." ' There were charges he was Clifford Sifton's candidate, particularly in November 1900 election, which Puttee again won, and it was true that he had much Liberal support. In 1904, he found labour sentiment had moved to the left and the Liberals no longer backed him. He was easily defeated and lost his deposit. Moderate labour leader, editor of *The Voice* in which he had financial interest from 1897 until its collapse in July 1918. One of

the strongest voices in favour of the organization of a Canadian Labor Party based upon the British Labour Party model. He and R. A. Rigg were nominated in early 1918 to meet with Prime Minister Borden on the conduct of the war, but neither apparently attended. Member of First Unitarian Church of Winnipeg. Address in 1919: 317 College.

Q

QUEEN, JOHN (1882–1946): Born in Lanarkshire, came to Winnipeg in 1906. Employed by North-West Laundry as driver of horse-drawn delivery wagon. Member of Social Democratic Party, cofounder of Winnipeg Socialist Sunday School. Alderman Ward 5 City of Winnipeg in 1919, having first been elected in 1916. Active in opposing Lord's Day Act in Winnipeg, which R. B. Russell regarded as a 'palliative', but one which resulted in giving some great pleasure. Chairman of Walker Theatre meeting of 22 December 1918. A cooper by trade. Elected member of the Manitoba legislature in 1920. Served as mayor of Winnipeg 7 times during Depression. Arrested on 17 June 1919 at home of Alderman Heaps, his family staying at Gimli for the summer. Advertising manager of *Western Labor News*. Found guilty of seditious conspiracy

on 28 March 1920 and sentenced to one year. Resided in 1919 at 317 Alfred.

R

RADICALISM: Movement toward rapid and (in some cases) total overhaul of the political, social, and economic system. In Canada most pronounced in the early twentieth century and in the west, although the western region had no monopoly. Radical ideology came to western Canada from Europe, from the United States, and especially from Great Britain's highly politicized labour movement. Western radicalism had at least three overlapping wings or tendencies: (1) the labourites, who sought reform of society within capitalism through political action; (2) industrial unionists, who sought to use industrial action, mainly the general strike, to bring down capitalism; (3) the socialists, who were Marxist revolutionaries insisting that there had to be a destruction of capitalism and a takeover by the proletariat. Unlike the industrial unionists, the socialists were committed to using the political process. But unlike the labourites, they sought total rather than partial reform of the system.

REAMES, A. E.: Royal North-West Mounted Police sergeant upon whose information and complaint the eight strike leaders were arrested in the early morning of 17 June. The strike leaders claimed that he 'led the riots. He was the chief provocateur.'

'RED FIVE': It is not clear who were the 'Red Five,' since five was a number frequently employed in labour organization. The Calgary Convention named five individuals to 'carry out the propaganda' in Manitoba: Russell, Lovatt, Scoble, Roberts, and Baker (of Brandon). Five members were elected by Trades and Labor Council (Russell, Queen, Winning, Veitch, McBride) to be central strike committee before delegates of affiliated unions appointed. This temporary committee included only one real radical (Russell), and three conservative trade unionists, so the sobriquet was quite illegitimate. The executive of the central strike committee also consisted of five individuals. Perhaps more to the point was the comment of R. J. Cromie, publisher of the *Vancouver Daily Sun*, on 31 May: 'It makes my blood boil to see five men, none of whom is Canadian born, or who has served overseas, run Winnipeg as they are at the present time.

RED FLAG: Vancouver-based radical journal found at Labour Temple on 17 June. Replaced *Western Clarion* when it was banned by the federal government.

RED SCARE: Postwar hysteria, especially in the United States, that the International Workers of the World would combine with socialists and radical trade unionists, to overthrow authority and replace it with a revolutionary government.

RESTALL, ELIZA (MRS): Arrested in connection with 21 June riot, arraigned on 23 June. Resided in 1919 at 809 William.

RICHARDSON, R. L. (1860–1921): Born Balderson, Canada. Founded Winnipeg *Tribune* in 1889. Well-regarded Canadian novelist. Regularly elected to House of Commons, last time as conscriptionist in 1917.

RIGG, RICHARD ALLEN (DICK) (1872– 1964): Secretary of Trades Council before War. Born in Todmorton, Lancashire, worked in cotton mill while in grade school and a full-time worker at age 12. Began theological studies in 1891 and had abandoned the Methodist ministry on coming to Canada in 1903. By 1909 local representative of Bookbinders' union. First nominee of Labor Representation Committee to win a seat on city council in 1913. In 1914 was sent to represent the Trades and Labor Council at the American Federation of Labor convention in

Philadelphia, a fact both Rigg and *The Voice* thought was important in view of the strength of his socialist convictions. Elected to provincial legislature of Manitoba in 1915 from Winnipeg North. Agreed to co-operate with the government's national registration programme in 1916 when assured that registration was not a prelude to conscription, but subsequently withdrew his support. Joined army in 1917, and insisted on being sent overseas. In late 1917 resigned his seat in the provincial legislature to contest federal election in Winnipeg North as nominee of Manitoba section of Canadian Labor Party. Nominated in early 1918 with A. W. Puttee to attend conference with Prime Minister Borden about the conduct of the war, but apparently never attended. Described by *Manitoba Free Press* in 1918 as 'the outstanding figure in the labour and radical world of Winnipeg.' Not prominent in the Winnipeg strike, although he drafted the motion of support for strike approved by Great War Veterans' Association on 15 May. Wanted city council to modify its position on police contract, but was unsuccessful in his arguments. Spoke for half an hour against Winnipeg Trades and Labor Council secession from national Trades and Labor Congress and international unions at meeting of 15 July 1919. Subsequently served as Canadian Trades and Labor Council troubleshooter against One Big Union. Resided in 1919 at 495 Carlaw.

RILEY, ARTHUR: Manager of Canada Bread Company plant; remanded on charges of disorderly conduct following disturbance at plant 30 May.

RIVER HEIGHTS: Residential district of south Winnipeg (south of the Assiniboine River) developed in years immediately before World War One. Home of many of city's professionals and middle managers.

ROBERTSON, SENATOR GIDEON (1874– 1933): Born Welland County, Ontario, raised in Portage la Prairie. Railroad telegrapher and leader of Telegraphers' Union. Called to Senate in 1917. Described by *The Labor News* as 'a big good-looking clean shaven Canadian, one of the statesmen among the ranks of the railway labour officials.' Minister of Labour in Ottawa in 1918 and 1919. In 1918 persuaded Winnipeg City Council to abandon the Fowler Amendment denying civic employees the right to strike. Met with A. J. Andrews in Thunder Bay in late May 1919. Told his deputy minister on 27 May that 'the motive behind this strike undoubtedly was the overthrow of constitutional Government.'

Pressured postal workers in city. Returned to Winnipeg on 11 June to deal with railway dispute threatening walkout by running trades in sympathy with strike. Decided in conjunction with A. J. Andrews to arrest strike leaders on 17 June.

ROBINSON, ERNEST: Secretary of Winnipeg Trades and Labor Council in 1919. A moderate. Attacked by socialist members of Council for sabotaging a protest meeting at Walker Theatre. Member of Central Strike Committee. Issued press release on 13 May that 'every organization but one has voted overwhelmingly in favour of the general strike.' Told strikers' meeting on 18 May: 'We have withdrawn labour from all industry, and it will stay withdrawn until the bosses realize that they cannot stand against the masses of labour. If we can control industrial production now, at this time, we can control it for all time to come, and we can control the Government of this country too.' Later told the Robson Commission that the procedure used for taking the strike vote was improper. Address in 1919: 1475 Ross. Regarded by most militants as weak. Did something during strike that got him the nickname 'rancid butter.'

ROBOCHNY NAROD (WORKING PEOPLE): Ukrainian socialist paper, a major force behind attempt of unskilled slavic workers to secure better working conditions through collective bargaining in 1917. Founded in 1909 as the organ of the Ukrainian Social Democratic Federation. Its purpose was to 'propagate socialist ideas among Ukrainian citizens of this country, and to organize our working masses for battle against our exploiters, for a socialist Canada.' The paper's control passed into more radical hands in 1916. The newspaper was always committed to the class struggle and to the eventual victory of the proletariat, but it printed far more Bolshevik material after 1916. It supported bilingual schools, insisting 'We recognize the official language of the state but we insist that all parents who wish to educate their children in their native language, have the right to do so.' Suppressed by the Canadian government in 1918.

ROBSON, H. A., K.C. (1871–1945): Born in Furness, England, of Scottish parents. Came to Canada in 1882. Kept journal of Riel treason trial, which he attended. Appointed to the bench in 1910, and to many investigative commissions. Head of Royal Commission to enquire into strike. Led provincial Liberal Party 1927–1930. Resided in 1919 at 321 Dromore.

ROSS, CHRISTINA: Arrested in connection with 21 June riot, arraigned on 23 June and remanded. Nurse at the General Hospital, where she resided in 1919.

ROUND TABLE CONFERENCE: called 23 May by Mayor Gray to discuss causes of strike and seek a solution.

ROUTLEDGE,_____: Assistant Commissioner of Royal North-West Mounted Police in Regina.

ROWELL, NEWTON (1867–1941): President of the Privy Council in Ottawa. A former leader of the Liberal Party in Ontario, had joined Union government because of its commitment to conscription. Helped organize effective secret service at end of 1918. Was conciliatory to labour and did not believe in a Bolshevik conspiracy in Canada. Royal North-West Mounted Police reported to him.

ROYAL ALEXANDRA HOTEL: A Canadian Pacific Railway hotel, one of Winnipeg's luxury hotels patronized by various dominion officials and frequent site of meetings with crowds, delegations, &c. Subscribed to Citizens' Committee fund raising. Located on Main Street.

ROYAL COMMISSION TO ENQUIRE INTO AND REPORT UPON THE CAUSES AND EFFECTS OF THE GENERAL STRIKE WHICH RECENTLY EXISTED IN THE CITY OF WINNIPEG FOR A PERIOD OF SIX WEEKS, INCLUDING THE METHODS OF CALLING AND CARRYING ON SUCH STRIKE (ROBSON COMMISSION): Robson appointed by letters patent from Lieutenant Governor dated 4 July 1919. Held open sittings in Winnipeg on 16, 22, 23, 24, 29, 30, 31 July, August 1, September 2, 8, 10. Commission assisted by C. P. Wilson, K.C., and C.H. Locke. T. J. Murray appeared on behalf of labour interests. J. Preudhomme held watching brief for City of Winnipeg. W. J. Moran appeared on behalf of Manitoba Bridge and Iron Works. No other employers appeared. The Citizens' Committee of One Thousand did not appear, but filed a statement. The commission's report found a high level of discontent among labour in Winnipeg, concerned about unemployment and the cost of living. It also found an aggressive Socialism in Winnipeg, often from those of Russian and Austrian origin although it had some headway among British subjects. It denied that the socialist leaders were true labour leaders, but 'genuine labour was given the appearance of being linked up with the movements of these men.' Denied that workers of British and Canadian origin ever intended to elevate labour to a state of dictatorship or to endorse the course that would lead to the Russian condition, although they readily responded to a strike call. It offered no real evidence for this assertion. The strike was in Robson's view a protest against conditions and a demand for general relief. Insisted that the question of the cause of the strike and the issues in the trials were not identical. Argued that the strike leaders attempted to close down businesses, however unsuccessfully, adding 'It should be said that the leaders who had brought about the General Strike were not responsible for the parades or riots which took place, and, in fact, tried to prevent them. Turbulent persons affected by this extraordinary condition broke loose.' Costs of strike were heavy to everyone. Commission distributed questionnaire to larger industries and businesses in Winnipeg, 602 answers received. Had Industrial Conditions Act of Manitoba of 1919 been implemented, it might have prevented trouble. Robson's report 'has been widely respected as an objective and accurate assessment of the strike, free of the rancour and extremism that marked other interpretations that appeared at the time.' (Kehler and Esau, 11–12.)

ROYAL COMMISSION ON INDUSTRIAL RELATIONS IN CANADA (MATHERS COMMISSION):
Appointed by Order-in-council PC 670 on 22 March 1919. Headed by Justice T. G. Mathers of Manitoba. Toured Canadian cities for hearings between April and June 1919. In Winnipeg it was boycotted by the Winnipeg Trades and Labor Council. Its final report submitted two days after the collapse of the strike. It argued that both industry and labour moving toward larger bargaining units. Did not matter what kind of body represented workers, so long as they were represented. Recommended a package of labour reform. (See also Mathers Commission)

ROYAL NORTH-WEST MOUNTED POLICE (RNWMP):
Dominion police force charged with law enforcement and domestic security west of the Lakehead. Headquarters in Regina. Commanded in Winnipeg by Colonel Cortlandt Starnes, who was required to provide daily reports of conditions in the city for his superiors. In the spring of 1919, the mounted police detachment in Winnipeg was increased gradually to over 300 men, in response to a formal request

from the Attorney-General of Manitoba on 17 May for assistance from the Mounted Police. The federal government refused for strategic reasons to use the Mounted Police to replace the regular Winnipeg police force dismissed at the end of May, leading to Winnipeg's use of 'special police', but the Canadian authorities were always prepared to employ the Mounted Police — if necessary — to suppress the strike. Before, during, and after the strike the Royal North-West Mounted Police employed men from its ranks as spies and infiltrators of labour ranks. It was the Mounted Police which executed the federal warrants arresting the strike leaders on 17 June. It was also the Mounted Police who charged the crowd on horseback on 21 June. Some of the mounted men employed at this time were Royal North-West Mounted Police who had been seconded to the Canadian army for Russian duty and were returning to Canada at the right time to be added to the Winnipeg detachment; they were the police in the 'khaki' uniforms complained about by the strikers, who charged that soldiers had been transferred by the government to the Mounted Police. The Police were convinced throughout the strike that Winnipeg's unrest was the result of revolutionary agitation. The strike leaders arrested on 17 June

were probably those identified by the Royal North-West Mounted Police as the most influential agitators. Merged with Dominion Police shortly after the strike to form the Royal Canadian Mounted Police, headquartered in Ottawa.

RUNNING TRADES MEDIATION COMMITTEE:
Officers of six railway unions connected with Canadian Railway Adjustment Board Agreement in early June 1919 offered their services as a mediation committee to the General Strike Committee and metal trades employers. On 4 June the Mediation Committee submitted a memo to both sides suggesting what it thought was a fair solution. Out of their own experience mediators agreed essentially with the strikers and endorsed the need to recognize the Metal Trades Council. Prepared report which strike leadership was prepared to endorse. Government sought to prevent 'prejudicial action by the Running Trades Committee', since Minister Robertson preferred to destroy nascent revolutionary 'syndicalism.' Instead, Robertson got the Ironmasters to agree to a compromise definition of 'collective bargaining' (which did not insist on the need for employers to bargain with the Metal Trades Council), and then pressured the mediation committee to endorse that definition as acceptable in the

railway industry. This compromise was released to the media on 16 June and was rejected by the strikers, leading the government to take the next step of arresting strike leaders.

RUPPELL, FREDERICK: Driver for J. E. Manning. Arrested on 21 June and charged with intimidation. Convicted December 1919 and fined $25 and costs.

RUSSELL, MATILDA: Committed for trial on 5 June on charges of intimidation of employees of a local department store.

RUSSELL, ROBERT B. (1888–1964): Leader of International Association of Machinists Local 122, secretary (a paid position) of district no. 2 at time of arrest. Of Scottish origin, raised in the Springburn district of Glasgow, came to Canada in 1911. Member of Socialist Party of Canada. Not active in labour's opposition to the war or conscription. Declared at Walker Theatre meeting that 'Capitalism has come to a point where she is defunct and must disappear.' At Calgary Convention chosen one of five Manitoba delegates to 'carry on the propaganda' for the One Big Union. Main leader of the general strike. Member of Central Strike Committee. Committee of 1000 claimed that he

had declared at City Hall, 'five individuals are responsible for this strike.' A Socialist and leader of One Big Union until its merger with the Canadian Labor Congress. Arrested 17 June 1919. *Toronto Star* commented, 'Russell was not worsted until Andrews was given the opportunity to use the powers of the State to put Russell in custody and eliminate him as a factor in the strike.' Fellow Socialist Alex Shepherd later insisted he was 'the real brains in the conduct of the strike.' Secretary-treasurer of Winnipeg Labor Council formed by One Big Union on 5 August 1919. Trial began 25 November and verdict of guilty delivered on 23 December 1919. The court was not sympathetic to Russell's insistence that he was only acting as a paid agent of the rank-and-file strikers, and sentenced him on 28 December to two years in prison. His appeal to the Manitoba Court of Appeal was unanimously dismissed, the court finding that his actions amounted to a seditious conspiracy. He appealed all the way to the Judicial Committee of Privy Council but his conviction was upheld, the beginning of a reluctance of that committee to interfere in Canadian matters. A new junior vocational school in Winnipeg was named after him in 1966. Resided in 1919 at 1415 Ross.

RYDER, W. S.: Author of unpublished M. A. thesis, *Canada's Industrial Crisis of 1919* (University of British Columbia, 1920), first scholarly study of strike.

S

SALISBURY, _____: Charged with intimidation and convicted December 1919. Fined $25 and costs.

SALTZMAN, HERMAN (CHAIM) (1882–): Born in Kamanetz-Dodolsk. Arrived in Winnipeg in 1906. Studied law and engineering at the University of Manitoba, sitting his B.Sc. finals in 1912. Jewish labour leader, helped found Socialist Party of Canada in Winnipeg in 1906. Secretary of Jewish Branch of Socialist Party of Canada in 1909. Argued in 1910 that impossiblism was only for the 'English comrades, while the foreign born were more interested in reform work, in progress, in democracy, in immediate demands which will palliate existing conditions.' One of founders of Social Democratic Party in 1910 and helped draft its program. Ran for office municipally in 1911 and provincially in 1914. Helped found the Hebrew Immigration Aid Society in 1912. Sent to Europe by Western Canadian Relief Conference in November 1920.

SCHAPPELLRI, OSCAR:
American-born, warrant issued 17 June. Deported for irregularities in papers. Applied to Court of Appeal for relief from deportation order by way of habeas corpus and certiorari. Court rejected application on grounds that the Immigration Act precluded review by a higher court unless person seeking relief was a Canadian citizen or had a Canadian domicile.

SCHEZERBANOWES, STEVE:
One of the two men who died as a result of the 21 June proceedings. He had been shot in both legs and died subsequently of gangrene.

SCOBLE, ANDREW (1882–1981): Born in London, England. His father was a gasfitter for the Midland Railway. Came to Winnipeg in 1904 because his father believed there was no future for gas in England. Became a motorman for Winnipeg Electric Railway, and later, a business agent for the Street Car Men's Union. At Calgary Convention chosen one of five Manitoba representatives to 'carry out the propaganda' for the One Big Union, but later claimed did not believe in the One Big Union, writing that while the Metal Trades workers had a legitimate case, it 'gave the opportunity for the proponents of the One Big

Union to bring into effect all the arguments that they were expounding for some time past and with the unsettled conditions of the returned men it all tended to make things difficult.' Member of central strike committee. Owned an automobile and drove members of the strike committee around the city. Met with F. G. Thompson and Canon Scott sometime around 5 June, 1919. Resigned his position with union rather than join One Big Union in 1920. Entered city service in 1919, City Weights & Measures Department, and retired as market superintendent in 1947. Address in 1919: 43 McAdam, which he owned, having purchased it for $1900 to be paid at $20 per month principal and interest. Later involved in Co-operative Commonwealth Federation and New Democratic Party.

SCOTT, REV. CANON FREDERICK GEORGE (1861–1944): Rector St Matthew's Church, Quebec, and canon of the cathedral. Popular soldier's 'padre' came to Winnipeg to support returned soldiers. Former first chaplain of Canadian Expeditionary Force's first division in France. Despite comments by strike committee and its newspaper, it is not clear that he supported the strike. More likely Scott saw himself as a mediator

who proved unable to mediate. Presided in early June at meeting between anti-strike soldiers headed by F. G. Thompson and four members of the strike committee. Thompson later claimed that he asked whether strike committee endorsed the principles of the One Big Union, and received four different answers.

SCZAURSKI, _____: Arrested and charged with unlawful assembly. Convicted 27 November 1919 and sentenced to one year in prison.

SEDITIOUS CONSPIRACY: chief charge against arrested strike leaders. Sedition was defined by Judge Metcalfe in his charge to the jury in the trial of Robert B. Russell through a quote from the English legal authority Archbold: 'It embraced all those practices, whether by word, deed or writing, which fall short of high treason, but directly tend to have for their object to excite discontent or dissatisfaction; to excite ill-will between different classes or the King's subjects; to create public disturbances, or lead to civil war, to bring into hatred or contempt the Sovereign or the government, the laws or constitution of the realm. . . to incite people to unlawful associations, assemblies, insurrections, breaches of the peace.' This definition, it should be noted, included as sedition considerably less 'revolutionary' behaviour than the specific charges against the strike leaders. The definition, said Mr Justice Metcalfe, did not stand in the way of free discussion provided that discussion did not take place *'under circumstances likely to incite tumult.'* He insisted, 'A torch applied to a green field may not be likely to cause a fire, yet when the grass is ripe and dry a spark may cause a conflagration.' Metcalfe also pointed out that there must be seditious intent: 'When a man is charged with a crime, the essence of the crime is the guilty mind; that is not peculiar to sedition.' But, he insisted, it was not necessary that the conspirators had actually joined in concert or had even met one another. He maintained that since the Canadian code did not define sedition, it was necessary to turn to the English cases, which 'show how wide the legal notion of seditious conspiracy is.' His broad definitions helped prepare the way for the jury to convict the accused in most cases.

SEDITIOUS LIBEL: charge against F. J. Dixon and J. S. Woodsworth. More specific than seditious conspiracy since it did not include actions and could not be interpreted to incorporate the secondary behaviour of others.

Seditious libel was the classic Anglo-Canadian charge used by those seeking to muzzle public criticism, and Dixon, like others before him, turned his trial into one over the issue of freedom of speech and press. He concluded by telling the jury, 'You are the last hope so far as the liberty of the subject is concerned. . . In your hands is placed the question of liberty of speech. Whether a man has a right to criticize government officials or not.' The prosecution had included in Woodsworth's 'seditious libels' two passages from the biblical Book of Isaiah, which suggested how dubious the charge could be.

SHEPHERD, ALEX (1897–1970): Born London, England. Apprenticed as machinist. Came to Winnipeg with mother around 1910. Delegate Winnipeg Trades and Labor Council 1916–1922. In December 1918 became secretary of the Winnipeg branch of the Socialist Party of Canada. Also secretary of Metal Trades Machinist Lodge 457, which struck against the city's ironmasters and provoked the Winnipeg general strike. Delegate to General Strike Committee during strike. Moved to Chicago in 1920s and returned to Winnipeg to found Shepherd Machine Tool & Die Works. A lifelong socialist, Shepherd believed in overthrowing capitalism by peaceful means.

SHERWOOD, COLONEL SIR ARTHUR PERCY (1854–1940): Born Ottawa. Career soldier cum policeman. Chief Commissioner of Dominion Police from 1913, retired at the end of 1918 as head of the nation's security forces. While in charge of Canada's secret service was also Chief Commissioner of the Boy Scouts' Association of Canada (1910–1918).

SIFTON, CLIFFORD (1861–1929): Born near Arva, Ontario. Sifton moved to Manitoba in 1875, settling at Brandon to practise law. He was elected to the Manitoba legislature in 1891 and moved to federal politics in 1896. Was most famous as federal minister of immigration who encouraged the settlement of eastern Europeans. Purchased The *Manitoba Free Press*. Sifton was an active businessman and investor, suspicious of organized labour.

SIMKIN, FAIVEL, "FRANK", (1885–1983): Came to Winnipeg in 1906. An active opponent of the pogroms in Russia, he became an anarchist in Winnipeg and founded *The Israelite Press* in 1914.

SMITH, A. E. (1872–1947): Born Guelph, Ontario. Ex-president of Manitoba Methodist Conference. Organized Labour Church in Brandon. Elected to Manitoba legislature in 1920, later president of Ontario section of Canadian Labor Party. Member of Communist Party arrested in 1934 on charge of sedition under section 98 of criminal code and was acquitted. Spoke to mass meeting at Victoria Park on 12 June, criticized churches and described Bankers' Association as One Big Union. Argued the strike was as religious a movement as a church revival. In his autobiography (1947) he dismissed the strike as a mere labour dispute.

SMITH, _____ : Member of central strike committee as telegrapher.

SOCIAL DEMOCRATIC PARTY (SDP): Organized in Winnipeg around 1904 as the Manitoba Social Democratic Party. Merged in 1911 with Canadian Socialist Federation as a result of a unity convention held in Port Arthur, Ontario; the new party was called the Social Democratic Party of Canada. Party's programme drafted by R. A. Rigg, Jacob Penner, and Herman Saltzman. By 1913 the party was the largest socialist party in Canada with 3,500 members in 133 locals, and by 1915 it had 5,300 members. The Social Democratic Party's membership was largely composed of immigrant workers: Finns, Ukrainians, Poles, Russians, and Jews. Many had memories or knowledge of the 1905 Russian revolution. Its largest centre was in Winnipeg's North End, particularly among the ethnic communities. Although the Social Democratic Party was Marxist and suspicious of trade unionism, it was not as militant as the Socialist Party about these matters, and never cut itself off entirely from organized labour. It was less dogmatic and closer to the interests of its members. Nevertheless, in 1917 the Social Democratic Party of Manitoba held a convention which rejoiced about the overthrow of the capitalists in Russia by the Bolsheviks, and indicated a willingness to unite with the Socialist Party of Canada on the basis of the Bolshevik programme. Nationally, however, the party was less enthusiastic, partly because some provincial branches were less radical than that in Manitoba. A number of prominent strike leaders in Winnipeg, including Richard Johns, John Queen, F. G. Tipping, and A. A. Heaps, were members of the Social Democratic Party at the time of the strike.

SOCIAL GOSPEL: A version of Christianity based on premise that it was a social religion concerned with human relationships through which men and women found meaning for their lives by attempting to realize the Kingdom of God on earth. Many of its leaders were former Methodist ministers active in the labour movement, often as socialists. One of social gospel's manifestations was the Labour Church. Social gospellers active in the Winnipeg Strike included: J. S. Woodsworth, William Ivens, and A. E. Smith.

SOCIALIST PARTY OF CANADA (SPC): Organized in Winnipeg around 1904. On a national level, the party began with a mistrust of trade unionism because it 'diverted working men from the true cause of revolution', and its hostility only became more extreme as the years went on. It disapproved of strikes and general strikes. This stance made cooperation with organized labour fairly difficult. Its function was educational and consciousness-raising rather more than to engage in practical politics. It was not internationally affiliated. Ideologically, the Socialist Party of Canada was Marxist — some said 'crudely' Marxist, and many of its members were followers of Daniel DeLeon. It was 'impossiblist' in its beliefs, arguing that capitalism could not be reformed and class-conscious political action was the only route for the proletariat to take on their way to the co-operative commonwealth. The Socialist Party of Canada refused to include reform in its platforms — only the destruction of the wage system.

However, the party was not necessarily syndicalist in its beliefs, since it did not seek disruptive acts to bring the revolution into being. A number of strike leaders in Winnipeg, particularly R. B. Russell, George Armstrong, and William Pritchard (of Vancouver), were members of the Socialist Party of Canada. The Party nominated Russell, Armstrong, Pritchard and Richard J. Johns, in the 1920 Manitoba provincial election .

SOKOLOWISKI, MIKE: Tinsmith. Killed instantly in the 21 June melee. Resided at Balmoral Apartments at 540 Balmoral. Survived by a widow and three children. *Free Press* claimed he was one of the more active 'missile throwers' in the crowd.

SOLDIERS' AND SAILORS' LABOR PARTY: Petitioned Meighen on 24 June with 356 signatures, complaining that government had acted contrary to 'those principles of Liberty and Democracy for which we volunteered to fight.' Concluded by demanding that government deport them to their mother countries, since government was not governed by democratic spirit. Petitioned again (with Labour Church, Dominion Labor Party) in September of 1919 claiming that

strike leaders were within their legal rights. This petition contained more than 2,400 names and addresses.

SOLDIERS' PARLIAMENT: Mass meetings of returned soldiers in Victoria Park during strike. Passed a number of resolutions, including one supporting government's attempt to deport 'undesirable aliens' and opposing new immigration from enemy lands. Echoed cry that legislation to halt immigration was 'called for by the blood of 55,000 Canadian dead.'

SPANISH INFLUENZA: Pandemic that struck Canada in late 1918 and early 1919. As many Canadians died from the flu as did in the trenches of the Great War. The flu hit Winnipeg in the spring of 1919.

SPARLING, JOHN KERR (1872–1941): Born Montreal, came to Winnipeg in 1888. Alderman 1917–1922, chairman of Police Commission. Partner in Hull, Sparling and Sparling. Later chaired Board of Governors of United College. Lawyer. A pioneer Boy Scout leader in Manitoba. Address in 1919: 957 Dorchester.

SPARTACANS: The Bolshevik radicals in Germany who became the Communist Party of Germany in 1919.

SPEERS, _____: Returned soldier, told premier Norris on 31 May that soldiers had fought for democracy and returned to find Committee of 1000 running city like autocrats.

STAPLES, WILLIAM: Arrested by bailiffs at sentencing of R. B. Russell on 28 December after calling for a 'tiger' for the convicted man. Address in 1919 at 482 Carlaw.

STARNES, COL. CORTLANDT: Commanding officer of Royal North-West Mounted Police in Winnipeg. Reported to commissioner of Royal North-West Mounted Police in Regina. Sent nightly telegrams during height of strike. He always treated the strike as a labour dispute although his submissions contained reports of rumours and inflammatory statements. On 10 June he reported 'the backbone of the strike is broken, and it should be only a matter of a few days before the majority of the strikers are back at work.'

STEINHAUER, MARGARET: Arrested on 5 June for inciting strikers on Main Street near Market Square. One of the women incited by Helen Armstrong in late June to assault *Tribune* employees selling papers on street. Fined $5 plus costs.

STEINKOPF, MAX: Born in Bohemia in 1881. Came to Winnipeg in 1898. Founder of local B'nai B'rith. Prominent Jewish lawyer and businessman. President of Talmud Torah in 1919. Member of Citizens' Committee of 1000, and defeated in several subsequent elections (1919, 1927) because of this affiliation. Elected to Canadian Jewish Congress in 1919 as a Zionist.

STONY MOUNTAIN PENITENTIARY: Federal prison north of Winnipeg to which arrested strike leaders were taken and where they ultimately served their prison terms.

STRATHCONA HOTEL: Initial home of food kitchen set up by Women's Labor League to provide women strikers with food. Located on corner of Rupert and Main.

STUBBS, LEWIS ST. GEORGE (1878–1958): Born in West Indies, moved to Manitoba in 1902, settled as lawyer in Birtle. Assisted F. J. Dixon in preparing his defense.

SWEATMAN, WILLIAM A. TRAVERS: (1879-1941) Prominent lawyer and member of Committee of 1000. Partner in Richards, Sweatman, Kemp & Fillmore. Assisted in prosecution of eight arrested strike leaders. In 1920 recommended the deportation of the principal leaders of the One Big Union. Resided in 1919 at 266 Kingsway.

SWIFT COMPANY: Packing plant scene of attack by angry mob on 28 January 1919 to protest employment of alien workers.

SYMPATHETIC STRIKES: Strikes in support of comrades taking labour action. Most of the workers in Winnipeg were sympathetic strikers supporting those in the Metal and Building industries who had begun the strike. There were sympathy strikes in other Canadian cities, including Vancouver, Calgary, Edmonton, Prince Albert, Regina, Toronto, Sydney, and Amherst. Sympathy strikes, although often 'general' in nature, should not be confused with 'general strikes', which are part of the strategic arsenal of radicalism and syndicalism, and are intended to force a massive and permanent shift in economic and political power from capital to labour by toppling the capitalistic state. Part of the trouble in Winnipeg was that the very terminology of the strike, as well as its logic, led opponents to see it as part of a proto-revolution. As Mr Justice Metcalfe put it in his charge to the jury in the trial of R. B. Russell, 'How can a general sympathetic strike, the object of which is to tie up all industry, to make it so inconvenient for others that they will cause force to be brought about, to stop the delivery of food, to call off the bread, to call off the milk, to tie up the wheels of transportation — how can such a strike be carried on successfully without a breach of all these matters likely to endanger human life?'

SYNDICALISM: A political theory involving the takeover of industry and government by labour unions through general strikes or other direct means, including violence. There is considerable disagreement among historians over whether either the One Big Union or the Socialist Party of Canada were truly syndicalist, and many historians would argue that syndicalism was not very important in the Winnipeg general strike, despite the assertions and actions of the Canadian government. As with so much of the strike, the issue revolves around one's interpretation of 'intention.'

T

THOMPSON, FREDERICK GEORGE: Born in Winnipeg, educated at Manitoba College and Manitoba Law School. Member of law firm of Waller, Thompson and

Crawford. A returned soldier from the 78th Battalion of the Winnipeg Grenadiers, he had been wounded at Amiens 8 August 1918 and returned to Winnipeg to recuperate at Deer Lodge Hospital, where he had several operations. He organized Loyalist Returned Soldier Association after failing to convince Great War Veterans' Association to abandon its policy of neutrality. He later denied that he was a Captain, as described by the strikers' newspaper, and he vehemently denied that he was ever a member of the Committee of 1000. 'I went out', he subsequently testified, 'and knowing a lot of returned men, around town, I put my views to them — that something had to be done, and I got an auto and chased around to other places . . . and preached the word from mouth to mouth that we would have to parade as a counter to this other parade and set a time and place.' In early June met with four members of strike committee (Winning, Russell, Scoble, and Pritchard) under chairmanship of Canon Scott. Later testified that he asked whether strike committee endorsed the One Big Union principles, and got four different answers. Practised law in Winnipeg. Later elected an honorary fellow of St John's College.

TIPPING, F. G. (1885–1973): Englishman who was a Baptist preacher upon his arrival in Manitoba in 1905. Drifted from preaching into carpentry and then into industrial education as a schoolteacher at Lord Roberts School, retiring as associate principal. Moderate socialist and member of Social Democratic Party. Elected President of Winnipeg Trades and Labor Council in late 1917, deposed as president in late 1918 because as member of Mather Industrial Commission signed report more critical of labour than of management; he particularly objected to Metal Trades Union going on strike while matter before commission, which intended to settle dispute. Vote calling for his suspension passed on 5 September 1918 by 49 to 10. His resignation accepted on 19 September. The movement to depose him was led by R. B. Russell, and was indicative of a growing split between moderates and radicals on the Trades and Labor Council. Later founder of Manitoba Co-operative Commonwealth Federation. Received Manitoba Centennial Medal in 1970. A senior citizens' block on Osborne St was named after him in 1974. A frequent source for later interviews with historians about the strike, although many of his contemporaries regarded him as discredited and outside the mainstream of events during the strike period. Resided in 1919 at 490 Beresford.

TORONTO GENERAL STRIKE: Began with a dispute in the metal trades. The workers wanted an eight-hour day and a forty-four hour week, and voted overwhelmingly to strike, in a vote sponsored by the Toronto Trades and Labor Council. A committee of 15 was empowered to call a strike on 28 May of as many unions as it felt were necessary to back up the metal workers. Negotiations under the auspices of the federal government delayed strike action, which began on 30 May. The strike call was heeded by a far smaller proportion of workers than in Winnipeg, but the possibility of expansion was present, leading to the organization of a citizens' committee of ten thousand modelled on the Winnipeg example. The strike collapsed when the street railwaymen on 1 June refused to participate, and it was officially called off on 3 June. The existence of the Toronto strike, and its threat, helps explain the concern of the authorities, particularly the Dominion government, in Winnipeg at the end of May to bring their local situation under control. And the collapse of the Toronto strike was one of the reasons observers like John Dafoe were convinced that the Winnipeg strike would fail without extreme repressive measures.

TRADE UNIONISM: Labour organization based upon the craft or trade. By the 1880s many local unions in particular crafts and trades had begun organizing into 'international' (i.e., in both the United States and Canada) bodies, particularly those affiliated with the American Federation of Labor led by Samuel Gompers, and many Canadian unions had joined in the Trades and Labor Congress of Canada. The international unions and the Trades and Labor Council tussled for years. Both organizations tended to be bread and butter unions which preferred to keep free of political organizations, although willing to endorse specific candidates from any party who offered support to labour. Gradually in the early 20th century, both labourism and socialism muddied the waters of non-partisan trade unionist politics. Many scholars would insist that traditional trade unionism was strongest in eastern Canada, while in western Canada labourism, socialism, and especially industrial unionism made far greater inroads.

TRADES AND LABOR CONGRESS OF CANADA (TLC): Founded in 1883 and originally dominated by the Knights of Labor, the *TLC* became national around 1900. Controlled by craft unionists, the Trades and Labor

Council was moderate and gradualist in its policy, although it never overtly rejected socialist ideas. Nevertheless, its policy was to stress negotiation and to avoid strikes except as a very last resort. It had fallen out with many in the labour movement, especially in the west, over the questions of registration and conscription. By 1919 the Trades and Labor Council was facing a serious challenge from the One Big Union. It viewed the Winnipeg strike as a line of action 'in harmony' with the policies of the One Big Union and in direct challenge to its own, and it was not very helpful in protesting the arrests of the strike leaders or the suppression of the strike by the authorities. Among other complaints, the Trades and Labor Council saw the Winnipeg example as repudiating 'the autonomy of each craft union to decide for itself whether its members would take part in a sympathetic strike.' It saw the mass action of industrial unionism as 'mob rule.'

TRADES AND LABOR COUNCIL: Composed of elected representatives from every Winnipeg union that decided to affiliate. Affiliated membership about 12,000 in 1919. Split in 1918 between conservative trade unionists and more radical socialists, who favoured industrial organization. Resignation of

President F. G. Tipping forced by radicals in September 1918. In January 1919 a stormy meeting fought over the failure to acquire the Walker Theatre as another venue for a protest gathering desired by the Socialists, Social Democrats, and Dominion Labor people on the council. George Armstrong, R. B. Russell, and R. J. Johns attacked Secretary Ernest Robinson. 'In Winnipeg tonight we are fighting with ideas', commented Johns, 'but we shall soon be fighting with rifles.'

TRIBUNE, THE: Winnipeg daily often sympathetic to labour but unalterably opposed to the general strike as a tactical weapon.

TRUEMAN, WALTER H. (1870-1951): Manitoba judge who defended William Ivens and John Queen. Clashed frequently with Judge Metcalfe. Insisted in his address to the jury, 'you cannot indict ideas. You cannot take away from Labor the right to organize.' Retained by Defence Committee to take R. B. Russell's appeal to the Privy Council, but could not get an appeal judge to register a dissenting judgment, and the Judicial Committee of the Privy Council would not hear the appeal, saying 'The Judicial Committee is not a Court for Criminal appeal. It is only to be used if justice is violated.'

U

UKRAINIAN SOCIAL DEMOCRATIC PARTY: Pro-Soviet revolutionary Marxist party claiming 2,000 members, which was outlawed by the Canadian government in September 1918. In 1917, its second national congress, held in Winnipeg, passed a resolution stating that 'no branch of the U.S.D.P. may cooperate with any group of people who do not recognize the class struggle and the necessity of abolishing the capitalist order.'

UKRAINIAN TEMPLE: Searched for seditious literature on 17 June.

UNLAWFUL ASSEMBLY: Defined by section 87 of the Criminal Code of 1919 as 'an assembly of three or more persons who . . . assemble in such a manner or so conduct themselves when assembled as to cause persons in the neighbourhood of such assembly to fear, on reasonable grounds, that the persons so assembled will disturb the peace tumultuously, or will . . . provoke other persons to disturb the peace tumultuously.' Use of force to disperse such an assembly is entirely legitimate. Whether the parade of 21 June constituted an 'unlawful assembly' was much debated at the time and has been ever since.

V

VANCOUVER GENERAL SYMPATHETIC STRIKE: The most serious of the various strikes that sprang up in the wake of the Winnipeg strike, because it was located in the west and especially in a British Columbia which had an extremely militant labour movement and socialist presence. The Vancouver Trades and Labor Council monitored the Winnipeg situation closely from the beginning, and threatened a general strike vote if the government suppressed the Winnipeg strike with armed force. On 28 May it ordered a strike vote, partly for local issues, partly in support of Winnipeg. Its seven demands included three specifically concerned with Winnipeg, two connected with the returned soldiers, and two connected with general grievances (food hoarding and unemployment). The vote was much closer than in Winnipeg, but the Council called the strike on the evening of 2 June. The response of the Vancouver workers was considerably greater than the close vote had suggested. Estimates of numbers on strike varied from 12,000 to 60,000. Anti-strike leadership was taken by a Citizens' Law and Order League backed by the provincial premier John Oliver, who stated that the strike was organized by men seeking to overthrow constituted authority. The strike gradually collapsed and was formally ended by the Council on 3 July. The returned soldiers had never become involved and there was no government repression, although everyone was obviously aware of the Winnipeg example.

VEITCH, HARRY GEORGE (1881–1960): Born in Scotland, came to Winnipeg in 1910. President of Wallingford Press, printer, member of Typographical Union. Member interim central committee and Central Strike Committee. President of Winnipeg Trades and Labor Council in 1916. An orthodox trade unionist. Advised workers in 1916 to refuse to fill out their registration cards. Resided in 1919 at 632 Arlington.

VENICE CAFE: Restaurant at 330 Smith, the favourite eating place of radical socialists in Winnipeg.

VERENCHUCK, MIKE: Russian-born youth arrested on 17 June at home of B. Davieatkin without warrant. Had volunteered for the army in 1915, was wounded several times including once at the Somme in 1916. Honourably discharged in 1917. Held for some time without charges. Government attempted briefly to have him declared insane, possibly so that his citizenship could be revoked.

VICTORIA PARK: Downtown Winnipeg Park used for many rallies. Site of Soldiers' Parliament. Later renamed 'Liberty Park.'

VOICE, THE: A weekly newspaper described by Robson Commission as a conservative advocate of trade unionism, published by a private company in the interests of labour until succeeded by *Western Labor News* in August 1918. *The People's Voice* began publication in 1894. *The Voice* published from 1896 to July 1918 with the endorsement of the Winnipeg Trades and Labor Council. It was edited during the war by A. W. Puttee. It saw the war as a capitalistic one that should cease. It opposed conscription, profiteering, and the curtailment of civil rights. It also opposed the civic workers' strike of 1918 as 'too precipitate', arguing *The Voice* 'believes that there is a time to strike, but that time is after all efforts of conciliation and arbitration have failed.' As a result, the strike committee broke with *The Voice* and turned to publishing its own newspaper. [An interesting question whether there was a sharp ideological break after paper came directly under Winnipeg Trades and Labor Council in August 1918]

VULCAN IRON WORKS: A firm dependent on outside contracts that had a bad reputation for labour relations going back to the early years of the century. A strike occurred there in 1906. One of eight Winnipeg metal fabrication shops awarded Canadian government

VULCAN IRON COMPANY WAREHOUSE, 1903

contracts for shell manufacture in 1915. At height of shell crisis paid hourly wages plus a bonus to some of its workers, a practice labour regarded as discriminatory. By 1916 efforts to unionize the Vulcan shop were met with the introduction of labour spies. There was so much labour discontent at Vulcan that head of Munitions Board (Joseph Flavelle) was forced to examine the problems personally.

W

WALKER THEATRE: 'Canada's finest theatre', built in 1907 on Smith St. Its curtain had the motto: 'Finds tongues in trees, books in the running brooks, sermons in stones, and good in everything.' Recently refurbished as theatrical venue.

WALKER THEATRE MEETING: Called by Winnipeg Trades and Labor Council in association with Socialist Party of Canada on Sunday 22 December 1919. Passed resolutions protesting against orders in council (especially 'War Measures Act') limiting freedom of speech, calling for withdrawal of troops from Russia, and calling for the release of political prisoners.

WALLBAK, _____: Arrested 21 June and charged with intimidation. Convicted December 1919 and fined $25 and costs.

WAR MEASURES ACT: One of the first actions of the Borden government, after war was declared, gave the executive (The Governor in Council) virtually unlimited power 'to do and authorize such acts and things, and to make from time to time such orders and regulations, as he may by reason of the existence of real or apprehended war, invasion or insurrection deem necessary for the security, defence, peace, order, and welfare of Canada.' It provided for censorship, arrest, detention, exclusion, and deportation. The legislation had no autonomous mechanism for termination, but would be ended only when the executive decided the crisis was over. The War Measures Act made it possible to replace parliamentary government for the duration of the emergency with government by order-in-council. Many of the chief critics of this legislation were radical labour leaders who had felt its sting.

WARREN, N. W.: Representative of Metal Trades Employers.

WARTIME ELECTIONS ACT OF 1917: Stripped former citizens of enemy countries who had been naturalized Canadians of their vote in federal elections.

WATSON, GEORGE A.: Telephone commissioner of Manitoba Telephones from 1912. Advertised for new employees on 27 May 1919, insisting later that he was not looking for strike breakers but permanent new employees. Announced when workers returned after strike that not all would be rehired and all would lose their seniority. Resided in 1919 at 758 Macmillan.

WEBB, MRS: Chairman of relief committee of Women's Labor League.

WELLINGTON CRESCENT: Street and district along the south side of the Assiniboine River running from near Osborne Street to Tuxedo. Contained large lots and some of Winnipeg's largest houses. The developer required that Wellington Crescent homes had to have a value of at least $6,000 when completed and be set back at least one hundred feet from the street. The home of many of Winnipeg's richest and most prominent citizens, 'the Crescent' became the symbol of the plutocracy (at that time mainly Ontario-born of British origin) in the city.

WESTERN LABOR NEWS: Official organ of the Trades and Labor Council, succeeded *The Voice* (a privately published paper in the interests of labour) in August 1918. Edited by William Ivens. This paper advocated socialism instead of trade unionism. Robson Commission claimed that 'it played a large part in fanning the discontent of the working class, and bringing this discontent to such a pitch that, as a class, the working people of Winnipeg were in an extremely receptive mood when the proposal of the General Strike was brought before them.' (Robson, p. 11) Masthead of non-strike issues read: 'We must control all we produce – We produce all.' Central Strike Committee wrote and published a *Special Strike Edition* from

18 May to 23 June which structured a language of 'working class entitlement' growing out of the war recently ended.

WESTERN STAR: Successor to *Strike Bulletin* edited by F. W. Dixon and first published 24 June under motto 'ON TO VICTORY.'

WESTMAN, CLARA: Arrested in connection with 21 June riot, arraigned 23 June.

WESTON DISTRICT: Working-class section of Winnipeg located around the Canadian Pacific Railway shops and yard between McPhilips and Keewatin.

WHEELER, CAPTAIN: An organizer of the Returned Soldiers' Loyalist Association.

WILLIAMS, ESTEN KENNETH (1889–1970): Born Parkhill, Ontario. Called to bar in 1911 and came to Winnipeg. Lawyer (in 1919 member of firm of Williams and O'Grady) and prominent member of Committee of 1000. Appointed Chief Justice of Manitoba Court of King's Bench in 1946. Resided in 1919 at 728 Dorchester.

WILLING, H. B.: Salesman at Eaton's, secretary-treasurer of

Imperial Veterans' Association. Resided in 1919 at 492 Marjorie.

WILSON, CLIFFORD PARNELL, K. C.: Assisted H. A. Robson on royal commission to investigate strike.

WILTON, JOHN (1879–1942): Born High Bluff, Manitoba. Liberal lawyer, supporter of T. J. Norris in the legislature. Introduced Workmen's Compensation Bill, which provided for private coverage

JOHN WILTON

by insurance companies rather than state funding, into Manitoba legislature in February 1916. Then enlisted as private in Canadian army, returning as captain. His unpublished auto-

biography is critical of the Citizens' Committee. Resided in 1919 at 9–74 Spence.

WINNING, JAMES: Alderman, city of Winnipeg. President, Trades and Labor Council at the time of the strike. Scotborn, he worked in London as a bricklayer and migrated to Winnipeg in 1906 where he worked at the same trade. Member of Central Strike Committee. Served as member of Manitoba Minimum Wage Board 1918–1941. Testified before Robson commission and was principal witness that strike was not revolutionary in intent. Resided in 1919 at 298 Ferry in St James.

WINNIPEG BOARD OF TRADE: Founded in 1879, the major umbrella organization of Winnipeg businessmen, the equivalent of what in other cities would be called the 'Chamber of Commerce.' Staunch supporter of conscription.

WINNIPEG CITIZEN: Daily paper put out by Citizens' Committee and distributed free on street. First issue on 19 May, which declared 'Among the objects of this committee may be mentioned the maintenance of law and order, the carrying on of the essential services necessary to preserve the lives and health of the whole community, including the strikers,

but more particularly, the little children, invalid soldiers, and the sick.' According to strikers it 'Bottomlied the one and only Horatio.' The *Western Labor News* declared on 21 May, 'a terrorist paper has been published in this city. While proclaiming itself to be neither for nor against the strikers, it proceeds to paint the strike "Red." ' Strikers complained it was distributed from fire halls.

WINNIPEG DEFENCE COMMITTEE: Set up to raise money to support costs of defending strikers. Advertised in newspapers for funds. Admitted in 24 Feb. 1920 *Western Labor News* that defence had not raised its goal of $50,000. Also published trial documents and original writings. Pamphlets included a comparison of judge's charge to jury in King v. Russell and in Rex v. Burns (1886), Dixon's address to jury, Pritchard's address to jury, 'King v. J. S. Woodsworth'. Also published *The Winnipeg General Sympathetic Strike* (reprinted in 1973), costing 50 cents.

WINNIPEG PRINTING & ENGRAVING COMPANY: Printer of *Strike Bulletin*. Told to stop printing on 23 June 1919.

WINNIPEG TELEGRAM: Called the Winnipeg 'Yellowgram' by the strikers. Most hostile of Winnipeg dailies against the strike, particularly virulent on the 'alien' question.

WINTERS, FRANK: Hostler, Canadian National Railways. Remanded on charges of disorderly conduct following disturbance at Canada Bread Company on 30 May. Address in 1919: 573 Warsaw.

WOLSELEY DISTRICT: Middle-class housing area developed in the years immediately before World War One, between the north bank of the Assiniboine River and Portage Avenue, bounded to the east by Maryland St and to the west by Omand's Creek.

WOMEN'S LABOR LEAGUE: Chicago-based women's organization with a feminist agenda. Wanted equal pay for equal work, an 8-hour day, and a living wage. Winnipeg branch led by Helen Armstrong and Helen Anderson. Organized kitchen and dining room at Strathcona Hotel on Main Street, later moved to Oxford Hotel which had larger dining room and more modern kitchen. Financed kitchen with funds raised by a Relief Committee headed by Mrs Webb and donations from appeals made in *Western Labor News*, as well as from dances and benefit performances.

WOODSWORTH, JAMES SHAVER (1874–1942): Born in Ontario, Woodsworth moved to Brandon with his family in 1885. After some time as a Methodist circuit rider and study at Victoria College and Oxford, Woodsworth began work with immigrants at All People's Mission, and became a prominent exponent of the social gospel. He resigned from the ministry in 1918 over the Methodist Church's support of the war, working in Vancouver as a longshoreman. He returned to Winnipeg on 8 June 1919, speaking to crowds at the Labour Church and Soldier's Parliament. Assumed editorship of *Strike Bulletin* after William Ivens arrested. Arrested on 23 June. Charges of seditious libel were stayed by crown, but were never actually withdrawn after the Dixon acquittal. Woodsworth was one of the few personal beneficiaries of the Winnipeg General Strike, since he acquired (without so attempting to do) much of the aura of martyrology that came to surround the strike and the strikers without most of the accompanying pain and emotional stress. He organized the Manitoba Independent Labor Party, which helped elect him as Winnipeg North Centre's representative to the House of Commons in 1921 under the slogan 'Human Needs before Property Rights.' He held the seat until his death in 1942. From 1933 he led the Co-operative Commonwealth Federation. The party rejected his pacifism in 1939, and he stood alone in opposing the Canadian declaration of war against Germany.

X, Y, Z

YOUNG WOMEN'S CHRISTIAN ASSOCIATION (Y.W.C.A.): Provided emergency accommodation for women, 'strikers or not, who are temporarily in want on account of the strike.'

ZANETH, F. W.: Royal North-West Mounted Police constable who, posing as Harry Blask (an American International Workers of the World leader), infiltrated labour movement and Socialist Party of Canada. Was delegate at the Calgary Conference of March 1919. Became a prime source of intelligence on security matters in months before Winnipeg strike, and was a star witness for the prosecution at the strike trials. Blask had himself arrested and released in Regina under Wartime Regulations in order to prove that he was not a police spy.

Abella, Irving, ed., *On Strike: Six Key Labour Struggles in Canada 1919-1945* (Toronto, 1981).

Allen, A. Richard, *The Social Passion* (Toronto, 1971).

Angel, Eric, 'Restoring Order: The RMWMP and the Winnipeg General Strike of 1919,' unpub. paper, Queen's University, no date.

Angus, Ian, *Canadian Bolsheviks* (Montreal, 1981).

Artibise, Alan F.J., *Winnipeg: A Social History of Urban Growth, 1874-1914* (Montreal, 1975).

Artibise, Alan F.J., 'The Divided City: The Immigrant in Winnipeg Society, 1874-1921', Gilbert Stelter and Alan F.J. Artibise, eds., *The Canadian City: Essays in Urban History*, 300-336.

Artibise, Alan, *Winnipeg: An Illustrated History* (Toronto, 1977).

Artibise, Alan F.J., 'Patterns of Population Growth and Ethnic Relationships in Winnipeg, 1874-1974', *Histoire Sociale/Social History*, 9, No. 18 (November 1976).

Avery, Donald, 'The Radical Alien and the Winnipeg General Strike of 1919', Ramasy Cook and Carl Berger, eds., *The West and the Nation*, 209-231.

Avery, Donald, *Dangerous Foreigners: European Immigrant Workers and Labour Radicalism in Canada, 1896-1932* (Toronto, 1979), 65-89.

Avery, Donald, 'Ethnic Loyalties and the Proletarian Revolution', Jurgen Dahlie and Tissa Fernando, eds., *Ethnicity, Power and Politics in Canada* (Toronto, 1981).

Avery, Donald, 'Ethnic and Class Tensions in Canada, 1918-1920: Anglo Canadians and the Alien Worker', Frances Swyripa and John Herd Thompson, eds., *Loyalties in Conflict: Ukrainians in Canada During the Great War* (Edmonton, 1985), 79-98.

Balawyder, A., ed., *The Winnipeg General Strike* (Vancouver, 1967).

Baxter, T.C., 'Selected Aspects of Canadian Public Opinion on the Russian Revolution', unpub. M.A. thesis, University of Western Ontario, 1973.

Bellan, Ruben, *Winnipeg's First Century: An Economic History* (Winnipeg, 1978).

Bercuson, David Jay, *Confrontation at Winnipeg: Labour, Industrial Relations, and the General Strike* (Montreal, 1974, rev. ed., 1990)

Bercuson, David, *Fools and Wise Men: The Rise of the One Big Union* (Toronto, 1978).

Bercuson, David and Kenneth McNaught, *The Winnipeg Strike: 1919* (Toronto, 1974).

Berkowski, Gerry, 'A Tradition in Jeopardy: Building Trades Workers Responses to Industrial Capitalism

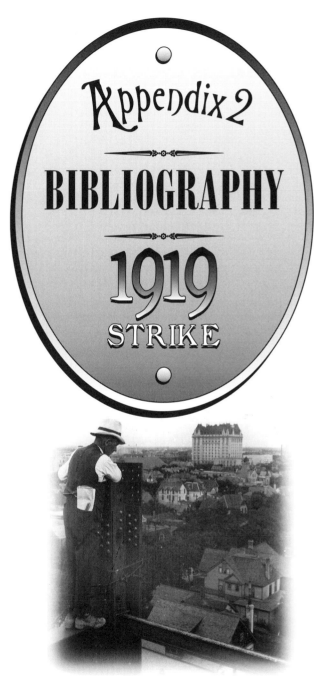

Appendix 2

BIBLIOGRAPHY

1919 STRIKE

CONSTRUCTION OF T. EATON CO. MAIL ORDER BUILDING, 18 JULY 1916

in Winnipeg, 1880-1914,' unpub. M.A. thesis, University of Manitoba, 1986.

Boudreau, Joseph, 'Western Canada's Enemy Aliens in World War I', *Alberta History*, 12:1 (1964), 1-9.

Brown, Desmond II., 'The Craftsmanship of Bias: Sedition and the Winnipeg General Strike', *Manitoba Law Journal*, 14 (1984) 1-33.

Brown, R.C. and Ramsay Cook, *Canada 1896-1921: A Nation Transformed* (Toronto, 1974).

Brown, Robert Craig, *Robert Laird Borden, A Biography*, vol. 2 (Toronto, 1980).

Brown, R.C., ' "Whither are we being shoved?" Political Leadership in Canada During World War I,' J. L. Granatstein and R. D. Cuff, eds., *War and Society in North America* (Toronto, 1971), 104-119.

Buck, T., *Canada and the Russian Revolution* (Toronto, 1967).

Buck, T., *Yours in the Struggle* (Toronto, 1977), 73-86.

Carlyle, W. J., 'Growth, Ethnic Groups and Socio-economic Areas of Winnipeg', T.J. Kuz, ed., *Winnipeg 1874-1974: Progress and Prospects* (Winnipeg, 1974), 27-41.

Cashmore, Ernest, 'The Social Organization of Canadian Immigration Law', *Canadian Journal of Sociology*, 3 (1978), 409-429.

Cherwinski, J., 'Saskatchewan Organized Labour and the Winnipeg General Strike, 1919' unpub. paper, 1976.

Chisick, Ernie, 'The Development of Winnipeg's Socialist Movement, 1900-1915', unpub. M.A. thesis, University of Manitoba, 1972.

Conley, James Robert, 'Class Conflict and Collective Action in the Working Class of Vancouver, British Columbia, 1900-1919', unpub. Ph.D. dissertation, Carleton University, 1986.

Cook, Ramsay, *The Politics of John W. Dafoe and the Free Press* (Toronto, 1963), 8-101.

Crook, Wilfrid H., *The General Strike; A study of Labour's Tragic Weapon in Theory and Practice* (Chapel Hill, 1931).

Cruikshank, Douglas and Gregory S. Kealey, 'Canadian Strike Statistics, 1891-1950', *Labour/Le Travail*, 20 (1987), 85-145.

Dick, Lyle, 'Politics and Discourse: A Review of "1919: The Winnipeg General Strike: A Driving and Walking Tour," ' *Manitoba History*, 13 (1987), 33-38.

Durkin, Douglas, *The Magpie* (Toronto, 1923).

Drystek, Henry, 'The Simplest and Cheapest Mode of Dealing with Them: Deportation from Canada before World War II', *Histoire*

Sociale/Social History, 14 (1982), 407-41.

Emery, G.N., 'The Methodist Church and the "European Foreigners" of Winnipeg: The All Peoples Mission, 1889-1914', *Manitoba Historical Society Transactions*, ser III, no. 28 (1971-71), 85-100.

Entz, W., 'The Suppression of the German Language Press in September 1918', *Canadian Ethnic Studies*, 8:2 (1976), 56-70.

Ewen, Geoffrey, 'La Contestation a Montreal en 1919', *Histoire des Travailleurs Quebecois Bulletin de R.C.H.T.Q.*, 36 (autumn 1986), vol. 12, no. 3, 37-62.

Friesen, G.A., *The Canadian Prairies* (Toronto, 1984).

Friesen, G.A., ' "Yours in Revolt": Regionalism, Socialism, and the Western Canadian Labour Movement', *Labour/Le Travailleur*, 1 (1976).

Geary, Roger, *Policing Industrial Disputes: 1893 to 1985* (Cambridge, England, 1985).

Graham, Roger, *Arthur Meighen; The Door of Opportunity* (Toronto, 1960), 236-7.

Grenke, Art, 'The German Community of Winnipeg and the English-Canadian Response to World War I', *Canadian Ethnic Studies*, 20, no. 1 (1988), 21-44.

Hall, David, 'Times of Trouble: Labour Quiescence in Winnipeg 1920-1929,' unpub. M.A. thesis, University of Manitoba, 1983.

Heaps, Leo, *The Rebel in the House: The Life and Times of A.A. Heaps* (London, 1970).

Heron, Craig, 'Labourism and the Canadian Working Class', *Labour/Le Travail*, 13 (Spring 1984), 45-76.

Heron, Craig and Brian Palmer, 'Through the Prism of the Strike: Industrial Conflict in Southern Ontario, 1901-1914', *Canadian Historical Review*, 58 (1977), 423-458.

Hogan, Brian F., *Cobalt: Year of the Strike 1919* (Cobalt, 1978).

Horodyski, Mary, 'Women and the Winnipeg General Strike of 1919', *Manitoba History*, 11 (1986), 28-37.

Horrall, S.W., 'The Royal North-West Mounted Police and Labour Unrest in Western Canada, 1919' *Canadian Historical Review*, 61 (1980), 169-190.

Irvine, Duncan Norman, 'Reform, War, and Industrial Crisis in Manitoba: F.J. Dixon and the Framework of Consensus', unpub. M.A. thesis, University of Manitoba, 1981.

Jewish Historical Society of Western Canada, *Personal Recollections: The Jewish Pioneer Past on the Prairies*, vol VI, Jewish Life and Times, Winnipeg (1993), 58-60.

Johnson, Albert, 'The Strikes in Winnipeg in May 1918: The Prelude to 1919', unpub. M.A. thesis, University of Manitoba, 1978.

Jordan, Mary W., *Survival: The Trials and Tribulations of Canadian Labour* (Toronto, 1976) [biography of R.B. Russell].

Katz, Leslie, 'Some Legal Consequences of the Winnipeg General Strike of 1919', *Manitoba Law Journal*, 4 (1970), 47.

Kealey, G.S., '1919: The Canadian Labour Revolt', *Labour/Le Travail*, 13 (1989), 11-44.

Kealey, Gregory, 'State Repression of Labour and the Left in Canada, 1914-1920: The Impact of the First World War', *Canadian Historical Review*, 73 (Sept. 1992), 281-314.

Kealey, Gregory, 'The Surveillance State: The Origins of Domestic Intelligence and Counter-Subversion in Canada', *Intelligence and National Security* 7:3 (1992), 179-210.

Kealey, Gregory, 'The Royal Canadian Mounted Police, the Canadian Security Intelligence Service, the Public Archives of Canada, and the Access to Information Act: A Curious Tale', *Labour/Le Travail*, 21 (1988), 199-226.

Kealey, Gregory and R. Whitaker, eds., *RCMP Security Bulletins: The Early Years 1919-1929* (St. John's, 1992).

Kealey, Linda, 'No Special Protection—No Sympathy: Women's Activism in the Canadian Labour Revolt of 1919', D. Hopkins and G. Kealey, eds., *Class, Community and the Labour Movement: Wales and Canada, 1850-1930* (Llafur, Wales, 1989), 134-159.

Kealey, Linda, 'Canadian Socialism and the Woman Question, 1900-1914', *Labour/Le Travail*, 13 (1984), 77-100.

Kealey, Linda, 'Women and Labour During World War I: Women Workers and the Minimum Wage in Manitoba', Mary Kinnear, ed., *First days, Fighting Days: Women in Manitoba History* (Regina, 1987).

Kehler, Ken and Alvin Esau, *Famous Manitoba Trials; The Winnipeg General Strike Trials—Research Source* (Winnipeg, 1990).

Keshen, Jeff, 'All the News That Was Fit to Print: Ernest J. Chambers and Information Control in Canada, 1914-19', *Canadian Historical Review*, 73:3 (1992), 315-343.

Kuz, T.J., ed., *Winnipeg, 1874-1974: Progress and Prospects* (Winnipeg, 1974).

Labour Gazette, July 1969.

Laycock, David, *Populism and Democratic Thought in the Canadian Prairies, 1910-1945* (Toronto, 1990).

Lipton, Charles, *The Trade Union Movement of Canada, 1827-1959* (Toronto, 1973), 185-217, 219-220.

Lysenko, Vera, *Yellow Boots* (New York, 1954), 211-242.

MacInnis, Grace, *J.S. Woodsworth: A Man to Remember* (Toronto, 1953).

McCormack, A.R., *Reformers, Rebels, and Revolutionaries: The Western Canadian Radical Movement, 1899-1919* (Toronto, 1977).

McKay, Ian, 'Strikes in the Maritimes, 1900-1914', *Acadiensis*, 13 (1983), 3-46.

Mackenzie, J.B., 'Section 98, Criminal Code, and Freedom of Expression in Canada', *Queen's Law Journal*, I (1972), 469-483.

McKillop, A.B., 'Citizen and Socialist: The Ethos of Political Winnipeg, 1919-1935', unpub. M.A. thesis, University of Manitoba, 1970.

MacLaren, Roy, *Canadians in Russia, 1918-1919* (Toronto, 1967).

McNaught, Kenneth, *A Prophet in Politics* (Toronto, 1959), 99-154.

McNaught, Kenneth, 'Political Trials and the Canadian Political Tradition', *University of Toronto Law Journal*, 24 (1947), 149-169.

Madiros, Anthony, *William Irvine: The Life of a Prairie Radical* (Toronto, 1979).

Manitoba Labor Education Centre, *1919 The Winnipeg General Strike*, Manitoba Labor Series (Winnipeg, reprint 1994).

Martynowich, Orest T., 'Village Radicals and Peasant Immigrants: The Social Roots of Factionalism among Ukrainian Immigrants in Canada, 1896-1918' unpub. M.A. thesis, University of Manitoba, 1978.

Martynowich, Orest T., 'The Ukrainian Socialist Movement in Canada, 1900-1918', *Journal of Ukrainian Graduate Studies*, 1 (1976), 27-44 and 2 (1977), 22-31.

Masters, D.C., *The Winnipeg General Strike* (Toronto, 1950).

Melnycky, Peter, 'A Political History of the Ukrainian Community in Manitoba, 1899-1922', unpub. M.A. thesis, University of Manitoba, 1979.

Melnycky, Peter, 'The Internment of Ukrainians in Canada', Frances Swyripa and John Herd Thompson, eds., *Loyalties in Conflict: Ukrainians in Canada During the Great War* (Edmonton, 1985), 1-24.

Millar, F. David, 'The Winnipeg General Strike, 1919: A Reinterpretation in the Light of Oral History and Pictorial Evidence', unpub. M.A. thesis, Carleton University, 1970.

Mills, Allen, *Fool for Christ: The Political Thought of J.S. Woodsworth* (Toronto, 1990).

Mills, Allen, 'Single tax, Socialism, and the Independent Labour Party of Manitoba: The Political Ideas of F.J. Dixon and S.J. Farmer', *Labour/Le Travailleur*, 5 (1980).

Mitchell, Tom, 'A square Deal for All and No Railroading: Labour and Politics in Brandon, 1900-1920', *Prairie Forum*, 15 (1990), 45-65.

Mitchell, Tom, ' "To Reach the Leadership of this Revolutionary Movement": A.J. Andrews, the Canadian State and the Suppression of the Winnipeg General Strike', *Prairie Forum*, 18 (1993), 239-255.

Montgomery, David, 'Immigrants, Industrial Unions, and Social Reconstuction in the United States, 1916-1923', *Labour/Le Travail*, 13 (1984), 111-113.

Morton, Desmond, 'Sir William Otter and Internment Operations in Canada during the First World War', *Canadian Historical Review*, 55:1 (March 1974), 32-58.

Morton, W.L., *Manitoba: A History* (Toronto, 1957), 356-379.

Mott, Morris, 'The "Foreign Peril": Nativism in Winnipeg, 1916-1923', unpub. M.A. thesis, University of Manitoba, 1970.

Murray, Robert K., *Red Scare: A Study in National Hysteria* (New York, 1964).

Naylor, James, *The New Democracy: Challenging the Social Order in Industrial Ontario, 1914-1925* (Toronto, 1991).

Naylor, James, 'Toronto, 1919', *Canadian Historical Association Historical Papers*, 1986, 33-55.

Orlikow, Lionel, 'A Survey of the Reform Movement in Manitoba, 1910-1920', unpub. M.A. thesis, University of Manitoba, 1955.

Osborne, Kenneth, *R.B. Russell and the Labour Movement* (Agincourt, 1978).

Palmer, Bryan D., *Working-Class Experience: The Rise and Reconstitution of Canadian Labour, 1800-1980* (Toronto, 1983), esp. 173-179.

Palmer, Bryan D., *Working-Class Experience: Rethinking the History of Canadian Labour, 1800-1991* (Toronto, 1992). (revised edition of above).

Penner, Jacob, 'Recollections of the Early Socialist Movement in Winnipeg', *Marxist Quarterly*, (1962), 29-30.

Penner, Norman, ed., *Winnipeg 1919: The Strikers' Own History of the Winnipeg General Strike* (Toronto, 1973).

Penner, Norman, *The Canadian Left: A Critical Analysis* (Scarborough, 1977), 28-29.

Pentland, H.C., 'Fifty Years After', *Canadian Dimension*, (July 1969), p. 14.

Peterson, Larry, 'The One Big Union in International Perspective: Revolutionary Industrial Unionism 1900-1925', *Labour/Le Travailleur*, 7 (1981), 41-66.

Peterson, Larry, 'Revolutionary Socialism and Industrial Unrest in the Era of the Winnipeg General Strike: The Origins of Communist Labour Unionism in Europe and North America', *Labour/Le Travail*, 13 (1984), 115-131.

Peterson, T., 'Ethnic and Class Politics in Manitoba', Martin Robin, ed., *Canadian Provincial Politics* (Scarborough, 1972), 81-6.

Prang, Margaret, *N.W. Rowell: Ontario Nationalist* (Toronto, 1975).

Preston, William, Jr., *Aliens and Dissenters: Federal Suppression of Radicals, 1903-1933* [in the United States], (Cambridge, Mass., 1963).

Pringle, Jim, *United We Stand: A History of Winnipeg's Civic Workers* (Winnipeg, 1991).

Rae, J.E., 'The Politics of Class: Winnipeg City Council, 1919-1945', Ramsay Cook and Carl Berger, eds., *The West and the Nation*, 232-249.

Rae, J.E., 'The Politics of Conscience: Winnipeg after the Strike', Canadian Historical Association Historical Papers, 1971.

Reimer, Chad, 'War, Nationhood and Working-Class Entitlement: The Counterhegemonic Challenge of the 1919 Winnipeg General Strike', *Prairie Forum*, 18 (1993), 219-239.

Reilly, Nolan, 'The General Strike in Amherst, Nova Scotia 1919', *Acadiensis*, 9 (1980), 56-77.

Roberts, Barbara, *Whence They Came: Deportation from Canada 1900-1935* (Ottawa, 1988).

Roberts, Barbara, 'Shovelling out the "Mutinous": Political Deportation from Canada before 1936', *Labour/Le Travail*, 18 (1986) 77-110.

Roberts, Barbara, 'Purely Administrative Proceedings: The Management of Canadian Deportation, 1890-1935', unpub. Ph.D. thesis, University of Ottawa, 1980.

Robin, Martin, *Radical Politics and Canadian Labour* (Kingston, 1968).

Robin, Martin, 'Registration, Conscription, and Independent Labour Politics, 1916-1917', *Canadian Historical Review*, 47:2 (June 1966), 101-118.

Royal Commission to Enquire into and report upon the causes and effects of the general strike which recently existed in the City of

Winnipeg for a period of six weeks, including the methods of calling and carrying on such Strike (n.p., n.d., published 1920).

Ryder, Walter Scott, 'Canada's Industrial Crisis of 1919', unpub. M.A. thesis, University of British Columbia, 1921.

Seager, Allen, 'Nineteen Nineteen: Year of Revolt', *Journal of the West*, 23, no. 4 (October 1984), 40-47.

Scott, Joan W., 'On Language, Gender, and Working-Class History', *International Labor and Working Class History*, 31 (1987), 1-13.

Skwarok, J., *Ukrainian Settlers in Canada and Their Schools* (Toronto, 1959), 60-67.

Smith, A.E., *All My Life* (Toronto, 1949).

Smith, David Edward, 'Emergency Government in Canada', *Canadian Historical Review*, 50 (1969), 429-448.

Smith, Doug, *Let Us Rise!* (Vancouver, 1985).

Socialist Party of Canada, Local no. 3, *Causes of Industrial Unrest* (Winnipeg 1919).

Steinhart, Allan L., *Civil Censorship in Canada During World War I* (Toronto, 1986).

Stubbs, Lewis St. George, *A Majority of One: The Life and Times of Lewis St. George Stubbs* (Winnipeg, 1983).

Sutcliffe, J.H., 'The Economic Background of the Winnipeg General Strike: Wages and Working Conditions', unpub. M.A. thesis, University of Manitoba, 1977.

Swettenham, John, *Allied Intervention in Russia, 1918-1919, And the Part Played by Canada* (Toronto, 1967).

Taylor, Jeffrey, 'The Language of Agrarianism in Manitoba, 1890-1925', *Labour/Le Travail*, 23 (1989), 91-118.

Thomas, Lillian Jean, 'A Test of Social Conflict Theory: The Case of the Winnipeg General Strike', unpub. M.A. thesis, University of Manitoba, 1977.

Thompson, John Herd, *The Harvest of War: The Prairie West, 1914-1918* (Toronto, 1978).

Tranfield, Pam, 'Girl Strikers', *NeWest Review*, 14, no. 5 (June/July 1989).

Usiskin, Roseline, 'Towards a theoretical reformulation of the relationship between political ideology, social class and ethnicity: a case study of the Winnipeg Jewish community, 1905-1922', unpub. M.A. thesis, University of Manitoba, 1978.

'Winnipeg General Strike: Looking Back', *Canadian Dimension*, 6 no. 2 (July 1969) [interview with Fred Lange, interview with Fred Tipping].

J. Wormsbecker, 'The Rise and Fall of the Labour Political Movement in Manitoba, 1919-1927', unpub. M.A. thesis, Queen's University, 1977.

DETAIL OF STRIKERS AND FRIENDS, 1919